Christ and His Communities

Reginald H. Fuller
M.A. (Cantab.), S.T.D., D.D.

Christ and His Communities
Essays in Honor of
Reginald H. Fuller

Edited by
Arland J. Hultgren
and
Barbara Hall

Forward Movement Publications
Cincinnati, Ohio

Published by Forward Movement Publications
412 Sycamore Street
Cincinnati, Ohio 45202.

Copyright © 1990
Forward Movement Publications

This volume is also published by
The Anglican Theological Review.
Evanston, Illinois, as Number 11
in its Supplementary Series.

Library of Congress Catalog Card Number: 89-82579
ISBN 0-88028-104-9

Printed in the United States of America

CONTENTS

Preface

This volume of essays is presented as a gesture of esteem and friendship for the honoree, Professor Reginald H. Fuller, on his 75th birthday, March 24, 1990. The essays have been written by persons who are indebted to Professor Fuller as teacher and scholar. Some of the authors are his former students. Some are former colleagues. All have learned from his published books and essays.

The title of the volume has been chosen because it suggests areas in which the essayists, and countless others, have profited from the works and activities of Professor Fuller. His insightful studies in the traditions about Jesus of Nazareth, his magisterial work in New Testament Christology, and his illumination of the life, literature, and mission of early Christian communities come to mind immediately. Beyond his more technical scholarly contributions, Professor Fuller has also been a leading teacher and interpreter of the Scriptures for the sake of proclamation in the communities of Christ today—not only communities within the Anglican Communion, which he has served so faithfully and well, but also communities of other communions and confessions throughout the world.

The editors, both former students of Professor Fuller, express their gratitude to many persons who have made this volume possible. Above all, Dr. Richard Reid, Dean of Virginia Theological Seminary, has gone to great lengths to see that the volume gets produced. It would not have been possible for the book to appear without his strong support and his opening of doors behind the scenes. Gratitude is also expressed to the Corporation of the *Anglican Theological Review* and its Editor, Dr. Richard E. Wentz, for including this volume in the *ATR* Supplementary Series. Finally, gratitude is expressed to Dr. Charles Long, Editor in Chief of Forward Movement Publications, with whom the book is being co-published, for his support and advice at various stages along the way.

Arland J. Hultgren
Luther Northwestern Theological Seminary

Barbara Hall
Virginia Theological Seminary

Reginald H. Fuller: A Tribute

RICHARD REID*

This volume of essays has been designed as a tribute by colleagues and friends to the Reverend Professor Reginald H. Fuller. That Professor Fuller deserves such a tribute and also the thanks of the community of New Testament scholars cannot be disputed. Anyone who knows the literature in the field will be aware of the many contributions Dr. Fuller has made to our understanding of the New Testament.

He brings to all of his study a carefully developed knowledge and appreciation of the insights of all the various methods of study which have been developed to help us understand the New Testament. He also brings balance, wisdom, and the ability to make careful and thoughtful judgments. And finally he gives us always the great gift of presenting the results of his scholarship and the conclusions he has reached in clear and lucid prose.

This volume contains a bibliography of Dr. Fuller's works. A careful reading of it will give a clear picture of the range of his scholarship. The depth of that scholarship can only be discerned by reading the works themselves. That he has a broad and deep command of the totality of New Testament scholarship is attested by his *Critical Introduction to the New Testament* published in 1966. It is a concise yet thorough overview of New Testament scholarship presented in a form readily available to students.

Dr. Fuller's work and writing has extended over many areas of new Testament criticism and theology. He has written on the miracles of Jesus, on the resurrection narratives, and on Christology, as well as many other subjects. Always his works reflect a thorough knowledge of scholarly literature on the subject as well as the author's own careful study and creative insights.

The debt which New Testament scholarship owes to Dr. Fuller is a great one. But perhaps even greater is the debt owed by the church. Without ever compromising scholarly integrity, Dr. Fuller has always remembered that the Bible is the church's book. He has repeatedly shown how careful New Testament scholarship can serve the preaching ministry of the church. His book *Preaching the New Lectionary* continues to be a helpful guide to countless preachers. Based on careful, critical

---

* Richard Reid is Dean of Virginia Theological Seminary, Alexandria, Virginia.

study, informed by a deep sense of the liturgy and the role of preaching within it, and inspired by the power of the gospel, it is a model work.

Dr. Fuller's concern for preaching, however, is reflected not only in this work, but in many of his other writings as well. It is a part of his own deep commitment to our Lord and to the church. There is never any sense in his work that the "academy" and the "church" are in conflict. Rather, careful and honest academic study which seeks the truth will always serve the church, for the church too is grounded in the truth.

His contributions to the life and ministry of the church include also his gifts as a teacher. He has taught in seminaries in Great Britain, in the United States, in Canada, and in Australia. In keeping with his deep ecumenical concern, reflected also in his writing, he has taught students from many Christian traditions. His teaching has included not only those preparing for ordination, but clergy in continuing education programs, and many lay people as well. He has helped many, many people to a deeper knowledge of Scripture.

As a colleague deeply indebted to Dr. Fuller for my own under-standing of the New Testament, it is my privilege to express on behalf of the community of New Testament scholars our profound thanks for the work which Reginald Fuller has shared with us all. As the Dean of one of the seminaries where he taught, it is my happy task to thank him on behalf of countless students for the quality of his teaching, for his concern, for the growth and support of those whom he taught, and for assisting so many to a deeper understanding of the Bible. As a preacher, it is my pleasure to thank him on behalf of so many for the example and stimulus he has given to all of us as we go about the task of proclaiming the gospel. As one concerned for the unity of the church, it is my welcome duty to thank him for his writing and efforts which have contributed to better understanding among various parts of the Christian community. And finally as a friend and fellow Christian, it is my joy to thank him for the friendship he gives to us all and for the witness and example he offers to us as a faithful servant of our Lord.

Reginald H. Fuller
Curriculum Vitae

BACKGROUND AND EDUCATION:

Born March 24, 1915, Horsham, Sussex, England, son of Horace Fuller, agricultural engineer, and Cora L. Fuller.

Educated at Collyer's School, Horsham, 1925–1934.

Scholar of Peterhouse, Cambridge, 1934.

First Class Honours, Classical Tripos, Part I, 1936.

Morgan Scholar, study under Sir Edwyn Hoskyns, 1936.

B.A., 1937.

First Class Honours, Theological Tripos, Part II (New Testament), 1938.

Study at Tübingen University under Gerhard Kittel, 1938–39.

Study at the Queen's College, Birmingham, 1939–40.

PROFESSIONAL ACTIVITIES:

Ordination to the diaconate by A. E. J. Rawlinson, Bishop of Derby, 1940.

Assistant Curate at Bakewell, Derbyshire, 1940–43.

Ordination to priesthood by A. E. J. Rawlinson, Bishop of Derby, 1941.

1941 M.A. (Cantab).

Marriage to Ilse Barda, 1942. Three daughters: Caroline, Rosemary, and Sarah.

Assistant Curate at Ashbourne-with-Mapleton, Derbyshire, 1943–45.

Assistant Curate at Edgbaston, Birmingham, 1946–50 (part time).

Lecturer at the Queen's College, Birmingham, 1946–50.

Recognized Lecturer, Birmingham University, 1946–50.

Professor of Theology and Hebrew, St. David's University College, Lampeter Wales, 1950–55.

Examining Chaplain to Bishop of Monmouth, 1950–55.

Professor of New Testament Literature and Languages, Seabury-Western Theological Seminary, Evanston, Illinois, 1955–66.

Baldwin Professor of Sacred Literature, Union Theological Seminary, New York, 1966–72.

Mollie Laird Downs Professor of New Testament, Virginia Theological Seminary, 1972–83; Professor Emeritus, 1985 —.

AWARDS AND HONORS:

>Schofield Prize and Crosse Student, University of Cambridge, 1938.
>
>AATS Fellowship, 1961.
>
>Honorary Canon, St. Paul's Cathedral, Burlington, VT, 1988.

PROFESSIONAL SOCIETIES AND ECUMENICAL ACTIVITIES:

>Member, Chicago Society of Biblical Research, 1956–66.
>
>Member, Society of Biblical Literature, 1966— .
>
>>Committee on Honorary Membership, 1979.
>
>Member, Studiorum Novi Testamenti Societas.
>
>>Committee, 1969–72.
>>
>>Editorial Committee, 1976–79.
>>
>>President, 1983–84.
>
>Revised Standard Version Revision Committee, 1981—.

CHURCH ACTIVITIES:

>Lectionary Committee of the Liturgical Commission, ECUSA.
>
>Lutheran-Episcopal Dialogue I and II.
>
>Anglo-German Theological Conferences, 1951 and 1955.
>
>Anglican-Lutheran Dialogue (International).
>
>Consultant, Anglican-Roman Catholic Dialogue (US).
>
>Task Force on Peter in the New Testament, Lutheran-Catholic Dialogue.
>
>Task Force on Mary in the New Testament, Lutheran-Catholic Dialogue.

VISITING PROFESSORSHIPS:

>The Queen's College, Birmingham, and the University of Birmingham, 1969.
>
>Church Divinity School of the Pacific and Graduate Theological Union, Berkeley, California, 1975.
>
>Summer School, University of the South, Sewanee, Tennessee, 1960, 1962, 1968, 1970, 1973, 1982, 1988.
>
>College of Emmanuel and St. Chad, Saskatoon, Saskatchewan, Canada, 1978, 1988.
>
>Episcopal Seminary of the Southwest, 1986.
>
>Nashotah House, 1986.
>
>St. Mark's College of Ministry, Canberra, Australia, 1987.

HONORARY DEGREES:

>S.T.D., General Theological Seminary, 1960.

S.T.D., Philadelphia Divinity School, 1962.
D.D., Seabury-Western Theological Seminary, 1983.

ACADEMIC LECTURES:

Boston College; Catholic University of America; College of Preachers; The Divinity School, Cambridge University; Eden Theological Seminary; Episcopal Theological Seminary of Kentucky; Episcopal Seminary of the Southwest (three times); Garrett Theological Seminary; Lutheran Theological Seminaries at Columbus, OH, Dubuque, IA, and St. Paul, MN (Hein Lectures); Iliff School of Theology; Howard Divinity School; Immaculate Conception College, NY; Kiel University, Germany; Lancaster Theological Seminary; Lancaster University, England; Lexington Seminary; Lutheran Seminary, Philadelphia; Lutheran Seminary, Waterloo, ON, Canada; Lynchburg College, Naperville Evangelical Seminary; Newcastle University, NSW, Australia; Notre Dame University; Nottingham University, England; Perkins School of Theology; Philadelphia Divinity School (twice); St. Anne's College, Oxford; St. Augustine's College, Canterbury (twice); St. John's College, Auckland, New Zealand; St. John's College, Morpeth, NSW, Australia; St. Michael's College, Winooski, VT; St. Michael's College, Worcester, MA; St. Stephen's College, Edmonton, AB, Canada; Salisbury and Wells Theological College; Seabury-Western Theological Seminary (Hale Lectures); Shenandoah College; Trinity College, Burlington, VT (twice); University of Richmond; United Theological Seminary, Dayton, OH (Showers Lectures); Valparaiso University; Vancouver School of Theology; Villanova University; Virginia Theological Seminary (Zabriskie Lectures); Washington & Lee University; Wesley College, Dover, DE; Wesley Theological Seminary, Washington D.C.; Yale Divinity School.

Reginald H. Fuller
Bibliography, 1940–89

ROBERT M. KAHL, JR.

AND

GERALD P. BURKE*

I. Books and Monographs

1940–49

The Church of Rome: A Dissuasive (with R.P.C. Hanson). London: SCM Press, 1948; 2d ed., New York: Seabury Press, 1960.

1950–59

The Mission and Achievement of Jesus: An Examination of the Presuppositions of New Testament Theology. Studies in Biblical Theology 12. London: SCM Press; Naperville: Alec R. Allenson, 1954.

The Book of the Acts of God: Christian Scholarship Interprets the Bible (with G. Ernest Wright). Garden City, NY: Doubleday & Co., 1957.

Luke's Witness to Jesus Christ. London: Lutterworth Press; New York: Association Press, 1958.

What Is Liturgical Preaching? Studies in Ministry and Worship 1. London: SCM Press, 1957.

1960–69

The New Testament in Current Study. London: SCM Press; New York: Charles Scribner's Sons, 1962.

Interpreting the Miracles. London: SCM Press; Philadelphia: Westminister Press, 1963; German trans.: *Die Wunder Jesu in Exegese und Verkündigung.* Trans. Franz Joseph Schierz. Berlin: Evangelische Verlag, 1966 (also trans. into Dutch and Spanish).

The Foundations of New Testament Christology. London: Lutterworth Press; New York: Charles Scribner's Sons, 1965.

A Critical Introduction to the New Testament. London: G. Duckworth, 1966.

Christianity and the Affluent Society (with Brian K. Rice). London: Hodder and Stoughton, 1966.

* Robert M. Kahl, Jr., is Rector of the Church of the Advent, Cape May, New Jersey. Gerald P. Burke is Administrative Assistant at the same church. Special thanks are extended to the staff of the Speer Memorial Library, Princeton Theological Seminary, for their kind assistance and the use of the facilities.

Lent with the Liturgy. London: SPCK, 1968.

1970–79

The Formation of the Resurrection Narratives. New York: Macmillan, 1971; 2d ed., Philadelphia: Fortress Press, 1980.

Preaching the New Lectionary: The Word of God for the Church Today. Collegeville, MN: Liturgical Press, 1974; rev. ed., *Preaching the Lectionary: The Word of God for the Church Today.* Collegeville, MN: Liturgical Press, 1984.

Holy Week (with William C. McFadden). Proclamation: Aids for Interpreting the Lessons of the Church Year, Series B. Philadelphia: Fortress Press, 1975.

Longer Mark: Forgery, Interpolation, or Old Tradition? Berkeley, CA: Center for Hermeneutical Studies, 1976.

1980–89

The Use of the Bible in Preaching. Philadelphia: Fortress Press, 1981.

Advent-Christmas. Proclamation 2: Aids for Interpreting the Lessons of the Church Year, Series C. Philadelphia: Fortress Press, 1982.

Who Is This Christ?: Gospel Christology and Contemporary Faith (with Pheme Perkins). Philadelphia: Fortress Press, 1983.

Holy Week. Proclamation 3: Aids for Interpreting the Lessons of the Church Year, Series B. Philadelphia: Fortress Press, 1984.

II. Journal Articles

1940–49

"The Church in Württemberg, 1938–39." *Theology* 41 (1940): 219–26, 268–76.

"The Word of God." *Theology* 47 (1944): 267–71.

Baptism and Confirmation." *Theology* 49 (1946): 113–18.

"Reason: Jezebel and Magdalene." *Divinity* (1946): 269–75.

1950–59

"Prayer for the Departed." *Theology* 53 (1950): 122–28.

"Recent Books on Confirmation." *Ecumenical Review* 3 (1952): 329–32.

"Le Sceau de l'Esprit: Le Baptême et la Confirmation." *Bulletin Anglican* 2 (1952): 10–13.

"Some Problems of New Testament Christology." *Anglican Theological Review* 38 (1956): 146–52.

"The Virgin Birth: Historical Fact or Kerygmatic Truth?" *Biblical Research* 1 (1956): 1–8.

"Current Issues in German Theology." *Australian Church Quarterly* (April 1957): 3–16.

"The RSV Apocrypha." *The Living Church* 135 (1957): 16–18.

"The Church under the Lordship of Jesus Christ." *Encounter* 20 (1959): 446–50.

"The Draft Liturgy of 1953 in Anglican Perspective." *Anglican Theological Review* 41 (1959): 190–98.

1960–69

"The Veneration of the Saints in the Normal Life of the Church." *The Anglican* 17 (1960): 1–7.

"The Resurrection of Jesus Christ." *Biblical Research* 4 (1960): 8–24.

"What Is Liturgical Preaching?" *Church Quarterly Review* 161 (Ja–Mr 1960): 95–96.

"On Demythologizing the Trinity." *Anglican Theological Review* 43 (1961): 121–131.

"The People of God in the Bible." *Crossroads* 13 (1962): 20–57.

"The Double Origin of the Eucharist." *Biblical Research* 8 (1963): 60–72.

"Tongues in the New Testament." *American Church Quarterly* 3 (1963): 162–68.

"The Clue to Jesus' Self-Understanding." *Studia Evangelica* 3, ed. F. L. Cross, 58–66. Texte und Untersuchungen 88; Berlin: Akademie Verlag, 1964.

"Some Further Reflections on Heilsgeschichte." *Union Seminary Quarterly Review* 22 (1967): 93–103.

"The 'Thou Art Peter' Pericope and the Easter Appearances." *McCormick Quarterly* 20 (1967): 309–15.

"The Bible Study." *Midstream* 6 (1967): 113–22 (report of COCU Meeting, Cambridge, MA, 1967).

"The Exegete and the Preacher." *United Theological Seminary Bulletin* 67 (1967): 2–16 (Balmer Showers Lecture).

"The Critic and the Exegete." *Foot-Notes* (Waterloo Lutheran Seminary) 4 (1968): 9–19.

1970–79

"Worship, Sacraments and the Unity of the Church." *Anglican Theological Review* 52 (1970): 214–17.

"Advent Sunday Readings." *Worship* 45 (1971): 554–65.

"Lenten Scripture Readings." *Worship* 45 (1971): 92–101.

"Easter Season Scripture Readings." *Worship* 45 (1971): 220–36.

"Apostolicity and Ministry." *Concordia Theological Monthly* 43 (1972): 67–76; reprinted as "The Development of the Ministry," in

Lutheran Episcopal Dialogue: A Progress Report, 76–93. Cincinnati: Forward Movement Publications, 1974.

"The Choice of Matthias." *Studia Evangelica* 6, ed. Elizabeth A. Livingstone, 140–46. Texte und Untersuchungen 112. Berlin: Akademie-Verlag, 1973.

"Aspects of Pauline Christology." *Review and Expositor* 71 (1974): 5–17.

"The Jews in the Fourth Gospel." *Dialogue* 16 (1977): 31–37.

"Baur versus Hilgenfeld: A Forgotten Chapter in the Debate on the Synoptic Problem." *New Testament Studies* 24 (1978): 355–70.

"John 20: 19–23." *Interpretation* 32 (1978): 180–84.

"New Testament Roots to the Theotokos." *Marian Studies* 29 (1978): 46–64.

"The Conception/Birth of Jesus as a Christological Moment." *Journal for the Study of the New Testament* 1 (1979): 37–52.

"Anglican Continuity in the Proposed Book of Common Prayer." *The Anglican* (1979): 2–10.

1980–89

"What Is Happening in New Testament Studies?" *Saint Luke's Journal of Theology* 23 (1980): 90–100; reprinted in *A Companion to the Bible*, ed. M. Ward, 29–41. New York: Alba House, 1985.

"Jesus Christ as Savior in the New Testament." *Interpretation* 35 (1981): 145–56.

"The Nature of Anglicanism." *The Anglican* 11 (1981): 2–6.

"Pre-Existence Christology: Can We Dispense with It?" *Word & World* 2 (1982): 29–33.

"Mary and the Bilateral Dialogues." *Ecumenical Trends* 11 (1982): 126–28.

"The Three Year Eucharistic Lectionary." *Occasional Papers* 1. New York: Standing Liturgical Commission, 1982.

"New Testament Trajectories and Biblical Authority." *Studia Evangelica* 7, ed. E. A. Livingstone, 189–99. Texte und Unterschungen 126. Berlin: Akademie Verlag, 1982.

"The Historical Jesus: Some Outstanding Issues." *The Thomist* 48 (1984): 368–82.

"Sir Edwyn Hoskyns and the Contemporary Relevance of Biblical Theology." *New Testament Studies* 30 (1984): 321–34.

"I Cor. 6:1–11, An Exegetical Paper." *Ex Auditu* 2 (1986): 96–104.

"The Passion, Death, and Resurrection of Jesus according to John." *Chicago Studies* 25 (1986): 51–63.

"Facing Unity: Models, Form, and Phases of Catholic-Lutheran

Church Fellowship: An Anglican Comment." *Ecumenical Trends* 15 (1986): 53–55.

"Trends in New Testament Studies." *St. Mark's Review* 131 (1987): 16–20.

"Popes, Bishops, Academic Freedom." *Cross Currents* 36 (1987): 404–409.

"Anglican Odyssey." *The Rotunda* 51 (1988): 1–8; reprinted in *The Anglican* 18 (1988): 1–8 and in *Associated Parishes Bulletin* (December 1988): 1–4.

"Order in the Synoptic Gospels: Summary." *The Second Century: A Journal of Early Christian Studies* 6 (1987–88): 107–109.

"Jesus, Paul and Apocalyptic." *Anglican Theological Review* 71 (1989): 134–42.

"The Decalogue in the New Testament." *Interpretation* 43 (1989): 243–55.

III. Contributions to Books and Collected Essays

1940–49

"Weihnachten in der Anglikanischen Kirche." In Hans Asmussen et al., *Evangelische Weihnachten: Kirche und Welt unter der Botschaft des Christfests*, 131–44. Tübingen: Furche Verlag, 1949.

1960–69

"Liturgy and Devotion." In *The Place of Bonhoeffer: Possibilities in His Thought*, ed. Martin E. Marty, 167–96. New York: Association Press, 1962.

"The World Come of Age: A Second Look at Bonhoeffer." In *Conflicting Images of Man*, ed. William Nicholls, 133–63. New York: Seabury Press, 1966.

"Two Trial Liturgies Compared." In *Towards a Living Liturgy*, ed. Donald L. Garfield, 27–40. New York: The Church of St. Mary the Virgin, 1969.

"Gospels." In *The Encyclopedia Americana*, 13:99–102. 30 vols. New York: Americana Corporation, 1969.

1970–79

"The Eucharistic Lectionary." In *Worship in Spirit and Truth*, ed. Donald L. Garfield, 17–24. New York: Jarrow Press, 1970.

"Anglican Self-Understanding and Anglican Tradition." In *Oecumenica 1971/72: Tradition in Lutheranism and Anglicanism*, ed. Günther Gassmann and Vilmos Vajta, 175–90. Gütersloh: Gerd Mohn; Minneapolis: Augsburg Publishing House, 1971.

"The Ministry in the New Testament." In *Episcopalians and Roman*

Catholics: Can They Ever Get Together?, ed. Herbert J. Ryan and J. Robert Wright, 88–103. Denville, NJ: Dimension Books, 1972.

"Lectionary" and "Sermon." In *A Dictionary of Liturgy and Worship*, ed. J. G. Davies. London: SCM Press, 1972; also published as *The Westminster Dictionary of Liturgy and Worship*. Philadelphia: Westminster Press, 1972.

"The New Testament in Current Study." In *Contemporary Christian Trends*, ed. William M. Pinson, Jr., and Clyde E. Fant, 103–119. Waco, TX: Word Books, 1972; reprinted in *Perspectives in Religious Studies* 1 (1974): 103–19.

"Das Doppelgebot der Liebe: Ein Testfall für die Echtheitskriterien der Worte Jesu." In *Jesus Christus in Historie und Theologie: Neutestamentliche Festschrift für Hans Conzelmann*, ed. Georg Strecker, 317–29. Tübingen: J. C. B. Mohr (Paul Siebeck), 1975; English translation (with Ilse Fuller) appeared as "The Double Commandment of Love: A Test Case for the Criteria of Authenticity." In Reginald H. Fuller et al, *Essays on the Love Commandment*, 41–56. Philadelphia: Fortress Press, 1978.

"Christmas, Epiphany and the Johannine Prologue." In *Spirit and Light: Essays in Historical Theology in Honor of Edward Nason West*, ed. Madeleine L'Engle and William B. Green, 63–73. New York: Seabury Press, 1976.

"The Incarnation in Historical Perspective." In *Theology and Culture: Essays in Honor of Albert T. Mollegen and Clifford L. Stanley*, ed. W. Taylor Stephenson, 57–66. Anglican Theological Review Supplementary Series 7. Evanston: Anglican Theological Review, 1976.

"Pro and Con: The Ordination of Women in the New Testament." In *Towards a New Theology of Ordination: Essays on the Ordination of Women*, ed. Marianne Micks and Charles P. Price, 1–11. Somerville, MA: Grenno, Haddon, 1976.

"Christian Initiation in the New Testament." In *Made, Not Born: New Perspectives on Christian Initiation and the Catechumenate*, Murphy Center for Liturgical Research, 7–31. Notre Dame: University of Notre Dame, 1976.

"The Nature and Function of New Testament Christology." In *Emerging Issues in Religious Education*, ed. Gloria Durka and Joanmarie Smith, 29–37. New York: Paulist Press, 1976.

"Hebrews." In Reginald H. Fuller et al., *Hebrews, James, I and II Peter, Jude, Revelation*, 1–27. Proclamation Commentaries. Philadelphia: Fortress Press, 1977.

"The Pastoral Epistles." In Reginald H. Fuller et al., *Ephesians, Colossians, 2 Thessalonians, the Pastoral Epistles*, 97–121. Proclamation Commentaries. Philadelphia: Fortress Press, 1978.

"The Son of Man Came to Serve, Not to Be Served." In *Ministering in a Servant Church,* ed. Francis A. Eigo, 45–72. Villanova: Villanova University Press, 1978.

"Classics and the Gospels: The Seminar." In *The Relationships Among the Gospels: An Interdisciplinary Dialogue,* ed. William O. Walker, 173–92. San Antonio: Trinity University Press, 1978.

"The Resurrection Narratives in Recent Study." In *Critical History and Biblical Faith: New Testament Perspectives,* ed. Thomas J. Ryan, 91–107. The College Theology Society Horizons. Villanova: Villanova University Press, 1979.

"Luke and the Theologia Crucis." In *Sin, Salvation, and the Spirit,* ed. Daniel Durken, 214–20. Collegeville, MN: Liturgical Press, 1979.

"Was Paul Baptized?" In *Les Actes des Apôtres: Traditions, rédaction, théologie,* ed. Jacob Kremer, 505–508. Bibliotheca Ephemeridum Theologicarum Lovaniensium 48. Louvain: Leuven University Press, 1979.

1980–89

"The Authority of the Scriptures in Anglicanism." In *Queen's Essays,* ed. J. M. Turner, 109–25. Birmingham: The Queen's College, 1980.

"The Criterion of Dissimilarity: The Wrong Tool?" In *Christological Perspectives: Essays in Honor of Harvey K. McArthur,* ed. Robert F. Berkey and Sarah A. Edwards, 42–48. New York: Pilgrim Press, 1982.

"Confirmation in the Episcopal Church and in the Church of England." In *Confirmation Re-Examined,* ed. Kendig B. Cully, 12–22. Wilton, CT: Morehouse-Barlow, 1982.

"Sukzession oder Ordination? Zum anglikanischen-lutherischen Gespräch." In *Oekumene: Möglichkeiten und Grenzen heute: Festschrift für Oscar Cullmann,* ed. Karlfried Froehlich, 24–31. Tübingen: J. C. B. Mohr (Paul Siebeck), 1982; English translation in *The Anglican* 13 (1982): 2–6.

"The Conception of the Blessed Virgin Mary in Anglican Doctrine and Liturgy." In *Studies and Commentaries,* ed. Richard C. Martin, 18–21. McLean, VA: Society of Mary, 1982.

"Preaching from the Fourth Gospel." In *Biblical Preaching: Expositor's Treasury,* ed. James W. Cox, 280–95. Philadelphia: Westminster Press, 1983.

"Early Catholicism: An Anglican Reaction to a German Debate." In *Die Mitte des Neuen Testaments: Einheit und Vielfalt neutestamentlicher Theologie: Festschrift für Eduard Schweizer zum 70. Geburtstag,* ed. Ulrich Luz and Hans Weder, 34–41. Göttingen: Vandenhoeck and Ruprecht, 1983.

"Foreword." In *A Dubose Reader,* ed. Donald S. Armentrout. Sewanee, TN: University of the South, 1984.

"Historical Criticism and the Bible." In *Anglicanism and the Bible*, ed. Frederick H. Borsch, 143–68. The Anglican Studies Series. Wilton, CT: Morehouse-Barlow, 1984.

"A Note on Luke 1:29 and 38." In *The New Testament Age: Essays in Honor of Bo Reicke*, ed. William C. Weinrich, 1:201–6. 2 vols. Macon, GA: Mercer University Press, 1984.

"Theology of Jesus or Christology?" In *Christology and Exegesis: New Approaches*, ed. Robert Jewett, 105–16. Semeia 30. Decatur, GA: Scholars Press, 1985.

"Easter," "Lord," "Resurrection," "Savior," "Son of God," and "Theology of the New Testament." In *Harper's Biblical Dictionary*, ed. Paul J. Achtemeier. San Francisco: Harper & Row, 1985.

"The Son of Man: A Reconsideration." In *The Living Text: Essays in Honor of E. W. Saunders*, ed. Dennis E. Groh and Robert Jewett, 207–17. Lanham, NY and London: University Press of America, 1986.

"The Classical High Church Reaction to the Tractarians." In *Tradition Renewed: The Oxford Movement Conference Papers*, ed. Geoffrey Rowell, 51–63. London: Darton, Longman & Todd; Allison Park, PA: Pickwick, 1986.

"Lectionary" and "Sermon." In *A New Dictionary of Liturgy and Worship*, ed. J. G. Davies. London: SCM Press, 1986; also published as *The New Westminster Dictionary of Liturgy and Worship*. Philadelphia: Westminster Press, 1986.

"God in the New Testament." In *The Encyclopedia of Religion*, ed. Marcia Eliade, 6:8–11. 16 vols. New York: Macmillan, 1987.

"Scripture." In *The Study of Anglicanism*, ed. Stephen Sykes and John Booty, 79–91. London: SPCK; Philadelphia: Fortress Press, 1988.

"Scripture, Tradition and Priesthood." In *Scripture, Tradition and Reason: A Study in the Criteria of Christian Doctrine: Essays in Honour of R. P. C. Hanson*, ed. Richard J. Bauckham and Benjamin Drewery, 101–114. Edinburgh: T. & T. Clark, 1988.

"Peace in Our Time—eine Aussenansicht." In *Im Dienst an Volk und Kirche! Theologiestudium im Nationalsocialismus Erinnerungen, Darstellungen, Dokumente und Reflexionen zum Tübinger Stift 1930–50*, ed. Siegfried Hermle, Rainer Lächerle and Albrecht Nuding, 86–101. Stuttgart: Quell Verlag, 1988.

"New Testament Theology." In *The New Testament and Its Modern Interpreters*, ed. Eldon J. Epp and George W. MacRae, 565–84. Atlanta, GA: Scholars Press; Philadelphia: Fortress Press, 1989.

"Matthew." In *Harper's Bible Commentary*, ed. James L. Mays, 951–82. San Francisco: Harper & Row, 1988.

IV. Major Reviews

1950–59

Leivestad, Ragnar, *Christ the Conqueror*. Reviewed in *Journal of Theological Studies* n.s. 6 (1955): 131–32.

Munck, Johannes, *Paulus und die Heilsgeschichte*. Reviewed in *Journal of Theological Studies* n.s. 6 (1955): 284–87.

Munck, Johannes, *Christus und Israel: Eine Auslegung von Röm 9–11*. Reviewed in *Journal of Theological Studies* n.s. 9 (1958): 128–9.

Robinson, J. M., *A New Quest of the Historical Jesus*. Reviewed in *Anglican Theological Review* 51 (1959): 232–235.

1970–79

Leander E. Keck, *A Future for the Historical Jesus*. Reviewed in *Interpretation* 28 (1974): 221–22.

"The Synoptic Problem after Ten Years." *Perkins Journal of Theology* 28 (1975): 63–68 (a critical appraisal of the synoptic problem since the 1965 publication of William R. Farmer's *The Synoptic Problem*).

A. T. Hanson, *Studies in Paul's Technique and Theology*. Reviewed in *Virginia Seminary Journal* 27 (1976): 25–26.

"Die neuere Diskussion über das synoptische Problem." *Theologische Zeitschrift* 34 (1978): 123–48 (an extended version of the article in the *Perkins Journal*).

"The Role of Mary in Anglicanism." *Worship* 51 (1977): 214–24 (a review of John Satgé, *Down to Earth*).

Brown, Raymond E., *The Birth of the Messiah*. Reviewed in *Catholic Biblical Quarterly* 40 (1979): 116–20.

V. Translations

1940–49

Bonhoeffer, Dietrich, *The Cost of Discipleship*. New York: Macmillan, 1948.

1950–59

Bonhoeffer, Dietrich, *Letters and Papers from Prison*. London: SCM Press, 1953; New York: Macmillan, 1954. Published originally at SCM as *Prisoner for God*. 3d. ed. rev. and enl., London; SCM Press; New York: Macmillan, 1967.

Bartsch, Hans Werner, ed. *Kerygma and Myth: A Theological Debate with Contributions by Rudolf Bultmann, Ernst Lohmeyer (and others)*. 2 vols. London: SPCK, 1953 and 1962.

Bultmann, Rudolf, *Primitive Christianity in Its Contemporary Setting*. London and New York: Thames and Hudson, 1956; reprinted,

Cleveland: World Publishing Co., 1970; Philadelphia: Fortress Press, 1980.

Jeremias, Joachim, *The Unknown Sayings of Jesus*. London: SPCK, 1957; 2d ed., London: SPCK; New York: Macmillan, 1964.

Loewenich, Walther von, *Modern Catholicism*. London: Macmillan; New York: St. Martin's Press, 1959.

1960–69

Barth, Karl, *Church Dogmatics* III/2, 437–511. Edinburgh: T. & T. Clark, 1960.

Flender, Helmut, *St. Luke: Theologian of Redemptive History* (with Ilse Fuller). London: SPCK; Philadelphia: Fortress Press, 1967.

Moltmann, Jürgen, and Weissbach, Jürgen, *Two Studies in the Theology of Bonhoeffer* (with Ilse Fuller). New York: Charles Scribner's Sons, 1967.

Schweitzer, Albert, *Reverence for Life* (with Ilse Fuller). New York: Harper & Row, 1969.

1970–79

Schottroff, Luise, Reginald H. Fuller, et al., *Essays on the Love Commandment* (with Ilse Fuller). Philadelphia: Fortress Press, 1978.

1980–89

Schweizer, Eduard, *The Holy Spirit* (with Ilse Fuller). Philadelphia: Fortress Press, 1980.

Forthcoming

"Eternal Life" and "Gospel." In *Harper's Dictionary of Christian Education*, ed. Iris V. and Kendig B. Cully.

"New Testament Theology," "Resurrection," and "Jesus." In *Oxford Companion to the Bible*, ed. Bruce M. Metzger.

"Christology." In *Mercer Dictionary of the Bible*, ed. Edgar V. McKnight.

"Romans 9–11 and the Revision of Salvation History." In *Dimensions in the Human Religious Quest* (Joseph Papin *Gedenkschrift*), ed. D. J. Armenti.

ABBREVIATIONS
Ancient Sources

Philo

All.	*Legum Allegoriae*
Conf.	*De Confusione Linguarum*
Det.	*Quod Deterius Potiori insidiari soleat*
Fug.	*De Fuga et Inventione*
Lib. Ant.	*Liber Antiquitatum Biblicarum* (Pseudo-Philo)
Som.	*De Somniis*

Dead Sea Scrolls

CD	Cairo (Genizah text of the) Damascus (Document)
1QS	*Manual of Discipline*

Patristic Literature

Adv. Haer.	Irenaeus, *Adversus Haereses*
Cat. Lect.	Cyril of Jerusalem, *Catechetical Lectures*
Dial.	Justin, *Dialogue with Trypho*
Exc. Theod.	Clement of Alexandria, *Excerpta ex Theodoto*
1 Apol.	Justin, *First Apology*
Ignatius, *Eph.*	Ignatius, *Ephesians*
Pan.	Epiphanius, *Panarion*
Protrep.	Clement of Alexandria, *Protrepticus*
Ref.	Hippolytus, *Refutatio*
Strom.	Clement of Alexandria, *Stromata*

Nag Hammadi Tractates

Ap. Jas.	*Apocryphon of James*
Ap. John	*Apocryphon of John*
Apoc. Adam	*Apocalypse of Adam*
2 Apoc. Jas.	*Second Apocalypse of James*
Apoc. Pet.	*Apocalypse of Peter*
Ep. Pet. Phil.	*Letter of Peter to Philip*
Gos. Eg.	*Gospel of the Egyptians*
Gos. Thom.	*Gospel of Thomas*
Gos. Truth	Gospel of Truth
Hyp. Arch.	*Hypostasis of the Archons*
Orig. World	*On the Origin of the World*
Soph. Jes. Chr.	*Sophia of Jesus Christ*
Treat. Seth	*Second Treatise of the Great Seth*
Tri. Trac.	*Tripartite Tractate*

Trim. Prot.   *Trimorphic Protennoia*

Journals, Reference Works, and Serials

AB	Anchor Bible
ANF	*The Ante-Nicene Fathers,* ed. Alexander Roberts and James Donaldson, 9 vols. (Buffalo: Christian Literature Publishing Co., 1885–97)
ATANT	Abhandlungen zur Theologie des Alten und Neuen Testaments
ATR	*Anglican Theological Review*
BA	*Biblical Archaeologist*
BAGD	W. Bauer, W. F. Arndt, and F. W. Gingrich, *A Greek-English Lexicon of the New Testament and Other Early Christian Literature,* 2d ed., rev. F. W. Gingrich and F. W. Danker (Chicago: Univ. of Chicago Press, 1979)
BDF	F. Blass, A. Debrunner, and R. W. Funk, *A Greek Grammar of the New Testament and Other Early Christian Literature* (Chicago: Univ. of Chicago Press, 1961)
BTB	*Biblical Theology Bulletin*
CBQ	*Catholic Biblical Quarterly*
CG	*The Coptic Gospel Library* (Leiden: E. J. Brill, 1975–)
ConBNT	*Coniectanea biblica, New Testament*
EBib	*Etudes bibliques*
EKKNT	Evangelisch-katholischer Kommentar zum Neuen Testament
EvT	*Evangelische Theologie*
ExpTim	*Expository Times*
FBBS	Facet Books, Biblical Series
FTS	Frankfurter theologische Studien
FRLANT	Forschungen zur Religion and Literatur des Alten und Neuen Testaments
GCS	*Die griechischen christlichen Schriftsteller der ersten drei Jahrhunderte* (Leipzig: Hinrichs, 1897–)
GNT	Grundrisse zum Neuen Testament
HNTC	Harper's New Testament Commentaries
HTKNT	Herders theologischer Kommentar zum Neuen Testament
HTR	*Harvard Theological Review*

IB	The Interpreter's Bible, ed. G. A. Buttrick, 12 vols. (Nashville: Abingdon Press, 1952–57)
ICC	International Critical Commentary
IDB	The Interpreter's Dictionary of the Bible, ed. G. A. Buttrick, 4 vols. (Nashville: Abingdon Press, 1962)
IDBSup	The Interpreter's Dictionary of the Bible, Supplementary Volume, ed. K. Crim (Nashville: Abingdon Press, 1976).
IEJ	Israel Exploration Journal
Int	Interpretation
JAAR	Journal of the American Academy of Religion
JBL	Journal of Biblical Literature
JLW	Jahrbuch für Liturgiewissenschaft
JSNT	Journal for the Study of the New Testament
LCC	Library of Christian Classics
LCL	Loeb Classical Library
LXX	The Septuagint
NCB	New Century Bible
NHS	Nag Hammadi Studies
NIGTC	New International Greek Testament Commentary
NovTSup	Novum Testamentum, Supplements
NPNF(2)	The Nicene and Post-Nicene Fathers: Second Series, ed. Philip Schaff and Henry Wall, 14 vols. (New York: Charles Scribner's Sons, 1890–1900)
NTS	New Testament Studies
PG	Patrologia graeca, ed. J. P. Migne, 161 vols. (Turnhout, Belgium: Brepols, 1857–66)
PL	Patrologia latina, ed. J. P. Migne, 221 vols. (Turnhout, Belgium: Brepols, 1844–1963)
RNT	Regensburger Neues Testament
SBLDS	Society of Biblical Literature Dissertation Series
SBLFA	Studii Biblici Franciscani, Liber Annus
SBT	Studies in Biblical Theology
SJLA	Studies in Judaism and Late Antiquity
SNTSMS	Society for New Testament Studies Monograph Series
TDNT	Theological Dictionary of the New Testament, ed. G. Kittel and G. Friedrich, 10 vols. (Grand Rapids: Wm. B. Eerdmans, 1964–76)
TG1	Theologie und Glaube

THKNT	Theologischer Handkommentar zum Neuen Testament
TLZ	*Theologische Literaturzeitung*
TRE	*Theologische Realenzyklopädie,* ed. Gerhard Krause and Gerald Müller (Berlin: Walter de Gruyter, 1977–)
TS	*Theological Studies*
VC	*Vigiliae Christianae*
ZDMG	*Zeitschrift der deutschen morgenländischen Gesellschaft*
ZNW	*Zeitschrift für die neutestamentliche Wissenschaft*
ZTK	*Zeitschrift für Theologie und Kirche*

Reginald H. Fuller:
The Man, the Churchman, and the Scholar

ILSE FULLER

R. H. F. the Man

I have been asked by the editors to write a brief sketch of my husband's idiosyncrasies. Of course I am delighted to tackle the subject (not the husband—only his peculiarities!), for of idiosyncrasies there is a plethora indeed. In many ways RHF is the proverbial Englishman, a stickler for routine, especially where cups of tea are concerned. But he is also the proverbial professor with his absentmindedness and forgetfulness, and as I understand it from his late mother, he has had both these traits right from birth. For example, in the days when he still smoked his pipe (he does so no longer), he used a different one after each meal. The particular one was of course always mislaid, but he would not dream of using one that happened to be available if it was not the one designated for after that particular meal. So the whole family—we have three daughters—would swarm all over the house in our search, looking down crevices in arm chairs or in the bathrooms, under books piled high on his desk (known as "mining operations") until he was happily united with the missing pipe, could light up, and peace reigned once more.

One of his amazing abilities is his power of concentration, which enables him to read at airports while waiting for planes or during TV commercials, then returning with total recall to watching the news or mystery program once the interruption is over. This is very useful as he never wastes time, but it was not conducive to reliable baby-sitting when our girls were young. When I went out I used to leave our six-year-old in charge of her father and sister as we all knew he would never remember what to serve them for their meals, or burn the soup trying to stir it while reading his book.

In retirement RHF starts his mornings, after reading Morning Prayer of course and taking a walk, about 9:00 a.m. at the typewriter. This he tackles with enormous speed and great imagination. I, who do his typing, refer to him as the only person who can type illegibly! The one thing still harder to decipher, however, is his handwriting, so I am content to change the ribbons on his typewriter or take it to be fixed for him just so he doesn't get tempted to resort to writing his rough drafts by hand. When I am desperate and give up totally trying to find my way among

1

balloons, arrows, and crossed off sections, he will kindly come and dictate to me, but that is not an easy process since he rearranges his thoughts as he goes along, which is liable to make havoc out of sentence structures and paragraphs, thus leaving an occasional footnote in mid-air. Sometimes I point out to him some slight repetition or run-on sentence, but the only thing I might change by myself are items in his personal letters. There I try to convey more of his humanity and make the letters read less like a learned treatise on the decalogue in the New Testament! We both are scared of computers and flatly decline to adjust to anything as modern despite our children and grandchildren's persuasiveness, though we appreciate their concern, of course.

We are sometimes asked how we met. It was in 1940 in London at the occasion of the ordination of a fellow student of Reg's from Queen's College, Birmingham. This man had been a Lutheran pastor in Berlin, then became a refugee from Hitler, and was ordained deacon in the Church of England. I was friendly with another Berliner, a young woman who had belonged to his circle there. She asked me to go along with her for the experience, and when we all got together after the service Reg and I (who come from Vienna, Austria) were the only non-Berliners present. So while the others shared their memories, he and I got talking to each other, and that was the beginning! We exchanged letters and started an almost daily correspondence in German very soon. But what I could have written to him about I cannot imagine, as I was leading a very circumscribed domestic existence then. Reg was going to be ordained deacon by Bishop John Rawlinson in Derby Cathedral about that time, Trinity Sunday 1940, and started his first curacy at Bakewell, so he had much of interest to report. Anyway, after about three months of this, in reply to my description of a visit by a puppy, I got this letter from him: "I hope you realize that you won't be able to have a dog once we are married because of my asthma." I dashed off a letter at once: WHAT do you mean—married??? Luckily the English mails are pretty fast and I got his answer quite soon. His explanation was that he assumed that I would have known that he was going to marry me since he himself had known this from our very first meeting! By then we had actually met only three times, about eighteen hours in all, and no hint of any engagement had been mooted. Once I got over my surprise, I agreed that this sounded like a good idea. I was eighteen and got over the shock both happily and rapidly—but not so my father. As a medical doctor from Vienna, he definitely expected a somewhat more formal approach, more *à la* Jane Austen perhaps, from someone asking for the hand of his only child in marriage!

Back to the subject of owning a dog, which started all this, many years later at Virginia Seminary we were able to have a much beloved poodle who traveled with us all over this continent from one seminary campus to another as we accompanied Reg on his lecture tours. Reg's secretary was instructed to accept the invitations with the proviso that he could only come accompanied by his wife and his dog, and as long as it was in that order, I was quite happy. The dog was called Philo of Alexandria (Virginia, of course, not Egypt), as he came from the local dog shelter, and over the years he figured in many of Reg's lectures, sermons, and exam questions to everyone's amusement. We acquired him after the youngest of our daughters had left for college, which helped us greatly over any "empty nest" complexes. Reg was wont to discuss history with our eldest, music with the middle one, and nature conservation with our youngest. But Philo would listen attentively to the most abstruse dissertations and never gave a yawn!

Of our four grandchildren the middle grandson is very much like Reg in looks and manner. Another striking family resemblance is between Reg and a cousin several times removed living in New Zealand. We only met him last year when Reg was asked to teach for a term in Canberra, Australia. Reg's grandfather's brother went out to New Zealand in 1910 from the ancestral farm near Horsham, Sussex, England, which incidentally is still called "Fullers." They had been yeoman farmers and sometimes smugglers, as the legend goes, with tombstones still extant going back to the early 1700s.

R. H. F. the Churchman

The daily offices and clerical duties (celebrating the eucharist and preaching) have always been the mainstay in Reg's life. As he always says, he was married to the church before he married me, so the church takes precedence. When our daughters want us to visit them, especially for Christmas or Easter, they only have to line up their local rector to invite Reg, and we are sure to come. Of course they know that Reg would spend most of his time in church, but also that he would be happiest with this arrangement. He considers it a particular honor when occasionally he is asked to take part in an ecumenical service. Since his student days in Tübingen, Germany, he has been very aware of the Lutheran Church especially, and although he descended from generations of members of the Church of England, he realized and appreciated that parts of the Lutheran Chruch had shown great courage in standing up to Hitler during the Nazi period, and that many of its members were persecuted by that regime. Reg likes to refer to himself as "Pre-Tractarian High Churchman."

Since RHF was a choir boy from age 9 to 15 in the medieval church in his hometown of Horsham, he became familiar with church music early on. It is a part of him now, and he is especially knowledgeable about Anglican chant and plainsong, which he uses alternatively when singing his office privately at home. He enjoys discussing hymns and anthems with choir masters and organists and has been told frequently how helpful his advice has been to them. He especially favors Bach, Mozart, and Haydn—and in complete contrast also loves to sing pieces from any of the Gilbert and Sullivan comic operas, as he knows most of them by heart.

In 1930 Reg remembers hearing an appeal from the bishops at the Lambeth Conference for boys and young men to offer themselves for the ordained ministry, and he felt called to serve the church as a priest and scholar. Many people were influential in guiding him, perhaps particularly Sir Edwyn Hoskyns, who suggested the study year in Tübingen, and Principal J. O. Cobham whom Reg encountered first while a student at Queen's and then again seven years later when he returned to Queen's as a lecturer. "J. O. C." had introduced many innovations, particularly the westward position, due to his insights into the liturgical movement. Reg was thus one of the first to celebrate in this then novel way, now universally adopted in the Anglican Communion. Freestanding altars were practically unheard of then, but the chapel at Queen's College pioneered it.

In Cambridge, Noel Davey at St. Benet's introduced Reg to the ceremonial of the English use, and Alec Vidler encouraged him to write about his experiences in Germany, his first article to be published. It appeared in 1940 in *Theology*, a monthly publication. This leads me to the next section.

R. H. F. the Scholar

Also at Queen's, Birmingham, as Vice-Principal, was Richard Hanson (later a Bishop in Ireland), who taught Reg Hebrew in exchange for having Reg teach him German, and in untold ways by provocative and stimulating discussions opened up new horizons. He was a wonderful friend, and we all enjoyed his company. We spent two vacations in Ireland with him—one in a rather primitive cottage in a glorious part of County Kerry. There we had no electricity and used a contraption called a Tilley lamp which needed "pumping" 40 times before it worked. Now this proved almost unsurmountably hard—not the pumping as such, but for one of the men to count and the other to keep silent during that time! Usually the one doing the pumping would reach perhaps 34 when the other started off with some subject that could not wait another moment, thus thowing off the counting and exploding the mantle of the Tilley lamp.

We used to get these mantles by the box in Tralee, about one hour's drive, and finally gave up on that and just spent the evenings by candlelight and the peat fire which Richard was very good at tending. Our middle daughter, his godchild, was just a few months old, and Richard was quite heroic in sharing the household with us, as he had never been near a baby before. It was a very happy interlude, away from busy Birmingham and the food rationing then still going on in England. Another reason to remember Richard fondly—he died in December of 1988— in addition to the fact that he and Reg found themselves in agreement on almost every point, despite the distance which separated them geographically for so many years now, was that Richard suggested co-authoring *The Dissuasive*, and so started Reg writing books.

In 1950 we moved to St. David's College, Lampeter, where Reg was invited to the chair of theology and Hebrew, his first professorship. There he was fortunate to come under the guiding influence of H. K. Archdall, the Principal, who encouraged him to write *The Mission and Achievement of Jesus*. We were in Welsh-speaking Wales. Reg learned Prayer Book Welsh in order to take services, and he became active in the surrounding parishes. During this period his translations of Dietrich Bonhoeffer came out, and he started having speaking engagements. Books were hard to get during this post-war period, and we are happy to think that many people who might not have had a chance to do so otherwise heard about Bonhoeffer through Reg.

The next phase came again through Richard Hanson. Reg was offered the professorship of New Testament literature and languages at the Seabury-Western Theological Seminary in Evanston, Illinois. After some thought we accepted, pulled up stakes, and emigrated in 1955 to the United States, where we had a wonderful welcome and settled down very quickly. We loved walking by beautiful Lake Michigan—an entirely new experience, as we had never lived near such a great body of water before—and Evanston was a good place for the growing family. We spent eleven very happy years there, with highly motivated students and much scholarly growth. But in 1966 Reg was invited to be the Baldwin Professor of New Testament at Union Seminary, New York, and he felt it was time to move on, though we were sorry to leave Evanston. So we went from almost rural Evanston, where we never locked car or house during the day, to drug-ridden New York, where nothing was safe from addicts compelled to any measures in order to raise money to satisfy their cravings. This was a shock and things got worse during the student revolt of 1968 at Columbia University just across the street with the burning of students' records, the smashing of plate glass windows, and the general unrest triggered by the war in Vietnam. The Union students were never quite as violent, but the whole atmosphere was charged with tension, and only a handful of students were even remotely interested in studying the New Testament. Reg, who is in his element when teaching—which rates a close second to his priestly duties—was naturally not very happy. But there were other things to compensate. Many of the like-minded students became faithful friends and have remained so through the years. It was during that time too that Fr. Marx, O.S.B., of Collegeville, Minnesota, asked Reg to contribute to *Worship* a series of articles on "Preaching the New Lectionary" which have since been brought out in book form and gone into several editions, in fact became his best-seller, opening up many contacts with Roman Catholics. It occasionally causes surprises when they find out that it was written by a co-author of *The Dissuasive*, but of course Vatican II has changed all that.

While Reg was on the Lectionary Committee of the Episcopal Church and also on the Lutheran-Episcopal Dialogue, both national and international, he had many opportunities for meeting interesting people. Another positive factor about life in New York: we had the most marvelous guest list and a large apartment in which to entertain them. Having Archbishop Michael Ramsey and his congenial wife Joan was one highlight. Then there were two most outstanding dinner parties when Eric Mascall (the Anglican Thomist), John Macquarrie, and Hans Küng engaged in lively ecumenical discussion in which one would have thought Mascall was the RC and Küng the Anglican! On another occasion Hans Küng and Helmut Gollwitzer discussed the Reformation, and Gollwitzer asked Küng whether Luther's career served as a warning to him, to which he replied with fervor: "NO schism"—and all present felt he could have started one tomorrow had he chosen to do so. We had several German-speaking parties. During one of these, Oscar Cullmann mentioned casually how he had had lunch with the Pope (Paul VI) in the Vatican's private quarters where "Protestants" were not normally admitted, and what a pleasant time he had had there. Reg and I often wondered whether such fascinating conversations could really have taken place at our table. Of course we also enjoyed many parties with less eminent guests greatly and think of them fondly too.

In 1972 Reg was invited to be the Molly Laird Downs Professor in The Episcopal Seminary in Alexandria, Virginia, which started an entirely different chapter in our lives. The campus in suburban Washington was safe from muggers and car thieves. We lived once more in a single family home with no immediate neighbors, and Reg had congenial and highly motivated students who were interested in all Reg had to teach, rather than in radical politics. They wanted to be prepared for parish ministry and not for the next protest meeting! We could take almost-rural walks, which gave Reg back his zest for life, especially as it was now centered around the daily chapel services once more. The wonderful influence of

Dean Woods and later of Dean Reid created an environment conducive to scholarly activity. As was our wont, we had many dinner parties. The most outstanding guest who comes to mind was then Archbishop Coggan, among many others of lesser eminence. There were the usual frequent lecture tours and preaching engagements far and near. All this wonderful period was crowned by the never-to-be-forgotten retirement festivities: first a full choral Evensong, followed by a dinner with many guests, including our daughters and families, with speeches and gifts—a marvelous end of this chapter in his life.

After our move into our own home in Richmond, the real traveling began with guest professorships at several seminaries: Union Seminary in Virginia, Nashotah House in Wisconsin, and other theological schools at Austin, Texas; Canberra, Australia,; and Saskatoon, Saskatchewan, Canada—and with speaking/preaching engagements en route to all these delightful places! This gave us a chance to meet many old friends all over the world, to have a great variety of marvelous new experiences, and to make new friends in many places.

I go along with Reg, generally speaking, as I refer to myself as his "mobile catering and laundry service." Scholar that he is, he has resisted successfully ever learning how to use an automatic washing machine. He is really efficient at making cups of tea, and also peels his own apple, but that is the total of his domesticity. We love visiting but have been very fortunate to settle down so happily in our house—full of books, naturally! Now he can do whatever he chooses we to, but that turns out to be just what he has done all his life anyway. We have been very fortunate. . . .

Nazareth and Sepphoris:
Insights into Christian Origins

THOMAS R. W. LONGSTAFF*

You are the light of the world.
A city set on a hill cannot be hid.[1]

Ancient Nazareth was located in the hill country of the lower Galilee just north of the fertile Jezreel Valley. The village itself lay on the eastern slopes of one of those hills where water and good agricultural land were conveniently accessible. A short climb to the summit of the hill would have opened up a striking vista to one looking northwest toward Acco and the sea. There in the beautiful Beit Natofa Valley was Roman Sepphoris, which sat perched like a bird atop a hill in the center of the wide plain below, not more than four miles distant. It can be suggested that, if the saying attributed to Jesus in Matthew 5:14 is authentic, he may have had Sepphoris in mind as the city set on a hill which could not be hid.

Despite the close proximity of Nazareth to Sepphoris, few scholars have explored the significance of the relationship between these two for understanding the context of the life and teaching of Jesus or the emergence of Christianity.[2] At least since the mid-nineteenth century it has been commonplace to picture the Galilee of Jesus and his disciples as a rural backwater of Jewish culture, unspoiled by Hellenism or other aspects of urban life in the first century.[3] Furthermore, the cultural milieu within which Christianity was understood to develop, at least in its earliest stages in Palestine, was similarly thought to be a simple, rural

---

* Thomas R. W. Longstaff is Professor of Religion, Colby College, Waterville, Maine.
[1] Matthew 5:14 (RSV).
[2] Shirley Jackson Case is a notable exception in this regard; see his *Jesus: A New Biography* (Chicago: The University of Chicago Press, 1927), 201ff.; see also Richard A. Batey, "Jesus and the Theatre," *NTS* 30 (1984): 563–584. More typical are the comments of Günther Bornkamm, *Jesus of Nazareth* (New York: Harper and Brothers, 1960), 54; Martin Dibelius, *Jesus* (Philadelphia: Westminster Press, 1949); and Ethelbert Stauffer, *Jesus and His Story* (New York: Alfred A. Knopf, 1960).
It should be acknowledged that the same claim could be made about the importance of Sepphoris for Jewish history. Again, few scholars have explored the significance of this city for understanding developments in Judaism between the destruction of Jerusalem in 70 C.E. and the beginning of the Byzantine period in about 350 C.E. However, since this essay appears in a volume dedicated to Reginald H. Fuller to mark his monumental contributions to the study of the New Testament and early Christianity, it seems appropriate to focus attention on the importance of Sepphoris for those areas of concern.
[3] See especially Ernest Renan, *The Life of Jesus* (New York: Modern Library, 1927, 1955). Renan's *Vie de Jésus* was first published in 1863.

one. This new religious movement was assumed to have its appeal primarily to a relatively unlettered and unsophisticated population. It is the purpose of this essay to challenge that popular, prevailing view of Christian origins and to suggest instead that the life of Jesus and the first stages of Christian history in Palestine should both be seen against the background of a thoroughly urban environment which was a major component of Galilean life in the first century.[4]

While it is true that in these early years Nazareth was no more than a rather small village, it is virtually certain that this village lay well within the sphere of the urban influence of Sepphoris. It has been noted above that Sepphoris would have been clearly visible from the top of the hill on the slopes of which Nazareth was built. It may now be added that it would have been easy to walk from one settlement to the other in about an hour and a half. Furthermore, ancient sources indicate that the territory falling under the administrative control of Sepphoris extended southeast to Mt. Tabor. Nazareth, therefore, would have been within the region of Sepphoris' jurisdiction. The citizens of Nazareth undoubtedly would have turned to Sepphoris for such governmental services as they required. It is also likely that a considerable amount of the economic and cultural activity of those citizens was related to this nearby urban center as well. To understand the cultural milieu of ancient Nazareth, therefore, one must consider the influence of Sepphoris to which it was intimately related as a dependent village.[5]

I. Sepphoris and Its Influence

Sepphoris is never mentioned in the Bible; however, it is frequently referred to by Josephus and in later rabbinic literature.[6] The rabbis seem to have believed that Sepphoris was built as a walled city in the time of Joshua the son of Nun. Since archaeological excavation has consistently

---

[4] This view of Jesus and of early Christianity may well be, in part, the product of the tendency, both in America and in Europe, to romanticize the rural, pastoral environment and to contrast it sharply with the "sinful city." Certainly the idealization of rural life has made the prevailing understanding of Jesus and of early Christianity more comfortable and attractive. An interesting analysis of this tendency in American culture can be found in Leo Marx, *The Machine in the Garden* (Oxford: Oxford Univ. Press, 1964).

[5] The view that Nazareth was one of the dependent villages of Sepphoris is also suggested by Josephus' comment that "Sepphoris [was] situated in the heart of Galilee, surrounded by numerous villages, and in a position, without any difficulty, had she been so inclined, to make a bold stand against the Romans." *Vita* 346. All references to Josephus in this essay are to the text and translation published in the Loeb Classical Library by the Harvard University Press.

[6] Frederic Manns provides an excellent summary of references to Sepphoris in "Essais sur le Judeo-Christianism," *Studium Biblicum Franciscanum, Analecta 12* (Jerusalem: Franciscan Printing Press, 1977), 165–190.

yielded a small number of shards from every historical period beginning with Iron II, this tradition may be firmly grounded in history.[7] The first written mention of Sepphoris is to be found in Josephus' account of the Hasmonean period. He indicates that Ptolemy Lathyrus, King of Cyprus, was at war with Israel during the reign of Alexander Jannaeus in 103 B.C.E. After attacking Acco-Ptolemais, Ptolemy turned inland and captured Asochis which was not more than five miles distant from Sepphoris. Then he laid siege to Sepphoris itself but was unable to take this city.[8] If, as seems probable, Sepphoris was a strongly fortified city at this time, it is also likely, as James Strange has suggested, that it was Greek in character, as were other cities of the region, including Ptolemais, Shikmona, Dora, Strato's Tower, Joppa, and Azotus (Ashdod).[9]

Virtually nothing is known about the situation in Sepphoris at the time Rome annexed the area in 63 B.C.E. In about 55 B.C.E. Aulus Gabinius, the Proconsul of Syria, located one of the five Roman Councils of Judea at Sepphoris.[10] Since this was the only one of the five located in Galilee, it serves as solid evidence of the importance of the city at this time. Subsequently, in the winter of 39/38 B.C.E., Herod the Great seized the city after it was abandoned by his rival Antigonas in the civil war that marked his coming to power.[11] It is generally accepted and highly probable that Herod maintained the city as an administrative center in the north throughout his reign.

Herod's death in 4 B.C.E. was the occasion for anti-Roman factions in Palestine to muster support for a revolt against Rome. That many of the residents of Sepphoris were displeased by Herod's transformation of the city into a Roman administrative center, and therefore joined the rebellion, seems likely in view of the events that followed. Josephus reports that "at Sepphoris in Galilee Judas, son of Ezechias . . . , raised a considerable body of followers, broke open the royal arsenals, and, having armed his companions, attacked the other aspirants to power."[12] The revolt, however, was an unsuccessful one. Within a short period of time Rome was again in control of Palestine. Sepphoris fared particularly badly in these events. Varus, Legate of Syria, "sent a detachment of his army into the region of Galilee adjoining Ptolemais, under the command

---

[7] It must be acknowledged, however, that at the time this essay was written neither the University of South Florida's Excavations at Sepphoris nor the Joint Sepphoris Project of Duke University and the Hebrew University of Jerusalem had yet uncovered any structures which can confidently be dated prior to the Early Roman period.

[8] Josephus, *Antiquities* 13.338.

[9] James F. Strange, "Sepphoris," *The Anchor Bible Dictionary* (forthcoming, Garden City, NY: Doubleday & Company).

[10] Josephus, *The Jewish War* 1.170.

[11] *The Jewish War* 1.304.

[12] *The Jewish War* 2.56; cf. *Antiquities* 17.271. The presence of a royal arsenal at Sepphoris is further evidence of the importance of this center in Early Roman times.

of his friend Gaius; the latter routed all who opposed him, captured and burnt the city of Sepphoris and reduced its inhabitants to slavery."[13]

Sepphoris did not remain in ruins for long. Herod Antipas, appointed tetrarch of Galilee, at once rebuilt the city on a grand scale. Josephus indicates that Antipas "fortified Sepphoris to be the ornament of all Galilee, and called it Autocratoris."[14] Although there is some debate over the meaning of the term "autocratoris" (whether or not it should be interpreted as "capital"), it seems most likely that early in the first century of the Common Era Sepphoris did in fact serve as Herod Antipas' capital of Galilee. This distinction may have been transferred, for a time, to Tiberius. But during the administration of the Procurator Felix (52–60), shortly before the revolt of 66–70, Sepphoris again became the capital of Galilee, a change that produced some strongly negative reactions in Tiberius. Indeed, the very strength of the Tiberians' insistence that their city had always been superior to Sepphoris may lend some credence to the claim that Sepphoris had earlier been the capital.[15]

However the debate referred to in the previous paragraph is resolved, Sepphoris was undoubtedly an impressive city in Antipas' time. Josephus frequently refers to it as the "largest" or "strongest" city in Galilee.[16] Other texts indicate that Sepphoris was a walled city and contained a fortress (referred to by the rabbis of the period as a "castra"), a royal bank, archives, an upper and lower market, temples, synagogues, inns, academies, and, of course, the palace of Herod Antipas.[17] Although much remains to be done, archaeological excavation provides further evidence that Sepphoris was a thriving urban center in the Roman and Byzantine periods. In 1931 Leroy Waterman exposed the central vomitorium, the stage, and a portion of the cavea of a large theater with a seating capacity of approximately 3,500 persons.[18] Recent excavation has dated this structure to the Early Roman period and probably to the time of Herod Antipas.[19] Remains of other elaborate structures, public and private, dating to the Early Roman, Middle Roman, and Late Roman

---

[13] *The Jewish War* 2.68. Cf. *Antiquities* 17.289.

[14] *Antiquities* 18.27.

[15] Josephus, *Vita* 37–39.

[16] *Vita* 232, 346; *The Jewish War* 2.511.

[17] For a more complete discussion and lists of the relevant texts, the reader is referred to Stewart Miller, *Studies in the History and Tradition of Sepphoris*, SJLA 37 (Leiden: E. J. Brill, 1984), and James F. Strange, "Two Aspects of the Development of Universalism in Christianity: The First to the Fourth Centuries," *Religion and the Quest for Global Order* (forthcoming, New York: Paragon House, 1990).

[18] Leroy Waterman, et al., *Preliminary Report of the University of Michigan Excavations at Sepphoris, Palestine, in 1931* (Ann Arbor: The University of Michigan Press, 1931).

[19] James F. Strange and Thomas R. W. Longstaff, "Sepphoris (Sippori), 1985 (II)," *IEJ* 35 (1985): 297–299; "Sepphoris (Sippori), 1986 (II)," *IEJ* 37 (1987): 278–280; cf. Eric Meyers, Ehud Netzer, and Carol Meyers, "Sepphoris (Sippori), 1986 (I)," *IEJ* 37 (1987): 275–278.

periods have also been exposed and indicate that the city was an important one from the time of its reconstruction by Herod Antipas until its subsequent destruction in the mid-fourth century, probably after an unsuccessful revolt against the emperor Gallus Caesar in 351.

Herod Antipas' reconstruction of Sepphoris marked its transition from a Greek city to a Roman one. Antipas had been raised in Rome[20] and undoubtedly understood the character of a Roman city in some detail. The impressive building projects undertaken by him and his successors suggest that they wanted, to the degree that it was possible, to replicate Roman culture in Galilee. More important than the architecture, perhaps, was the social organization that this entailed. Rome extended the boundaries of her empire as much (perhaps more) by the implantation of Roman institutions as by military conquest. Thus, throughout her domain, Rome emphasized her presence and exerted her influence not only in the structures of government but also through the gymnasia, theaters, hippodromes, stadia, and temples. The degree to which Herod Antipas was successful in his attempt to transform Sepphoris into a Roman city may be indicated by the fact that throughout the first century Sepphoris is known for its pro-Roman, or at least pacifist, stance.[21] Although it has been suggested, with appropriate caution, that "Sepphoris may have changed its course of action by the time of the second revolt (132–135 C.E.) . . . [perhaps because] its population was enlarged after the first war by refugees from more nationalistic Jewish centers,"[22] any such change in attitude seems to have been short lived. Well before the end of the second century (when Sepphoris was known as Diocaesarea) good relationships between the citizens of Sepphoris and the Roman administration had been restored. These good relations seem to have continued without serious interruption until the eve of the downfall of Sepphoris in 351 C.E.

Throughout this period the population of Sepphoris, while mixed, was predominantly Jewish. This is suggested both by the literary evidence and archaeological excavation on the acropolis. A number of houses with water installations that may confidently be identified as *mikvaot* and a few artifacts, notably fragments of incense shovels found in the University of South Florida's Soundings at Sepphoris in 1983, provide evidence of Jewish occupation. At the same time pagan artifacts, particularly small statues or figurines, and an abundance of pig bone in domestic refuse indicate that the Jewish population lived in close

---

[20]   *Antiquities* 17.20.

[21]   Among the numerous passages in Josephus, see especially *The Jewish War* 2.511, 629, 645–646, and *Vita* 30, 37–39, 103–111, 123–124, 346–348, 384, and 411.

[22]   Eric M. Meyers, Ehud Netzer, and Carol L. Meyers, "Sepphoris: 'Ornament of All Galilee,'" *BA* 49 (1986): 155.

association with non-Jews.[23] During the first century the city was known for its Sadducean or priestly presence, but in the second century a more prominent Pharisaic or rabbinic element emerged. By the end of the second century Sepphoris was the seat of an influential academy; it was here that the famous Rabbi Judah ha-Nasi spent the last seventeen years of his life and here that the Mishnah was most likely compiled. It was not until after Sepphoris was rebuilt as a Byzantine city following the mid-fourth century destruction that a Christian population of any significant size was evident at this site. Nevertheless, a small, and not entirely uninfluential, Christian presence at Sepphoris in the earlier centuries is suggested in several texts.[24]

II. The Galilean Setting of Jesus' Ministry

If the life of Jesus and the origins of Christianity are at all to be related to Nazareth and its environs, these events must be seen against the backdrop of a culture that was both urban and urbane. Although some characteristics of rural life surely continued to be present in Galilee during the first three centuries of the Common Era, the effect of Roman urbanization was also a fact of everyday life throughout the region. The presence of Roman culture expressed both in institutions and ideals was a pervasive one throughout Lower Galilee and surely affected the dependent villages as well as the cities upon which they relied.

Although this is an essay on Nazareth and Sepphoris, it must be acknowledged that the gospels frequently place Jesus and his disciples in the vicinity of the lake (the Sea of Galilee) and particularly at Capernaum. Sites in this area also figure prominently in early Christian history. It is important to note that these places also lay within the sphere of influence of sizeable cities and must, therefore, have felt the influence of urban, Roman culture. Tiberius, on the western shore of the lake, has been mentioned above and was another thoroughly Roman city built by Herod Antipas in the early decades of the first century of the Common Era.[25] It vied with Sepphoris in Galilee for prominence and for a time also served

---

[23]   James F. Strange and Thomas R. W. Longstaff, "Sepphoris (Sippori), 1983," *IEJ* 34 (1984): 51–52; "Sepphoris (Sippori), 1985 (II)," *IEJ* 35 (1985): 297–299; "Sepphoris (Sippori), 1986 (II)," *IEJ* 37 (1987): 278–280; James F. Strange, Dennis E. Groh, and Thomas R. W. Longstaff, "Sepphoris (Sippori), 1987 (II)," *IEJ* 38 (1988): 188–190; "Sepphoris (Sippori), 1988," *IEJ* 39 (1989): 104–106; Eric Meyers, Ehud Netzer, and Carol Meyers, "Sepphoris (Sippori), 1986 (I)," *IEJ* 37 (1987): 275–278; "Sepphoris: 'Ornament of All Galilee," *BA* 49 (1986): 153–167.

[24]   For a useful summary of these, see Eric M. Meyers, Ehud Netzer, and Carol L. Meyers, "Sepphoris: 'Ornament of All Galilee,'" *BA* 49 (1986): 159–160.

[25]   *Antiquities* 18.36–38.

as the capital of the region. Magdala, just north of Tiberius, likewise seems to have been a city of some size and one which also served as a regional capital.[26] Even Bethsaida, on the northeast shore of the lake, must be reckoned a city and not a rural village.[27]

Recent attention to Galilee, both in the analysis of literary texts and the excavation of archaeological sites, has produced a clearer and more detailed understanding of this region. In this revised view, Galilee emerges as an area transformed by the presence of Roman cities and influenced by Roman institutions and ideals. Sepphoris, frequently mentioned in post-biblical texts and now under excavation, provides a particularly good example of how the process of urbanization affected a mixed population, both in the city itself and in its dependent villages. This information will inform those who seek to interpret the context in which rabbinic Judaism and Christianity took shape. It is no longer possible to think of Jesus as a simple peasant from Nazareth (dare one say "a good old country boy"?) nor to describe the disciples as "hillbillies from Galilee."[28] Their lives, and those of the many who followed them, were certainly affected by the all-pervasive presence of the Roman city.

III. Summary

This essay should end with a summary—and a note of caution. It has been proposed above that a romanticized picture of Galilee as a rural backwater of Jewish culture, unspoiled by Hellenism or other aspects of urban life, has been uncritically accepted as the background for understanding the life of Jesus and the context of early Christianity. In the discussion the urban character of Galilee has been emphasized, although it has been recognized that some aspects of rural life survived, especially in smaller villages. While this essay argues that the influence of Roman urbanization was all-pervasive, it should not be understood to romanticize urban culture. While urban culture offers many advantages, there are disadvantages as well. Urbanization often brings with it a measure of oppression. The gap between the wealthy and the poor is frequently widened. Those who thrive in the city often do so at the expense of those in the dependent villages who do not. This is not to suggest that these

---

[26] James F. Strange, "Magdala," *IDBSup* 561. See also Virgilio C. Corbo, "Scavi Archeologici a Magdala (1971–1973)," *SBFLA* 24 (1974): 1–37.

[27] *Antiquities* 18.28; cf. *The Jewish War* 2.168.

[28] Pinchas Lapide, *The Resurrection of Jesus: A Jewish Perspective* (Minneapolis: Augsburg Publishing House, 1983), 129. Lapide is here arguing that the disciples were not sophisticated theologians and that for them the resurrection was a simple and literal fact. Nevertheless, his choice of words probably does reflect the stereotypic perception that this essay seeks to dispel.

villages were unaffected by Roman urbanization. It is to suggest that the affects of that process are yet to be fully understood and assessed. The attention that has recently been focused on Galilee has yielded a better understanding of that region in the first centuries of the Common Era. But there is more to be done before the relationship of Roman cities to the surrounding territories is clearly understood. Defining the relationship between Nazareth and Sepphoris may well be a major key to understanding the life and teaching of Jesus and the setting of early Christianity.

The Message of Jesus to the Poor and the Powerful

SHERMAN E. JOHNSON*

This essay, offered in honor of a distinguished interpreter of the gospels, will attempt to test three hypotheses:

1. Jesus' *promises* are directed primarily to the weak, i.e., the poor, hungry, sorrowful, and rejected.

2. His *demands* are made on the strong. These can include persons of more or less power and prestige, but in this case the "powerful" may be anyone who summons enough strength to respond to Jesus' challenge.

3. Those who receive the promises are treated as though they have this strength, and thereby they become strong.[1]

It is necessary to identify, if possible, the persons or groups to whom Jesus made promises and upon whom he laid demands. There are two problems. (1) Who are the "poor" and the powerful? (2) In each case, when Jesus speaks an imperative or makes a demand, is he addressing his hearers generally or his intimate disciples?

The sources considered here are mainly the Synoptic Gospels and the *Gospel of Thomas*. The evangelists often indicate an audience, but this represents their own judgment and is usually in the light of their theologies and for the purpose of adapting Jesus' teaching to the church's needs. Their material came originally from Jesus' message. He spoke on many occasions to different people and perhaps said similar things in various ways, and the tradition was handed down orally, not only through intimate disciples (conventionally "the Twelve") but perhaps also by others, then mediated by teachers and by prophets who heard him speaking as the risen Lord, until something was written down. Who can imagine how many times the sayings were discussed in the course of the oral tradition?[2]

Therefore one must rely principally on the earliest recoverable form

---

* Sherman E. Johnson is Dean Emeritus and Professor Emeritus of New Testament, The Church Divinity School of the Pacific, Berkeley, California.
[1] It is not easy to find the right words. Here I use "power" and "strength" interchangeably in a good or neutral sense, as an equivalent of ἐξουσία, which I contrast with force, domination, and violence.
[2] Werner H. Kelber, *The Oral and the Written Gospel* (Philadelphia: Fortress Press, 1983), esp. pp. 19–21.

of the parables and the logia or aphorisms, which are sometimes embodied apophethegms and other narrative pieces.

I. The Address to the Poor in the Beatitudes

As a point of departure I take the beatitudes of Matthew 5:1–12 and Luke 6:20b–23. Luke's form probably represents a stage prior to that of Matthew, for the congratulations are expressed in the second person and are unconditional.[3] There is a further question about the beatitude on the persecuted, which is longer.[4] Therefore we concentrate on the first three—to the poor, the hungry, and those who mourn. They will be fed and laugh, and this is probably part of the first promise, participation in the Reign of God.

Matthew's beatitudes imply certain conditions, e.g., being poor in spirit, hungering for righteousness or vindication, etc., and here the "poor" are like the pious *anawim* or *aniyyim* of the Psalms.[5] This interpretation is not necessarily wrong, but it is necessary to ask what "poor" might mean in the context of Jesus' ministry. Here I depend on recent sociological and cultural-anthropological studies.[6]

The "poor" with whom Jesus was concerned can be defined only by contrast with the strong. In the first century world society had a hierarchical structure of rulers, priests, merchants, artisans, peasants, and outcasts who were outside of this structure. The basic unit was the family, in which the father was "owner" of his wife and children. The honor of any individual was bound up with that of his or her family.

Being respectable or self-respecting had little or nothing to do with one's financial status. One who belonged to a secure family in any class was thus "strong." From this point of view, James and John were such, πένηται, not really in poverty, for their father Zebedee owned boats and had hired men (Mark 1:19–20). The day laborers of Matthew 20:1–13 might be actually destitute. Mary and Martha were probably secure persons. At least one of the women who followed Jesus and served him

---

[3] Günther Bornkamm, "Der Aufbau der Bergpredigt," *NTS* 24 (1978):419–32.

[4] John Dominic Crossan, *In Fragments: The Aphorisms of Jesus* (New York: Harper & Row, 1983), 169–71. *Gos. Thom.* 68–69a contains beatitudes on the persecuted, and 69b on the hungry.

[5] See, e.g., Pss. 10:9, 17–18; 14:6; 25:9.

[6] Bruce J. Malina, *The New Testament World* (Atlanta: John Knox Press, 1981), esp. pp. 35, 83–85. The English word "poor" can translate either of two Greek nouns. The πτωχοί or indigent had nothing and lived a hand-to-mouth existence. The πένηται might include small shopkeepers, artisans, and farmers who used their own tools; see L. W. Countryman, *The Rich Christian in the Chruch of the Early Empire* (New York: Edwin Mellen Press, 1980), 25.

belonged in a higher social stratum, Joanna the wife of Chuza, Herod
Antipas' ἐπίτροπος (Luke 8:3).

The really weak or poor people were those who had fallen out of the
social structure. Some did not have enough to eat or drink. There were
beggars like Lazarus (Luke 16:19–31); others were burdened with debts
they could not pay. Widows and orphans might be among these; certainly
the blind, the deaf-mute, the maimed, the insane; in addition, lepers and
the woman with the hemorrhage—both of which were ritually unclean.
There were also prostitutes, though Mary Magdalene was probably not
one of these. The seven demons with which she had been afflicted may
have been physical and mental ailments.

In addition the Pharisees expressed contempt for certain groups
which from their point of view were outcasts: tax-collectors, prostitutes,
and perhaps shepherds. Indeed, "no country person is pious" (*Mishnah,
Aboth* 2:6). In antiquity the world's goods were perceived as limited, not
an infinitely expandable GNP; thus one who was self-made, like an
occasional tax-collector, or those who got rich through bequests, were
"malefactors of great wealth" and thus not respectable.

Gentiles, like Pilate, and Samaritans were entirely outsiders. Members of the family of Herod the Great, though powerful, were in an
ambiguous position.

It seems likely, therefore, that the "poor" of the beatitudes are those
who have suffered great calamities or are even outcasts from society.
Many of the persons in the miracle stories who have been healed of
physical or mental ailments are thus among "the poor." Blessings come to
them usually with no condition expressed.

The tradition contains other macarisms, and one is especially appropriate to mention here. "Happy are the eyes that see what you see" (Luke
10:23–24-Matt. 13:16–17). This is a new age, which prophets and kings
could not see. The blessing is not reserved to the future.[7]

II. Promises to the Poor in the Parables

The parables, which point to the Reign of God rather than describing
it, should give the best clue to what is promised to the poor in the new
age.

The parable of the Sower (Mark 4:3–8//Matt. 13:3–8//Luke 8:5–8;
Gos. Thom. 9) seems to contrast the smallness of beginnings with the

---

[7]   Luke 10:21//Matt. 11:25 is perhaps related to this: what was hidden from the wise and
prudent has been revealed to babes. The "comfortable words" of Matt. 11:28–30, which
suggest Ben Sira's invitation (Sir. 51:23–27) may not have been part of Q (cf. J. Crossan, *In
Fragments*, 193) but fit well with the other promises to the poor.

tremendous result. As Crossan says, it expresses the themes of gift and surprise. He regards the Hid Treasure (Matt. 13:44; *Gos. Thom.* 109) as the key parable, for it combines also the themes of hiddenness and mystery, and action. The Fig Tree (Mark 13:28) and the Leaven (Matt. 13:33//Luke 13:20–21) also exhibit hiddenness. Two others are closely related to the Treasure, the Costly Pearl (Matt. 13:45; *Gos. Thom.* 76), and the Great Fish (*Gos. Thom.* 8). In all these, the past is shattered and the future irrelevant, for in the real time of the present there is a new world of life and action. The Lost Sheep (Luke 15:3–7//Matt. 18:12–13) and the Lost Coin (Luke 15:8–10) are, like the Pearl, parables of discovery and joy.[8]

What these parables add to the beatitudes is the consciousness of a new era in the relationship between God and humanity, so glorious that ordinary words cannot describe it. Those who benefit from it are suggested by the pictures of a farmer sowing seed, a fisherman, a peasant digging in the field, a merchant who sells everything to buy a pearl and has nothing left, a poor woman who has lost a coin, and another woman baking bread. These figures are probably not chosen by accident.

Although the new age is so indescribably glorious, the parables of reversal, as Crossan calls them,[9] encourage no illusions and seem to teach this: "The Reign of God, the way in which God operates in the world, is not necessarily what you might think appropriate." Sometimes it is, but this cannot be guaranteed. In the parable of the Laborers in the Vineyard (Matt. 20:1–15) the boss acts in a way that might lead to labor troubles and to his being criticized by other vineyard operators. This overturns conventional ideas of justice, though it may suggest, as many commentators say, that God is more generous than we are.

Mention of a vineyard evokes the Old Testament metaphors of viticulture. If Crossan is correct, the original parable of the Wicked

---

[8] John Dominic Crossan, *In Parables* (New York: Harper & Row, 1973), 34–52. There are other approaches and ways of classifying the parables, but Crossan's work is especially illuminating with respect to the poor. In this essay I do not consider the opponents of Jesus, who are mainly the "strong" who rejected his message. Crossan holds that the parables are not responses to their criticism of Jesus; rather they evoked the opposition (pp. 74–75). Reginald H. Fuller, *The Mission and Achievement of Jesus*, SBT 12 (Chicago: Alex R. Allenson, 1954), 20–49, criticized C.H. Dodd's "realized eschatology"; the Reign of God is a future event. In *Preaching the New Lectionary: The Word of God for the Church Today* (Collegeville: Liturgical Press, 1974) he approaches the concept of "inaugurated eschatology": "Jesus' message is that God is beginning to act eschatologically—with his own appearance—and will consummate that action in the not too distant future" (p. 313, on Mark 1:15). Crossan's judgment, *In Parables*, 23–36, which I find persuasive, is that in the parables Jesus' concept of time is not linear; rather, "Time is . . . the present of God" (p. 31); the "normalcy of past-present-future is rudely but happily shattered" (p. 34). However one understands Jesus' eschatology, his first hearers heard the promises as something they could immediately grasp.
[9] Ibid., 53–78.

Vineyard Workers (Mark 12:1–12 and parallels; *Gos. Thom.* 63) told of a brutal murder that went unpunished.[10] The story of the Dishonest Manager (Luke 16:1–7) is almost as bad, for the rascal gets away with his scheme. If verse 8 is part of Jesus' parable, it suggests that the "sons of light" ought to be as intelligent though not as wicked. Luke was obviously puzzled and added several sayings about wealth (16:9–13).

Poor people who heard these parables could be led to reflect that they might not get equal justice in this life, though they might occasionally experience unexpected blessings. They are encouraged to seek the Pearl of Great Price; at the same time they are thrown back upon trust in God, who "sends the rain on the just and the unjust" (Matt. 5:45) and is "kind to the unthankful and the evil" (Luke 6:35).

III. Conditions for Receiving the Promises

Matthew's form of the beatitudes indicates certain qualities in those who are to benefit from the promises. One of the most significant of them is that they are πραεῖς, which means not so much that they are meek, but rather of lowly station. The beatitude form is found elsewhere in the synoptic tradition, several times in Q, never in Mark, and it usually involves some conditions. Macarisms on loyal and watchful slaves are found in parables to be discussed later. Jesus counts that person happy who invites to dinner those who cannot reciprocate the invitation (Luke 14:14).

Another macarism, contained in a short dialogue, "Happy are those who hear the word of God and keep it" (Luke 11:28; *Gos. Thom.* 79a), has the moral emphasis on doing which is found elsewhere in the Jesus tradition and is standard in Judaism. It is Jesus' answer to a woman who cries out a blessing on Jesus' mother. Similarly, at the visit of Jesus' mother and brothers (Mark 3:20–21, 30–35; *Gos. Thom.* 99), Jesus' true family consists of those who do the will of God.

Conditions are not usually stated in the parables, though they may be implied. In the parables of the Hid Treasure, the Pearl, and the Great Fish, the heroes have one quality of life or attitude of mind in that they are ready to renounce everything else to have their greatest desire. These parables are radical, and one asks if they have a special application to Jesus' intimate, full-time disciples.

Crossan's Parables of Action intrinsically presume a demand to act, to keep on praying, wait patiently, not to rely on wealth, to extend the invitation (or accept it), and make preparation before it is too late.

---

[10]   Ibid., 96.

Among these the Servant parables are a special sub-group which portrays good and bad servants or slaves.[11] A doorkeeper must be on watch because his master will return (Mark 13:33–37) or because of the danger of a burglar (Luke 12:29–30; Matt. 24:43). The reward of faithful slaves is that the master himself will serve them dinner (Luke 12:35–38). These parables might apply to any follower of Jesus, but Luke 12:41 applies them to persons in authority. The faithful majordomo who provides the daily ration for his fellows will be set over all the householder's property (12:42–44).

One can apply the parables of the Talents (Matt. 25:14–30) or the Minas (Luke 19:13, 15–26) to the "talents" which everyone may have. This is useful as far as it goes, but only an obvious piece of prudential wisdom. In the context of Jesus' ministry these parables best refer to stewards to whom the message of the Reign of God has been committed. The one who makes the most of what he or she has will be given greater responsibilities. The parable of the Unmerciful Slave (Matt. 18:23–38) could apply to anyone, but since Matthew 18:21–22 puts it in the context of a dialogue with Peter, the evangelist thinks of it as especially important for leaders in the church.

Reward, however, is not automatic or measurable. The true slave is not expecting it: "When you do all the things prescribed for you, say, 'We are [only] good-for-nothing slaves, we have done what we ought to do'" (Luke 17:10; cf. the parable in 17:7–9, which balances 12:35–38).

IV. Demands on Everyone

The recorded teaching of Jesus contains many imperatives.[12] We need not linger over those that are echoes of Old Testament and traditional Jewish teaching except to note that their selection discloses Jesus' interests and that he often develops or sharpens an element of proverbial wisdom; for example, action and not mere profession; repentance, faith and trust; be a light to the nations; judge as you would choose to be judged.

Jesus does not refrain from using the rough and ready distinction between "good" and "bad" people (cf. Matt. 5:45); thus he has not come to summon the "righteous" but "sinners" (Mark 2:17). But his distinction between the two groups is unconventional and almost ironical. Further, the sayings on good and bad trees and figs from thistles (Luke 6: 43–45//Matt. 7:16–20; 12:33–35; cf. Gos. Thom. 43b, 45; Sir. 27:6) do not

---

[11] Ibid., 96–111.

[12] Paul S. Minear, Commands of Christ (Nashville: Abingdon Press, 1972), is a form-critical study of the demands, including the radical ones.

imply that some are ontologically good or bad; rather, they have to do with the inner disposition or intention that determines one's action.

Thus the motive for prayer, fasting, and almsgiving must be service of God, not enhancement of one's reputation (Matt. 6:1–8, 16–18). The antitheses of Matthew 5:21–48 are a more radical expression of a similar theme. These sayings require a totally new attitude, not only to Torah but to one's whole existence. They are not law in any narrow sense but are Torah in the broad sense, and they describe the style of life of the Reign of God, or, as Krister Stendahl expresses it, "a messianic intensification."[13] Georg Kretschmar compares the great Sermon to the apodictic laws of the Old Testament, e.g., the Ten Commandments. Alt and von Rad understand these as defining the identity of the true Israelite; just so, the antitheses disclose what it is to be a disciple of Jesus.[14] They also cut the ground from under any self-righteousness.

Radical as these sayings are, they are not confined to any class or group of Jesus' followers. They are examples for all.

V. Radical Following

Three brief dialogues on the requirements for following Jesus appear in Luke 9:58–62. The first two have aprallels in Matthew 8:19–22.[15] These conditions are radical. One must accompany the Son of man who has no place to lay his head. A man is not permitted to fulfill the most sacred of obligations, burying one's father. Elijah permitted Elisha to say goodbye to his people at home (1 Kings 19:20), but there must be no turning back even for a moment.

These dialogues belong to an early stage of the gospel tradition. The first has a parallel in *Gos. Thom.* 86, "Foxes have holes and the birds have [their] nests, but the Son of Man has nowhere to lay his head and to rest." The occurrence of "sons of men" in *Gos. Thom.* 106 suggests that here "Son of man" is neither Christological nor eschatological. It is already fixed in the tradition, and Thomas does not use the phrase elsewhere. Jesus is a homeless wanderer and a rejected prophet, and those who follow him must share his lot. Crossan compares this with the enigmatic saying in *Gos. Thom.* 42, "Become passersby."[16]

---

[13] Krister Stendahl, "Matthew," in *Peake's Commentary on the Bible*, ed. M. Black and H. H. Rowley (London: Thomas Nelson & Sons, 1963), 776.

[14] Georg Kretschmar, "Ein Beitrag zur Frage nach dem Ursprung frühchristlicher Askese," *ZTK* 61 (1964): 27–67; see esp. p. 59.

[15] J. Crossan, *In Fragments*, 239, argues that all three stood in Q.

[16] Ibid., 241. On the whole passage, see pp. 238–44. Crossan refers also to *Gos. Thom.* 86, in which Jesus (the Son of man) is wisdom, seeking a place to rest. It is the kernel sayings

In this connection we may compare such sayings on rejection of Jesus as Luke 10:13–15//Matthew 11:21–24; Luke 13:34–35//Matthew 23:37–39; and also Mark 6:4, "There is no prophet who is without honor," etc., the earliest form of which is probably the double saying in *Gos. Thom.* 31.[17]

Two other sayings related to this theme have parallels in Thomas (Luke 14:26–27//Matt. 10:37–38; *Gos. Thom.* 101, 55; cf. Mark 8:34 and parallels): (1) no one who does not hate his family and even his own life can be Jesus' disciple; and (2) no one who does not carry his cross and follow him can be his disciple. The only mention of a cross in the *Gospel of Thomas* is in logion 55. The form of these aphorisms was already fixed prior to the *Gospel of Thomas* and Q, and these are a very early tradition.

Another Q saying, Luke 12:49–53//Matthew 10:34–36 (cf. *Gos. Thom.* 16) refers to the coming crisis. Jesus has not come to cast peace on the earth but fire, a sword, or war (or divisions). There is no demand here, but these imply conditions that disciples must face if they follow him. "Fire" has significant parallels also in *Gos. Thom.* 10, 82.

Almsgiving is a standard virtue in Judaism. The Q sayings on laying up treasure in heaven, and "where your treasure is, there will your heart be also" (Matt. 6:19–21//Luke 12:33–34) may make this a more radical demand, particularly in Luke's form, "Sell what you have." Certainly this is so in the stringent saying in Mark 10:25//Matthew 19:34//Luke 18:25, "It is easier for a camel to pass through the eye of a needle than for a rich person to enter the Reign of God." The woes on the rich, on those who are satisfied, and those who laugh (Luke 6:24–25) are just as severe. When all allowances are made for Jesus' hyperbolical language, this at any rate teaches the danger of wealth and the need to get rid of it.

Although the parable of the Rich Man and Lazarus (Luke 16:19–31) probably was told to make a different point, the contrast of the two men favors poverty over wealth. There is an early and varied tradition that Jesus recommended divesting oneself of wealth.

VI. The Intimate Disciples

Are the demands to follow the homeless Jesus and to sell and give directed especially toward his most intimate associates? It is often remarked that Zacchaeus refunded his ill–gotten gains at twice the rate commanded by the law, and was accepted; but there is nothing to indicate that he became a member of the inner group.

The mission discourses do not settle the problem. Their oldest form

themselves that are important; the reference to Elisha has developed the saying into a dialogue.

[17] Ibid., 284.

is probably the address to the seventy-two in Luke 10:1–12. Arland
Jacobson has pointed out that it reflects more an errand of judgment than
a plan of evangelization; the prophetic preaching of the Q community had
an ideal model in this portrayal of Jesus' commands.[18] The disciples, like
the homeless Son of man, were to carry no purse or knapsack and to
depend on the hospitality of "sons of peace" (10:4–7). It would not,
however, be strange if Jesus commanded his intimates to announce his
basic message, even though in Luke 9:60 the evangelist may have added
the words, "but as for you, go proclaim far and wide the Reign of God."

Certainly the passages we have discussed mark the beginning of a
long and important tradition of "following Jesus" which deeply influenced
the piety of Palestine and Syria. Luke, in his Central Section (especially
9:51–18:14), provides a model in which his (men and women!) disciples
follow "the way of the Lord"[19] to Jerusalem and are taught on the way.
The Book of Acts follows this with accounts of charismatic prophets and
evangelists: Philip in Samaria (Acts 8:5–8), and Philip and Peter in the
coastal plain of Palestine (8:26–40; 9:32–10:48), Agabus (11:28; 21:10–11),
Philip's four daughters (21:8–9), and prophets and teachers in Antioch
(13:1–3). The prophets of the *Didache* belong to the same tradition.[20]

The story of the Rich Man introduces a section in which divestiture
of wealth is coupled with following Jesus in his mission. This man has kept
the important commandments, but one thing is lacking; thus in this
context (Mark 10:17–31//Matt. 19:16–30//Luke 18:18–30) he is the example of one who refused an invitation to be added to the Twelve. If Mark
10:17–22 is an independent old story, one cannot argue that Jesus asked
all his followers to give up their wealth; this is only an example that one
follows as best one can. Crossan, however, regards the entire passage as
Mark's redactional creation intended to frame the aphorism on the camel
and the eye of the needle (10:25),[21] and Mark's interpretation fits well
with the radical sayings of Luke 9:57–62. Peter and the others have given
up family and possessions and in return will have a new family and
houses—with persecutions.

However much the traditions may be formulated in the light of the
ideals of early Christians, they converge at one point. Evidently, as Jesus
went through Galilee and finally to Jerusalem, he was accompanied by
several men and women who shared his homelessness and poverty.[22] But

---

[18] Arland D. Jacobson, "The Literary Unity of Q," *JBL* 101 (1982): 365–89.
[19] W. C. Robinson, Jr., "The Theological Context for Interpreting Luke's Travel
Narrative (9:51 ff.)," *JBL* 79 (1960): 20–31.
[20] G. Kretschmar, "Ein Beitrag," 36–7, 49–55.
[21] J. Crossan, *In Fragments*, 221.
[22] Gerd Theissen, "Itinerant Radicalism: The Tradition of Jesus' Sayings from the
Perspective of the Sociology of Literature," *Radical Religion* 2 (1975):84–93, argued that
those who preserved the sayings which commanded hatred toward family and home were

there were those who responded to his message but stayed at home, and these he invited to a style of life of simplicity, modesty, and generous sharing.

VII. Rank and Lowliness

The "Twelve" must have been prominent in the oral tradition. Mark emphasizes their stupidity and disobedience to such an extent that his gospel is almost an anti-Twelve document, but he has to acknowledge their prominence and deal with it.[23]

In the old tradition there are not many direct promises to the inner group except that they will have success in their mission, e.g., "I will make you fishers of human beings" (Mark 1:17; cf. Luke 5:10). They will heal and cast out demons and receive support in time of persecution.[24]

Matthew and Luke often eliminate or soften Mark's sharp criticisms. A saying on the power of faith to move a mountain or a tree appears in two forms: Mark 11:23//Matthew 21:21 and Luke 17:6//Matthew 17:20 (Q). Mark's saying applies this to the faith of anyone, while in the other cases it is a promise to the disciples, and the editorial work of Matthew and Luke is easily discernible.

Luke makes the Twelve prototypes of the later apostles and applies this title to them.[25] Matthew includes the special promise to Peter that he will be the rock of the church and hold the keys of the Kingdom of the heavens (16:17–19), and this is singular. Both evangelists transmit what is evidently a Q saying, Matthew 19:28//Luke 22:28–30. Those who have followed Jesus (Matthew) or have stayed by him during his trials (Luke) will sit on thrones judging the twelve tribes of Israel. In Luke this is in a dialogue at the Last Supper and is combined with the promise of a kingdom and partaking of the messianic banquet.[26]

But this is preceded by the powerful words of Jesus in which he contrasts the kings of the nations who lord it over their people with the

---

outcasts on the fringes of society, suspect in the eyes of others. Not all of the followers of Jesus, however, belong to this group and few were in favor of revolution. Although there was a "zealot" among the Twelve, and in Pilate's time there were occasional outbreaks of violence, most of the incidents related by Josephus belong to a later period.

[23] Theodore J. Weeden, *Mark—Traditions in Conflict* (Philadelphia: Fortress Press, 1971), gives an extreme treatment of the theme.

[24] Peter, James, and John are bracketed together in Mark, e.g., 5:37; 9:2; 14:33, and Andrew is added in 1:16; 13:3, probably because of a tradition that they were prominent; cf. the "pillars," James, Cephas, and John (Gal. 2:9).

[25] Mark does so only once, in 3:14, where the reading is doubtful; cf. Bruce M. Metager, *A Textual Commentary on the Greek New Testament* (Stuttgart: United Bible Societies, 1975), 80.

[26] J. Crossan, *In Fragments*, 204, believes that this was the last item in Q.

way of Jesus the servant, who must be the model for the disciples (Luke
22:24–27). In Mark 10:35–45 (//Matt. 20:20–28) similar forms of these
sayings are introduced by the request of James and John for special places
of honor in Jesus' "glory." Mark has probably used traditional material to
single these two disciples out for criticism, namely, a saying that his
followers must be ready to share Jesus' baptism, i.e., be overwhelmed by
danger and death as he will be; cf. Luke 12:50, "I have a baptism to
undergo." The combination of cup and baptism may be due to Mark; cf.
the cup in the Gethesemane story, Mark 14:36. The concluding saying,
"The Son of Man came not to be served but to serve, and to give his life
as a means of freeing the many," may however be traditional.[27] There can
be no rank among the disciples, only a proper competition to serve well.

This passage is anticipated by an earlier pericope regarding places of
honor (Mark 9:33–37) which may be Mark's composition and which
brings together the themes of 10:35–45 and the blessing of children in
10:13–16.[28] Jesus singles out a child and embraces it; the disciples should
accept such a little one. The disciples, however, do not learn the lesson;
when children are brought to Jesus to be touched, they do not wish Jesus
to be bothered with such insignificant creatures (10:13–16).

Here the kernel saying is, "Whoever does not receive the Reign of
God like a child will not enter it" (10:15). Matthew 18:4 has modified this
saying: "Whoever lowers himself like this child is the one who is greatest
in the Kingdom of the Heavens." But even this does not refer to a
supposed humble attitude of mind; normal children may accept loving
gifts but they are not necessarily meek. The verb ταπεινόω means to put
into a low station in society or to accept it; children were at the bottom of
the family hierarchy.[29]

The saying on children in Mark 10:15 in itself may look in more than
one direction, and I would not revise my previous judgment that the
particular quality of a child may be openness, wonder, and faith that
everything is possible.[30] As Mark understood it, the reference was to
humble status, and this fits with the other traditions regarding amibition
for prestige, which Jesus regarded as contemptible (cf. also Luke
7:25//Matt. 11:8).

There is additional evidence for Jesus' position. Luke 14:7–11
contains his advice to guests invited to dinner: take the least prestigious

---

[27] J. Crossan, ibid., 291–93, holds that Mark has introduced "Son of man" at this point,
but not the soteriological statement.

[28] Ibid., 109.

[29] L. William Countryman, *Dirt, Greed, and Sex* (Philadelphia: Fortress Press, 1988),
171: "One enters the reign of the heavens by 'lowering onself,' giving up all claim to social
status, security and respect."

[30] Sherman E. Johnson, *A Commentary on the Gospel according to St. Mark* (London:
A. & C. Black, 1977), 172.

place at table. This concludes with the aphorism: "Everyone who exalts himself will be humiliated, and one who lowers himself will be exalted"; this stands in various contexts; cf. Luke 18:14; Matt. 23:12.

The conclusion, then, is that Jesus called upon his intimate followers—and perhaps others also— to give up a secure place in society, as he himself had done, and to identify oneself with the lowly and the outcasts. At the same time, becoming like a child opened up the wonders of the dawning age, for in God's time everything is possible.

VIII. The Lowly Becomes Strong, the Strong Become Lowly

The message was that the Reign of God, a new age, was at hand. This was the inauguration of what Mircea Eliade has called sacred time (*ab origine, in illo tempore*).[31]

What Jesus announced and acted out was that God has taken the initiative. The notion that one must please God in order to be accepted is overturned. God accepts anyone who responds in faith and trust, and this makes it possible to do his will. Thus he liberates women and children and all who are at the bottom of the social order, the poor, the outcasts, and the ceremonially unclean. Often men and women are healed of physical and mental ailments. Gentiles and Samaritans are among them.[32]

Jesus behaves toward the lowly in a way that restores their dignity, and for the first time they have the power or strength (ἐξουσία) that every human being potentially possesses. This constitutes a community in which they have mutual support. Poor people are often relatively more generous than those who are well off. Jesus' fellowship with tax-collectors and sinners probably denotes a mutual sharing of goods, so that even the poorest practice something like *noblesse oblige*.

The relatively secure people who responded to Jesus already had some power, and it was necessary for them to divest themselves of it, to share it with others, and become lowly. In so doing, they liberated themselves from the conventional attitudes and folkways that had protected their status and stultified spontaneity. Men like Peter, James, and John, who had a definite place in society, however modest, became strong in a new sense through sharing equally with the most deprived people. The gospel tradition indicates that this re-education did not take place all at once.

---

[31] For example, Mircea Eliade, *The Sacred and the Profane* (New York: Harcourt, Brace & World, 1959), 68–72.

[32] Jesus associated freely with women and had special concern for widows. Women had no standing in society apart from their membership in a family.

If one asks about the process whereby the lowly became exalted and proud people humbled, we have to go beyond historical method and to some degree use our imaginations. When these different sorts of people heard the message of the parables and the beatitudes they could contemplate a new world of life and action. Jesus let them look at the world in a different way. Old ideas of what is appropriate, and even of God's justice, had to be reconsidered. The new view was realistic, evil and injustice were still rampant, and they could see the glory of kings and rulers in all its tawdriness, pettiness, and futility. But there was boundless hope in the goodness of God, and they could see signs of it in operation.

Even Jesus' stern demands could serve as a tonic and make one wish to respond by appropriate action. The antitheses of Matthew 5 might lead to reflection and repentance, so that the hearers understood their true situation, but that was not the sole purpose; rather, it revealed what was possible for a child of God and what entering the Reign of God was like. So a child of God will believe, abandon all self-righteousness, pray, keep alert, cease insisting on rights and privileges, accept the position of the lowly, be first by being last and serving one's fellows, rejoice in the good deeds and fortunes of others, and transform earthly wisdom into heavenly by making the most of talents and opportunities.

As Paul and other early Christians developed their Christology, they came to realize that God himself was the model for this discipleship in that he loved the unthankful and the evil, and through the Incarnation in Jesus lowered himself to the status of a slave and accepted a Cross. This was not the end; the one who had accepted shame was exalted.

Jesus and Women Exemplars

Frederick H. Borsch*

"Jesus' disciples marveled that he was talking with a woman" (John 4:27). Careful readers of the gospels will say, "they shouldn't have." In his pivotal story about Jesus' speaking with the woman at the well, the Johannine evangelist makes much of the fact that Jesus was not just talking about mundane matters but having a discussion regarding religious concerns with a woman who was also a Samaritan ("For Jews have no dealings with Samaritans," John 4:9). Although our evidence from this period can never be as definitive as we would wish,[1] it is clear that Jesus was effronting well established teachings and mores to have been holding such a conversation, especially in public. One scholar speaks of Jesus' associations with women being "without precedent in contemporary Judaism."[2]

---

* Frederick H. Borsch is Bishop of the Diocese of Los Angeles, California. He adds the following tribute:

Reginald Fuller helped me find my first position teaching New Testament, a post he had once held himself at the Queen's College in Birmingham, England. When he left Seabury-Western Seminary to go to Union Seminary in New York, I also followed him in that ministry in Evanston. Some thought that I must have been his nephew or at least a former student. But, although I never had the privilege of formally being a student of Reg Fuller, I was able to hear him lecture or talk on a number of occasions, joined in several seminars with him, and was always the beneficiary of his extensive writings and his generous friendship along with that of Ilse. It is a pleasure to offer this essay in tribute to such a distinguished mentor and friend.

[1] The nature of our sources and the problems with dating particular traditions make it difficult to reconstruct the world of early first century Judaism with certainty, but it seems sufficiently clear that women of the time were expected to have a role almost exclusively in the home and were to be passive in almost every public setting. There is some evidence that contact with Hellenism and Roman society may have given some impetus to an improved status for women. See Joachim Jeremias, *Jerusalem in the Time of Jesus: An Investigation into Economic and Social Conditions during the New Testament Period* (Philadelphia: Fortress Press, 1969), 358–376; Ben Witherington III, *Women in the Ministry of Jesus: A Study of Jesus' Attitudes to Women and their Roles as Reflected in His Earthly Life*, SNTSMS 51 (Cambridge: Cambridge Univ. Press, 1984), 1–10; Phyllis Bird, "Images of Women in the Old Testament," in *Religion and Sexism: Images of Women in the Jewish and Christian Tradition*, ed. Rosemary Radford Reuther (New York: Simon & Schuster, 1974), 41–88; Barbara J. MacHaffie, *Her Story: Women in Christian Tradition* (Philadelphia: Fortress Press, 1986), 6–9; Mary J. Evans, *Woman in the Bible* (Exeter: Paternoster Press, 1983), 33–43; and L. William Countryman, *Dirt, Greed, and Sex: Sexual Ethics in the New Testament and Their Implications for Today* (Philadelphia: Fortress Press, 1988), 151–167.

[2] Werner Förster, *From the Exile to Christ: A Historical Introduction to Palestinian Judaism* (Philadelphia: Fortress Press, 1964), 127. On the danger, however, either of making Jesus look better by painting the patriarchy of the Judaism of his time in the worst

The Synoptic Gospels as well as other material in the Fourth Gospel preserve a lively and memorable tradition that Jesus had a number of significant relationships with women. New Testament scholarship, and particularly the work of women scholars, has allowed this picture to reemerge with clarity. By any reckoning, what is to be marveled at in these first century documents is the frequent and regular role of women, especially in the context of a strongly patriarchal religion and androcentric cultures. Less noted, but of perhaps even more surprise and significance, is the fact that many of the stories and sayings in which women play a role are of great importance for advancing the distinctiveness of the gospel message. Women have no comparable role in rabbinical stories of the period. It is not just that Jesus associated and talked with and about women. In a number of cases they appear to have been deliberately chosen to carry important lessons. In some instances the women seem to have been selected because they were without much status or standing in society and in law. Theirs are stories of Jesus' ministry with and on behalf of the lowly and marginalized.[3] In other cases one can believe that there was a more general concern with the discipleship of women. As it becomes increasingly evident that at the heart of Jesus' ministry was a passionate desire to gather and reform the people of Israel in as inclusive a manner as possible for the coming of God's reign,[4] one recognizes how fully women were to be part of this renewed community. In a number of cases they are presented as witnesses and actors, helping to make the new community happen.

The most significant role given to women in the gospel's story was not directly within Jesus' control. Yet it is doubtful that women could have found their prominent place in the resurrection narratives unless Jesus had earlier drawn them into close and meaningful association with his ministry as those who "followed (ἀκολουθεῖν) him and ministered (διακονεῖν) to him in Galilee" (Mark 15:40–41//Matt. 27:55–56//Luke 23:49; and see Luke 8:2–3). The two Greek words have a quasi-technical meaning of discipleship and ministering in the New Testament.[5] The fact that a number of these women are given names, and that there were said

---

colors possible (there is evidence that practice was sometimes better than theory), or of separating him from his own people and culture which would have helped inspire his teaching, see Elisabeth Schüssler Fiorenza, *In Memory of Her: A Feminist Theological Reconstruction of Christian Origins* (New York: Crossroad, 1983), 106–110. Fiorenza then, however, goes on to stress the distinctiveness of Jesus' ministry and message regarding women.

[3] See Pheme Perkins, "Women in the Bible and Its World," *Int* 42 (1988): 33–44.

[4] See Gerhard Lohfink, *Jesus and Community: The Social Dimensions of Christian Faith* (Philadelphia: Fortress Press, 1982), 7–73; and E. P. Sanders, *Jesus and Judaism* (Philadelphia: Fortress Press, 1985), 61–119.

[5] See Elizabeth M. Tetlow, *Women and Ministry in the New Testament* (New York: Paulist Press, 1980), 97.

to be "many others," indicates both the specificity and strength of this tradition. What is particularly to be remarked upon is not that the women assisted Jesus in various ways (for this was true in case of other rabbis of the time) but that women of various stations in life (Joanna in Luke 8:3 is the wife of Chuza, Herod's steward) traveled with him.[6]

While the four gospels vary in indicating whether one, two, or three or more women followers of Jesus were the first to learn of Jesus' resurrection, they are all clear that women were first and that Mary Magdalene was one of them or the one. Dispirited and perhaps feeling guilty because they had either deserted or not been of any help to Jesus, the male disciples were led to resurrection faith by the women followers who, as is so often true of women, appear at first just to be attempting to pick up the pieces and help life to go on by visiting the grave to anoint and honor Jesus' body. Having come with Jesus from Galilee, they had been able only to look "on from a distance" while he was crucified. But they were there (Mark 15:40–41//Matt. 27:55–56//Luke 23:49; see John 19:25). They also waited, the narrative informs us, to see "where he was laid" (Mark 15:47; Matt. 27:61; Luke 23:55–56).

The questioning of the women's testimony in Luke 24:11 underscores the inferior status of women in that era as far as being legal witnesses was concerned,[7] but also further serves to emphasize the strength and unanimity of the early tradition in this regard. The women's crucial role was likely an embarrassment to a number of men and to all those concerned to demonstrate the truth of the resurrection by the standards of the time.

Mary of Magdala's foremost place as the prototype witness to the resurrection in all the gospel traditions[8] (particularly in the moving scene in John 20:11–18), along with her inclusion among those who "ministered to Jesus," has led to more than a little speculation about a special relationship with Jesus. In fact, however, we know very little about her. Luke informs his readers that she had once been possessed by seven demons which now had left her (8:2). One must assume she had been in a bad way whether physically or spiritually or both. Although there is no reason to link her with the immoral woman in the preceding passage (Luke 7:36–50), much less the woman taken in adultery (John 8:3–11), she must have had serious problems and been an important exemplar of Jesus' readiness to associate himself with those in difficult circum-

---

6 See B. Witherington, *Women in the Ministry of Jesus*, 116–118.

7 Cf. ibid., 9–10.

8 The earliest of the traditions in 1 Cor. 15:3–8 makes no mention of Mary Magdalene or any of the other women. Whether this was because Paul did not know of or here did not wish to present the empty tomb tradition, or whether it was due to his androcentricity, or some other reason, is not known.

stances—the poor, the sick, and the rejected. One can imagine the particularly harsh circumstances of a woman with several or all of these problems.

A number of commentators, discussing the scene between Jesus and the sinful woman in Luke 7:36–50, have suggested that she is not in fact the best illustration of the little parable embedded in the longer passage which instructs that those forgiven much will love much (7:41–43). Jesus only pronounces her forgiveness after she has cared so personally for him.[9] This criticism, however, misses the awareness that Jesus had already shown his acceptance and forgiveness by allowing the woman to minister to him. As so often in Jesus' ministry, actions spoke louder than words and likely brought him into much more trouble. It is one thing to talk about forgiveness and acceptance of those regarded by others as low in life and irreligious. It is another to do it. Strong in the reminiscence of the disciples was the awareness that Jesus did as he said and, in this as in a number of other significant instances, that a woman in difficult circumstances (yet more so if, in fact, she was a prostitute, since then as now almost all prostitutes came from impoverished conditions) was at the center of his controversial action, playing a critical role in his ground-breaking ministry.

Because they also picture a woman ministering lavishly to Jesus and both scenes have a figure named Simon (in Luke a Pharisee; in Matthew and Mark a leper), Mark 14:3–9//Matthew 26:6–13 are often regarded as coming from the same tradition which Luke 7:36–50 may have developed. While Mark's and Matthew's vignette has a different function with respect to foreshadowing Jesus' death and burial, the scene again conveys the strong memory of Jesus' association with women and their use as primary actors. In John's Gospel the story of the woman who anoints Jesus in preparation for burial (12:1–8) has more in common with Luke 7:36–50. (She anoints his feet and wipes them with her hair.) Here the woman is identified as Mary, the sister of Martha and Lazarus. (See below.)

While the uncertain textual history of the story of the women taken in adultery means that its direct association with Jesus' activity is problematic, one can still regard it as the kind of story which became linked with Jesus because of his other teaching and actions. The memory of his acts of forgiveness and his concern for the defenseless and women helped make the story part of the tradition. Similarly and correspondingly, the powerful words of Mary's song are meant to anticipate themes of Jesus' ministry:

---

[9]   On various interpretations of Luke 7:36–50, see B. Witherington, *Women in the Ministry of Jesus*, 53–57.

God has scattered the proud in the imagination
of their hearts;
God has put down the mighty from their thrones,
and exalted those of low degree;
God has filled the hungry with good things,
and the rich God has sent empty away.
(Luke 1:51–53)

Frequently noted is the place that women have in Luke's Gospel.[10]
On several occasions he seems deliberately to follow a story about a male
actor with one about a woman. Whether all of these stories are to be
traced to Jesus' historical ministry, whether they are all or in part the
result of Luke's special interest, or whether they stem from some other
period of the tradition's development, their place in the gospel can still be
regarded as resulting from Jesus' special concern for and the distinction
he gave to women.

Widows, of course, were of particular moral concern in Israel and to
Israel's God who is "Father of the fatherless and protector of widows" (Ps.
68:5). Without a husband to help them in a male-dominated society,
widows had few rights or protections and, therefore, the Bible urges
special care and fair treatment. That this was not always the case is rather
humorously illustrated in Jesus' story of the widow who persistently made
a nuisance of herself until a judge, who had no regard for God or human
opinion, finally granted her justice as a way of getting her off his back
(Luke 18:1–8).[11] The story may imply that the judge was waiting for some
kind of a bribe from the widow or her opponent, but the widow—
presumably without money or much legal clout—used her insistent
nagging to gain her rights. She becomes a hero in a story which Luke uses
to underline the importance of perseverance in prayer, though one can
guess it might have been used earlier to stress the importance of
steadfastedly and single-mindedly seeking God's justice and expecting to
receive it. If this uncaring judge would grant that widow her wish because
she was such a nuisance, how much more, the parable suggests, will God
give the good things of the reign of God to those who persist.

In a story which reaches beyond our modern-day understandings,
Jesus raises to life the only son of a widowed woman from the town of Nain

---

[10] See Hans Conzelmann, *The Theology of St. Luke* (New York: Harper & Brothers,
1960), who on pp. 46–47 suggests that Luke may have had a special interest in women
because of their importance as witnesses distinct from the male disciples. It is often thought
that women may have played important roles in the Lucan community. On the other hand,
there are also some indications in the lack of full comprehension by some of the women who
call out to or speak with Jesus that Luke may subtly be playing down aspects of women's
importance.
[11] For more on this story, see Frederick H. Borsch, *Many Things in Parables:
Extravagant Stories of New Community* (Philadelphia: Fortress Press, 1988), 111–116.

(Luke 7:11–17). The gospel presents the story in order to portray Jesus' compassion toward the widow and especially to help later disciples realize that the creative healing power of God's reign was ultimately greater than even the awesome power of death. "A great prophet has arisen among us!" the crowd exclaims, and "God has visited God's people" (Luke 7:16).

In Luke 13:10–17 a bent over woman is healed on the sabbath day and becomes an important example of Jesus' actions and teaching in this regard.[12] Similar to his description of Zacchaeus ("he also is a son of Abraham," Luke 19:9), she too is "a daughter of Abraham" and is to be fully included in God's restored people.

Women can play significant roles in Luke's Gospel while not fully comprehending Jesus or what is happening to him. The woman who calls out, "Blessed is the womb that bore you, and the breasts that you sucked!" is told, "Blessed rather are those who hear the word of God and keep it!" (11:27–28). The women who bewailing and lamenting follow Jesus on the way to the crucifixion (23:27–31) can be remembered for their compassion, but they do not really understand what is taking place.

In a parable closely linked with that of the shepherd who leaves the ninety-nine sheep in the wilderness to seek one that is lost, we hear of another woman in Luke's Gospel who, having lost one of ten silver coins, diligently searches for it until she finds it (15:8–10). The evangelist sees the incident as an illustration of how there will be joy before the angels of God over one repentant sinner. In another yoked parable found in both Luke (13:20–21) and Matthew (13:33) a woman puts leaven in three measures of meal, a simile for the apparent insignificance of God's inbreaking reign, which will yet transform all. The result is at least a half bushel of meal, enough for more than a hundred people and a festive occasion. In the Matthean parable of the wise and foolish maidens (25:1–10) some women are illustrations of unpreparedness for the reign of heaven while others will know its joy.[13] The fact that women could be portrayed in less favorable as well as favorable roles in situations both fictitious and real would seem to indicate that Jesus thought of women as persons and not idealized figures. Similarly, in addition to the two men, of whom at the time of judgment one will be taken and the other left, also "there will be two women grinding together; one will be taken and the other left" (Luke 17:34–35//Matt. 24:40–41). Women will share equally in

---

[12] E. Schüssler Fiorenza, *In Memory of Her*, 125, regards this as the oldest of the tradition's stories about sabbath healings.

[13] For more on the parable, see F. Borsch, *Parables*, 84–89. This is the only distinctively Matthean story about women, and one notes that he shortens several Marcan stories that portray women. While Matthew regularly shortens narratives, it has been suggested that Matthew is the Gospel least interested in women's roles, and that the evangelist may be deliberately limiting their place lest too much scope be given to women in his conservative community.

the blessing and judgment of God's reign. They apparently will also share in making judgment. Not only will the men of Nineveh arise at the judgment day to condemn this generation for its lack of repentance and readiness to live in hopefulness, but also "the queen of the South" (the Queen of Sheba who came to hear Solomon's wisdom: 1 Kings 10:1–13) will arise to offer her condemnation (Matt. 12:41–42//Luke 11:31–32).

Luke (21:1–4) and Mark (12:41–44) use the story of the widow and her donation of two coins to illustrate truly sacrificial giving. Similar stories are known from other cultures, but it is significant that the hero of Jesus' story is again a woman. It should also be noted that some scholars find in this illustration a critique of an attitude which would encourage a widow to donate the whole of her living.[14] (See Mark 12:40//Luke 20:47 on the condemnation of the religious officials who devour widows' houses.)

It is the daughter of Jairus who is raised from death or the point of death (Mark 5:21–24, 35–42//Matt. 9:18–19, 23–26//Luke 8:40–42, 49–56) into which story is interpolated the healing of the woman with an issue of blood (Mark 5:25–34//Matt. 9:20–22//Luke 8:43–48). The significance of the faith of this woman (impoverished by her medical expenses and no doubt without societal protection) for her healing is emphasized. Remarkable also, in this and similar stories where Jesus heals women, is his willingness to be touched or to touch when the women's illnesses would have caused others to regard them as unclean (cf. Lev. 15:25–30). Here he not only allows it to happen but calls attention to the fact. Peter's mother-in-law is another woman whose healing is specifically noted in the gospels (Mark 1:29–31//Matt. 8:14–15//Luke 4:38–39).

Of still more import for the development of the gospels' story is the healing of the daughter of the Syrophoenician or Canaanite woman (Mark 7:24–30//Matt. 15:21–28). Although the story was valuable to the early churches as one of the few examples of Jesus' reaching out to gentiles, the seeming coarseness of Jesus' dialogue with the woman and his hesitation in responding to her request may also have given the evangelists pause in using it.[15] It is often thought that Luke has declined to include it in his gospel for these reasons. But for those same reasons it is possible that aspects of the story reach deep into the tradition to a time when gentile sensitivities were of less importance and Jesus did indeed believe he was "sent only to the lost sheep of the house of Israel" (Matt. 15:24)—on a ministry to restore the people of Israel for the advent of God's reign. As

---

[14] See A. G. Wright, "The Widow's Mites: Praise or Lament?—A Matter of Context," *CBQ* 44 (1982); 256–65.

[15] For more on the story and its place in the gospels, see Frederick H. Borsch, *Power in Weakness: New Hearing for Gospel Stories of Healing and Discipleship* (Philadelphia: Fortress Press, 1983), 51–66.

it stands in the gospels the story now represents a kind of breakthrough on Jesus' part, his finding himself called to reach out beyond his own idea of his mission. In a sense he is being challenged to live up to his *sermon* which immediately precedes this story (Mark 7:1–23//Matt. 15:1–20), instructing in the importance of what is inside, rather than outside appearances. The one whose courage born of desperation and whose bold banter causes Jesus to reach out is not only a gentile but a woman. His healing of her daughter must, at least at first, have seemed even more surprising to many of the early followers of Jesus than the healing of the gentile centurion's servant (Matt. 8:5–13//Luke 7:10).

While they are now often employed as the gospels' one great legalism, some commentators suspect that Jesus' sayings on divorce originally were more concerned with the protection of women than insisting on the indissolubility of marriage *per se* (cf. Mark 10:2–12//Matt. 19:3–9; 5:31–32//Luke 16:18). "Moses allowed a man to write a certificate of divorce and to put his wife away." While certain protections were in place, evidently in Judaism at that time a man could obtain a divorce for almost any reason he chose.[16] "For your hardness of heart Moses wrote this commandment," Jesus responds. That is not God's purpose. A man is to "leave his father and mother and be joined to his wife, and the two shall become one. What therefore God has joined together, let not man put asunder." Men are not to divorce their wives, leaving them in many ways helpless, anything like that easily. Whoever does this, Jesus may well have said in the oldest version of these words, commits adultery against his wife when he marries another woman and also makes his wife an adulteress (i.e., he forces her to join herself to another man as the only way she can find protection).[17]

A parallel concern for women seems to be signified in the new teaching that "everyone who looks at a woman lustfully has already committed adultery with her in his heart" (Matt. 5:28). Many of the limitations on women in Jewish society seem to be based on a fear that men could not control their sexual desires. It was best, therefore, to control women socially and in other ways. Standard teaching of the time usually concentrates on the dangers of female seductiveness. This teaching of Jesus seems to expect that his male disciples can learn to control themselves. Perhaps, above all, there is found here a severe condemnation of thinking of women and relating to them only or even primarily in sexual terms.

---

[16]   On the issues generally and these sayings in particular, see B. Witherington, *Women in the Ministry of Jesus*, 2–6, 18–28.

[17]   Mark 10:12 speaks of the possibility of a woman divorcing her husband. Such a reference would have been unusual in Judaism of the time and may come from a later stage in the development of the tradition, perhaps under the influence of Roman society.

At several important points in the gospels Jesus seems among the first to be concerned with what we today would call inclusive language and its implications. When Jesus is told his mother and brothers are asking for him, he uses this as an occasion to teach about a still more important relationship: "Whoever does the will of God is my brother and sister and mother" (Mark 3:35//Matt. 12:50). By taking "it for granted that women, equally with men, can do the will of God, and thereby be his true kindred" Jesus is presenting "a radical redefinition of the Old Testament and Jewish relationship between women and men and God."[18] When Peter rather plaintively says, "Lo, we have left everything and followed you," Jesus responds:

> Truly I say to you, there is no one who
> has left house or brothers or sisters or
> mother or father or children or lands, for
> my sake and for the gospel, who will not
> receive a hundredfold now in this time,
> houses, and brothers and sisters and mothers
> and children and lands. . . .
> (Mark 10:29–30//Matt. 19:29//Luke 18:29)

That seems like a great deal of family, and it certainly is remarkably inclusive. It is particularly interesting that leaving sisters, who would usually have been seen at that time as a burden and responsibility, is considered a sacrifice.[19]

While Jesus' mission seems in the Synoptic Gospels to have required him to keep himself at some distance from his family, in the story of the wedding feast at Cana the Fourth Gospel gives his mother an important role. They are portrayed in frank, and on Jesus' part, even somewhat strained exchange. Mary appears to sense Jesus' authority and power for this occasion but not fully to realize the importance of timing for his mission. Mary's faithfulness, along with Jesus' concern for her, is demonstrated in the poignant scene at the foot of the cross (John 19:25–27). The later development of Mary's role in the birth narratives of Matthew and Luke is the result of several factors, but gives to her an exalted place in the reverence of the churches.

While it may not be right to call them his second family, Jesus appears to have been especially close to Martha, Mary, and Lazarus. Traditions about Martha and Mary form one of those intriguing links between the Third and Fourth Gospels and are often thought to go back

---

[18]   Joanna Dewey, "Images of Women," in *The Liberating Word: A Guide to Nonsexist Interpretation of the Bible*, ed. Letty M. Russell (Philadelphia: Westminster Press, 1976), 62–81, 75.
[19]   See M. Evans, *Women in the Bible*, 46.

to the churches' early memories.[20] The two sisters play vital roles in the final and greatest of Jesus' miracles in John's Gospel, the raising of Lazarus (11:1–44). Their hesitant coming to faith in Jesus and the power of resurrection, and the ways in which they do so, are meant to be models for all disciples.

Martha seems the more outgoing, her faith both trusting and questioning. "Even now I know that whatever you ask from God, God will give you" (John 11:22). When Jesus says, "Your brother will rise again," Martha responds with her belief in the general resurrection: "I know that he will rise again in the resurrection at the last day." But Jesus tells her the power for resurrection is here and now, with him. "I am the resurrection and the life; the one who believes in me, though dying, yet shall live; and whoever lives and believes in me shall never die." Then Jesus puts her faith to the test: "Do you believe this?" Martha is able to answer, "Yes, Lord, I believe that you are the Christ, the Son of God, the one who is coming into the world" (11:22–27). She has a personal trust in Jesus. Indeed, her witness is more powerful even than Peter's "confession" at Caesarea Philippi in the Synoptic Gospels and earlier in this gospel (6:68). Yet she does not fully answer Jesus' question. She knows Lazarus is quite dead, and in a moment she will warn Jesus that the body has already become odoriferous because it is decaying (11:39).

Mary comes to Jesus when she learns from her leading sister Martha that he is calling her. She simply repeats Martha's initial plaintive statement of trust in Jesus' power to heal: "Lord, if you had been here, my brother would not have died" (11:32; see 11:21). Then she can only weep. Her weeping and that of other Jews who are there brings Jesus to tears (11:33–35).

The picture of Martha as active and Mary as more quietly attentive to Jesus is further drawn in John 12:1–8 and yet more clearly in Luke 10:38–42. In John 12:1–8 Martha serves the supper while the woman who anoints Jesus' feet with costly ointment and wipes it with her hair is identified as Mary.

Many commentators focus on Mary in the Lucan story, her sitting and listening to Jesus (who is again teaching a woman, perhaps here either a group of women or a woman in mixed company) and being commended for that which is most important. It is Martha, however (in whose house this scene takes place), who is actually the more prominent figure in the story. Most people who feel that they take upon themselves more than their share of the world's work can identify with her in her resentment, because Mary seems to be enjoying herself instead of helping. In these

---

[20]   On the Mary, Martha, and Lazarus traditions, see Raymond E. Brown, *The Gospel According to John I–XII*, AB 29 (Garden City, NY: Doubleday & Co., 1966), xliv–xlvii, 432–435.

terms the story becomes a challenge to all hard-working disciplined followers of Jesus. Can they serve without resentment of others, while recognizing the importance of contemplation along with action, of listening and being as well as doing and accomplishment? As a result of all her activity, Martha, Jesus perceives, is troubled and anxious about many things, along with her resentment. But Jesus stresses what is most needful and, in what appears to be a little word-play at this meal, tells Martha that Mary has chosen the good portion, the main dish that is needed.[21]

In recent years a number of women have voiced their concern with aspects of Luke's presentation of the Mary and Martha story. Whatever is said about the significance of the two women, the story remains male-centered in that Jesus is the main actor, and the narrative clearly is told to preserve his decisive words. The story sets two women against each other and seems to see them only in domestic roles.[22] It is important to remember, however, that Jesus is the central figure throughout the gospels in which male disciples also play lesser and frequently far from flattering parts. Mary and Martha may be somewhat caricatured in Luke's vignette, but the narrative still recalls the vital place in his ministry of two sisters whose roles as disciples and witnesses may emerge more clearly in John's Gospel.

Finally we return to the story of the Samaritan woman at the well (John 4:7–42)—still a surprising narrative, although by now readers have grown accustomed to stories of Jesus' deliberate efforts to make clear the full inclusion of many different women in the new offer of God's reign. With typical use of irony, misunderstandings based on overly-literal hearings of words, and the use of words of double meanings, the fourth evangelist employs this extended narrative and dialogue to advance several of his important themes. Indeed, one of his messages to hearers may well be, "Don't get stuck with overly literal understandings. Truth often lies deeper."

When Jesus speaks of his gift of "living water," the woman thinks he means water that is moving, running water. She advises him that the well is deep and that he has nothing to draw with. Uncomprehendingly she asks, "Are you greater than our father Jacob?" She soon comes to understand, however, that one greater than the patriarchs of Samaritans and Jews is here. She learns to ask for water that will cause her never to thirst again. To both the people of Israel and the Samaritans water was another of the symbols for Torah—the water of life. This Jesus himself

---

[21] On the textual problems with Luke 10:42 and the passage more generally, see B. Witherington, *Women in the Ministry of Jesus*, 100–103.

[22] See Elisabeth Schüssler Fiorenza, "A Feminist Critical Interpretation for Liberation: Mary and Martha: Lk. 10:38–42," *Religion and Intellectual Life* 3 (1986): 21–35.

now gives in his words and person, with perhaps an allusion to the water of baptism as well.

As the dialogue continues, Jesus slowly penetrates the woman's incomprehension, suspicion, and defensiveness. She is at first both fearful and surprised by his insights into her. While hearers may be meant to understand that she had five husbands in the literal sense, they are probably also intended to think of the five peoples with whom Samaritans were said to have intermarried and their gods. Never mind! Salvation can now come to Samaritans as well—beginning with this woman. She learns that true worship will no longer be identified with either this sacred mount in Samaria or with Jerusalem. It is not where people worship but how they worship and with what sense of God that matter. The woman learns that the one who is telling her these things is the Messiah.

The disciples return and marvel that Jesus is talking with a woman. But the woman is now a convert and through her witness brings many other Samaritans to faith. She is a prototype evangelist through whom others come to believe that "this is indeed the Savior of the world" (John 4:42).[23] Once again hearers of the gospels learn of Jesus' intention fully to include women in "the God movement."[24] They hear of his concern to show care for women as persons often disadvantaged in society, and to employ them in their variety and reality as crucial exemplars of the ways in which God through Jesus' ministry was breaking down old barriers and making a new community of God's people.

There is a sense in which stories like that of the Samaritan woman take on even greater significance when they are not regarded as coming from the early Jesus' traditions. Along with the stories of Mary and Martha of Bethany, Mary Magdalene, and others, these narratives may well give a glimpse of a time in the life of the young Christian communities when women had leading parts as evangelists, teachers, and witnesses,[25] in some cases because of their earlier association with Jesus. They played vital roles in carrying on his ministry and his concerns. Even the all male evangelists and the generations of male-dominated churches have not fully eclipsed that record.

---

[23]   Raymond Brown finds that the use of ἀποστέλλειν in John 4:37 tends to enhance the missionary function of the Samaritan woman, perhaps preserving a memory that women played an important role in the mission to Samaria. R. E. Brown, "Roles of Women in the Fourth Gospel," *TS* 36 (1975): 688–689, 691–692.

[24]   Clarence Jordan's translation of "the reign of God." See *The Cotton Patch Version of Luke and Acts: Jesus' Doings and Happenings* (New York: Association Press, 1969).

[25]   See Sandra M. Schneiders, "Women in the Fourth Gospel and the Role of Women in the Contemporary Church," *BTB* 12 (1982): 35–45.

The Bread Petition of the Lord's Prayer

ARLAND J. HULTGREN*

The fourth petition of the Lord's Prayer is notoriously difficult to translate and interpret. It is commonly translated into English as "Give us this day our daily bread" (based on Matt. 6:11), in which "daily" is used to translate the Greek word ἐπιούσιος. But the meaning of that Greek word has been a matter of dispute from ancient times to the present. The purpose of this essay is to offer an interpretation which seems to the writer to be the simplest and most plausible on the basis of etymological and other considerations. But first some observations will be made concerning the Greek texts of this petition, followed by a review of major interpretive proposals.

I. Textual Observations

The Greek texts for the bread petition in Matthew 6:11 and Luke 11:3 are as follows:

Matt.6:11, τὸν ἄρτον ἡμῶν τὸν ἐπιούσιον δὸς ἡμῖν σήμερον.

Luke 11:3, τὸν ἄρτον ἡμῶν τὸν ἐπιούσιον δίδου ἡμῖν τὸ καθ᾽ ἡμέραν.

The Greek text in Matthew has no variants. Luke's text has three, but none is to be preferred to any of the words printed here. The text of the petition in the *Didache* (8.2) is exactly the same as Matthew's.

1. The texts have a large degree of verbal agreement in the case of six words: τὸν ἄρτον ἡμῶν τὸν ἐπιούσιον . . . ἡμῖν. Whether this points to a common source (Q) for the two versions, or whether it simply attests how strongly fixed the clause was, so that it shows up in quite similar form in two traditions (so-called L and M), need not be an issue here. In any case, the word ἐπιούσιος, which appears in both texts, appears only at these places in the New Testament. Although there have been instances where investigators have claimed that the word has been detected in two sources independent of the Greek New Testament,[1] these have been

* Arland J. Hultgren is Professor of New Testament, Luther Northwestern Theological Seminary, St. Paul, Minnesota.
[1] For references see BDF 66 (#123); Ernst Lohmeyer, *The Lord's Prayer* (London: Collins, 1965), 141–42.

disputed as misreadings of the evidence.[2] All other instances of the term's appearance in Greek sources are in patristic quotations of and commentaries on the Lord's Prayer or the Gospels of Matthew and Luke. Origen remarked that the word "is not employed by any of the Greeks or learned writers, nor is it in common use among ordinary folk; but it seems likely to have been coined by the evangelists."[3] Origen's view that the word was not in common use in antiquity is important, and it has not been refuted. His view that the evangelists coined it, however, should probably be rejected. Since the word is so unusual, it is not likely that *both* Matthew and Luke coined it independently of one another. Both are more likely dependent on a Greek-speaking tradition that goes back to the threshold of Aramaic usage.

2. The Greek texts differ in their use of main verbs and adverbial modifiers. Matthew has the aorist imperative δός plus σήμερον. Luke has the iterative present imperative δίδου plus τὸ καθ᾽ ἡμέραν. Matthew's "give . . . today" calls upon God to provide provisions for the present— with little thought of provisions for tomorrow and the days to come, which is in agreement with what is to come later in the Sermon on the Mount (6:25–34), especially, "Therefore do not be anxious about tomorrow" (6:34). Luke's version can be translated, "Keep on giving . . . day by day" and therefore looks to God to provide provisions in a succession of days which could extend into an indefinite length of time.

Exegetes disagree on which evangelist has departed more from a hypothetical original. Robert H. Gundry has suggested that Matthew's use of the aorist verb coheres theologically with his emphasis on no anxiety about tomorrow, and that "σήμερον is a Mattheanism."[4] On the other hand, Joachim Jeremias, I. Howard Marshall, and Joseph A. Fitzmyer have suggested that Luke's outlook and style show up in his version of the petition.[5] Marshall, for example, says that "τὸ καθ᾽ ἡμέραν is a Lucan phrase."[6] It is also a phrase that is found in the story of the "bread from heaven" at Exodus 16:5 (LXX, τὸ καθ᾽ ἡμέραν), and one

---

[2]　Cf. Bruce M. Metzger, "How Many Times Does 'Epiousios' Occur outside the Lord's Prayer?," *ExpTim* 69 (1957–58):52–54.

[3]　Origen, *De oratione* 27.7; Greek text in *PG* 11:509; English text (quoted here) in *Alexandrian Christianity*, ed. John E. L. Oulton and Henry Chadwick, LCC 2 (Philadelphia: Westminster, 1954), 298.

[4]　Robert H. Gundry, *Matthew: A Commentary on His Literary and Theological Art* (Grand Rapids: Wm. B. Eerdmans, 1982), 107.

[5]　Joachim Jeremias, "The Lord's Prayer in the Light of Recent Research," in his *The Prayers of Jesus* (Philadelphia: Fortress Press, 1978), 91–92; I. Howard Marshall, *The Gospel of Luke*, NIGTC (Grand Rapids: Wm. B. Eerdmans, 1978), 459; and Joseph A. Fitzmyer, *The Gospel according to Luke*, AB 28–28A; 2 vols. (Garden City, NY: Doubleday and Co., 1981–85), 2:897.

[6]　I. H. Marshall, *The Gospel of Luke*, 459. He points to Luke 19:47 and Acts 17:11 as other instances where the phrase appears.

might argue that Luke (or his source) has provided a "biblical" phrase at this point.[7]

3. The adverbial modifiers (Matthew's σήμερον, Luke's τὸ καθ' ἡμέραν) stand at the end of the clause in each case. Could it be that both are interpretive additions to the clause to clarify the meaning of the obscure ἐπιούσιος? Sherman E. Johnson has proposed such, saying that ἐπιούσιος would probably not have been understood by Matthew's and Luke's readers, so they added the adverbial modifiers to explain the term.[8] Yet one must exercise caution here. To take the adverbial modifiers as self-evidently explaining the meaning of ἐπιούσιος would predetermine the outcome (e.g., "Give us *today* our bread *of today*" for Matthew; "Give us *day by day* our *day-by-day* bread" for Luke). It is possible that ἐπιούσιος does not have a temporal meaning at all, but rather a qualitative one, and that a temporal adverb (as in Matthew) or adverbial phrase (as in Luke) existed in the petition from the beginning.

II. Proposed Meanings: A Review

Various meanings of the term ἐπιούσιος have been proposed from antiquity. There are four major proposals[9]—although these do not exhaust all possibilities—based on etymological analysis. None of these four proposals accounts explicitly for the use of the traditional and enduring English word "daily." This latter term is used in the English translation of Tyndale (1525), and in most English versions ever since, and it may have been traditional already at the time of Tyndale. In any case, Tyndale had predecessors in other languages. The Old Latin versions have *cotidianum* (or the variations *cottidianum* and *quotidianum*, "daily") at both Matthew 6:11 and Luke 11:3. The Vulgate has this term at Luke 11:3 (but *supersubstantialem* at Matt. 6:11). Luther's translation (1522) reads *täglich*. The question concerning how this interpretation arose will not be a major issue in this essay, although we shall return to it at the end. Suffice it to say here that there were certain Greek fathers who wrote—without explanation—that the term is equivalent to ἐφήμερος.[10]

---

[7] The phrase is also found in classical Greek (e.g., Aristophanes, *Equites* 1126).

[8] Sherman E. Johnson, *The Gospel according to St. Matthew*, IB 7 (Nashville: Abingdon Press, 1951), 313.

[9] The four major interpretations are listed in BAGD 297 and are reviewed by various scholars, including E. Lohmeyer, *The Lord's Prayer*, 141–46, and Philip B. Harner, *Understanding the Lord's Prayer* (Philadelphia: Fortress Press, 1975), 85–86. The most thorough review of possible meanings and bibliography is by Jean Carmignac, *Recherches sur le 'Notre Père'* (Paris: Éditions Letouzey & Ané, 1969), 121–43.

[10] Basil, *Regulae breviorum tractate* 252 (PG 31:1252); Gregory of Nyssa, *De oratione dominica* 4 (PG 44:1168D); and Chrysostom, *Homiliae in Matthaeum* 19.5 (PG 57:280).

Proposal 1. One of the oldest proposals is that ἐπιούσιος is derived from a combination of the prefix ἐπί ("for") and the noun οὐσία ("being," "existence") and that it means "for existence," "for subsistence," or "necessary." This view was put forth by Origen.[11] Various other writers in antiquity—apart from questions of its precise etymological origins— understood the term in similar ways, so that in this petition one prays that God will give us today "our bread for subsistence," "our necessary bread."[12] That is also the meaning given in translation in the Syriac Peshitta and Harclean versions. It is a view that is held by various modern commentators as well.[13]

The most important objection to this etymological proposal was stated long ago by J. B. Lightfoot: one should expect an adjective created out of ἐπί and οὐσία to appear as ἐπούσιος, not ἐπιούσιος; i.e., the iota would be elided (as in the word ἐπουσιώδης, "accidental," Porphery, *Isagoge* 16).[14] It has been argued that this expectation is too rigid, but no evidence has been offered to dispute it.[15]

Proposal 2. The second major proposal is that ἐπιούσιος is derived from a contraction of ἐπὶ τὴν οὖσαν [ἡμέραν], meaning "for the existing day," and so the Matthean petition would read, "Give us today our bread for the present day," and Luke's would be, "Give us day by day our bread for the existing day." There is support for this proposed etymology in modern scholarship,[16] but surprisingly little.[17] The main objection is, again, that the iota should be absent in an adjective constructed from the prefix ἐπί and a participial form of the verb "to be." Attested forms of such a compound exist (e.g., ἐπόντος, Demosthenes, *Orations* 21.9

---

[11]   Origen, *De oratione* 27.7; 27.9 (*PG* 11:509); English texts in *Alexandrian Christianity*, ed. J. Oulton and H. Chadwick, 298–99.

[12]   Gregory of Nyssa, *De oratione dominica* 4.1 (*PG* 44:1176); Basil, *Regulae breviorum tractate* 252 (*PG* 31:1252); Cyril of Jerusalem, *Catechesis* 23 [*Mystagogica* 5] (*PG* 33:1120); Chrysostom, *De angusta porta et in orationem dominicam* 5 (*PG* 51:46); and Victorinus, *Adversus Arium* 2.8; text in *PL* 8:1094. It is also suggested as a possibility by John of Damascus, *Expositio fidei orthodoxae* 4.13 (*PG* 94:1152B).

[13]   Friedrich Hauck, "ἄρτος ἐπιούσιος," *ZNW* 33 (1934): 199–202; Werner Foerster, "ἐπιούσιος," *TDNT* 2:599; Henri Bourgoin, "'Επιούσιος expliqué par la notion de préfix vide," *Biblica* 60 (1979): 91–96; Francis W. Beare, *The Gospel according to Matthew* (San Francisco: Harper & Row, 1981), 175–76; J. A. Fitzmyer, *The Gospel according to Luke*, 2:900, 904–906; Alexander Sand, *Das Evangelium nach Matthäus*, RNT (Regensburg: Friedrich Pustet, 1986), 126–28; and Georg Strecker, *The Sermon on the Mount: An Exegetical Commentary* (Nashville: Abingdon Press, 1988), 118–19. Additional references are listed by J. Carmignac, *Recherches sur le 'Notre Père,'* 130–31.

[14]   Joseph B. Lightfoot, *On a Fresh Revision of the English New Testament*, 2d ed. (London and New York: Macmillan, 1872), 201–202.

[15]   Cf. W. Foerster, "ἐπιούσιος," *TDNT* 2:593–94 (and nn. 21 and 22).

[16]   Bernhard Weiss, *Das Matthäusevangelium und seine Lucas-Parallelen* (Halle: Verlag der Buchandlung des Waisenhauses, 1876), 185 (n. 1); BDF 66 (#123); other literature is cited by W. Foerster, "ἐπιούσιος," *TDNT* 2:594 (n. 26).

[17]   Cf. the few entries by J. Carmignac, *Recherches sur la 'Notre Père,'* 131–32.

[Against Meidias]; τὰ ἐπόντα, Plotinus, *Enneads* 2.4.10; and ἐπόντων, Arrian, *Tactica* 10.8), and the iota is lacking. Moreover, there is no evidence of ἡ οὖσα existing in ancient sources as an expression for "the present day."

Proposal 3. The third major proposal is that ἐπιούσιος is derived from a participial form of ἐπιέναι (ἐπιών, ἐπιοῦσα, ἐπιόν, etc.), a compound of ἐπί and the verb ἰέναι ("come," "go"), hence "to come upon." This possibility was recognized already by Origen,[18] although in the final analysis he favored another etymology, as indicated above. Participial forms of this compound are plentiful in ancient texts— classical, Hellenistic (including Jewish Hellenistic writers, e.g., Philo and Josephus), New Testament, and patristic. So, for example, participial forms exist in such phrases as ἐπιόντων Σκυθέων ("when Scythians advanced," Herodotus, *History* 4.11), στρατοῦ ἐπιόντος μεγάλου ("when a great army invaded," ibid.), τὸ ἐπιόν ("that which occurs," Plato, *Phaedrus* 238d; 264b), ἐπιόντος τοῦ χρόνου ("as the time passes," Plato, *Timaeus* 44b), and τοῖς ἔξωθεν ἐπιοῦσι ("to those coming from outside," Plutarch, *Coriolanus* 8.2.1). One of the most common expressions using the participle is ἡ ἐπιοῦσα ἡμέρα, "the coming day," which appears in the New Testament once (Acts 7:26) and abundantly in other ancient texts.[19] This phrase is sometimes abbreviated to ἡ ἐπιοῦσα, and the dative τῇ ἐπιούσῃ is widely attested for "the next day," "tomorrow" in various sources, including the New Testament (Acts 16:11; 20:15; 21:18).[20] Accordingly it has been proposed that the adjective ἐπιούσιος has been derived from this participle—the major part of it being επιουσ (as in the participle just cited), and the ending -ιος formed on analogy to περιούσιος ("chosen").[21]

This etymology is the basis for two closely related proposals. The first is that ἐπιούσιος means "for the coming day," "for tomorrow," and so we pray, "Give us today our bread for the coming day." That is what Jerome claims that the term meant in the Gospel according to the Hebrews (or Gospel of the Nazaraeans, as it is sometimes called): "In the so-called Gospel according to the Hebrews instead of 'essential to existence' I found '*mahar*', which means 'of tomorrow', so that the sense is: Our bread of

---

[18] Origen, *De oratione* 27.13 (*PG* 11:517); English text in *Alexandrian Christianity*, ed. J. Oulton and H. Chadwick, 302.

[19] E.g., Herodotus, *History* 3.85; Plato, *Crito* 44a; Philo, *De opificio mundi* 89.2; Josephus, *Life* 293; and Appian, *The Civil Wars* 1.13.110.

[20] Polybius, *History* 2.25.11; Aristophanes, *Ecclesiazusae* 105; LXX Prov. 3:28; 27:1; Josephus, *Life* 280.

[21] BDF 62 (#113) and 67 (#123). Cf. Origen, *De oratione* 27.7 (*PG* 11:509): "There is a word similar to *epiousion*, in the writings of Moses, spoken by God: 'And ye shall be unto me a peculiar [*periousios*] people'"; English translation quoted from *Alexandrian Christianity*, ed. J. Oulton and H. Chadwick, 298.

tomorrow—that is, of the future—give us this day."[22] Jerome did not,
however, follow this rendering in the translation of the Vulgate. It has not
been until modern times that the etymology discussed here (and existing
already in the works of Origen) has been put forth as a serious proposal in
the works of several interpreters.[23] A. H. McNeile may be quoted as
perhaps typical: "In liturgical use 'bread for the coming day' could denote
either 'bread for the day then in progress,' or 'bread for the morrow,'
according as the Prayer was used in the morning or in the evening."[24]

   Proposal 4. The fourth proposal is closely related to the third. Based
on the same etymological proposal for the origins of ἐπιούσιος, it picks up
the broader implications of a future reference. J. Jeremias, commenting
on the words of Jerome just quoted, says, "As a matter of fact, in ancient
Judaism *maḥar*, 'tomorrow', meant not only the next day but also the
great Tomorrow, the final consummation."[25] Accordingly, the petition is
a call upon God to give not only "daily bread" for physical sustenance but
"the bread of life," "the powers and gifts of God's coming age."[26] This
proposal—the eschatological interpretation—can be found in the ancient
church,[27] and it has become a major proposal in contemporary
scholarship.[28] Generally its proponents do not deny that the petition for

---

[22]   Quoted from the text in *New Testament Apocrypha*, ed. Edgar Hennecke and
Wilhelm Schneemelcher, 2 vols. (Philadelphia: Westminster Press, 1963), 1:147. The text is
from Jerome's *Commentary on Matthew* 6:11, which is in *PL* 26:44.
[23]   These include J. B. Lightfoot, *On a Fresh Revision of the English New Testament*,
199–205; Alan H. McNeile, *The Gospel according to St. Matthew* (London: Macmillan,
1915; reprinted, Grand Rapids: Baker Book House, 1980), 79; Alfred Plummer, *A Critical
and Exegetical Commentary on the Gospel according to S. Luke*, 5th ed., ICC (Edinburgh:
T. & T. Clark, 1922), 296; James M. Creed, *The Gospel according to St. Luke* (London:
Macmillan, 1930), 157; E. F. Scott, *The Lord's Prayer: Its Character, Purpose, and
Interpretation* (New York: Charles Scribner's Sons, 1951), 98; Walter Grundmann, *Das
Evangelium nach Matthäus*, THKNT 1 (Berlin: Evangelische Verlagsanstalt, 1968), 202;
Floyd V. Filson, *The Gospel according to St. Matthew*, 2d ed.; HNTC (New York: Harper
& Row, 1971), 96; Eduard Schweizer, *The Good News according to Matthew* (Atlanta: John
Knox Press, 1975), 153–54; R. H. Gundry, *Matthew*, 107; and Colin J. Hemer,
"ἐπιούσιος," *JSNT* 22 (1984): 81–94. For references to still other scholars, cf. W. Foerster,
"ἐπιούσιος," *TDNT* 2:592 (n. 16) and J. Carmignac, *Recherches sur le 'Notre Père,'* 132–36.
Frederic H. Chase, *The Lord's Prayer in the Early Church*, Texts and Studies 1/3
(Cambridge: Cambridge Univ. Press, 1891), 44–53, can be included here, but he concludes
that the terminology refers to "the bread of the day" (which is coming on) within the context
of a morning prayer.
[24]   A. H. McNeile, *The Gospel according to St. Matthew*, 79.
[25]   J. Jeremias, "The Lord's Prayer in the Light of Recent Research," 100.
[26]   Ibid., 102.
[27]   Athanasius, *De incarnatione Verbi Dei et contra Arianos* 16 (*PG* 26:1012); Theodoret,
Interpretatio Epistolae ad Philippenses 4.19 (*PG* 82:589); the view is held as a possibility by
John of Damascus, *Expositio fidei orthodoxae* 4.13 (*PG* 94:1152B).
[28]   E. Lohmeyer, *The Lord's Prayer*, 141–46, 156–57; J. Jeremias, "The Lord's Prayer
in the Light of Recent Research," 100–102; C. F. Evans, *The Lord's Prayer* (London:
SPCK, 1960), 44–56; Raymond E. Brown, "The Pater Noster as an Eschatological Prayer,"
in his *New Testament Essays* (Milwaukee: Bruce Publishing Co., 1965), 238–43; C. W. F.
Smith, "Lord's Prayer," *IDB* 3:156–57; David Hill, *The Gospel of Matthew*, NCB (London:

bread includes earthly, material bread, but they stress in any case that it has an eschatological reference beyond the day to come.

As with the first two proposals, so there are difficulties with proposals three and four, which propose the same etymology. First, it is difficult to assess the significance of *maḥar*, which Jerome claimed to find in the so-called Gospel of the Nazaraeans. J. Jeremias has claimed that the term attests an "Aramaic wording of the Lord's Prayer . . . older even than our gospels,"[29] which the Greek ἐπιούσιος seeks to represent in Greek-speaking Christianity. But that can be challenged. If the familiar term *maḥar* ("of tomorrow") was the traditional expression in Aramaic-speaking Christianity, why was it not translated into the equally familiar αὔριον ("tomorrow") known to both evangelists (Matt. 6:30//Luke 12:28; Matt. 6:34; Luke 10:35; 13:32–33)? Or if it meant not necessarily "tomorrow" but "the coming day" (from the perspective of early morning prayer), why was it not translated into any of the familiar expressions which have this meaning, e.g., τῆς ἐπιούσης ἡμέρας,[30] τῆς ἐπιούσης,[31] εἰς τὴν ἐπιοῦσαν,[32] τῇ ἐπιούσῃ,[33] etc.? Further, it must be said that having two temporal references ("today," "of tomorrow") in so short a sentence seems unusual, even unnatural.[34] It is surely possible, as Philipp Vielhauer has argued, that the Gospel of the Nazaraeans presupposes the Greek text of Matthew at this point and that *maḥar* "is the earliest attempt to explain" the meaning of ἐπιούσιος.[35]

There is difficulty also with the eschatological interpretation in particular. As indicated, J. Jeremias suggests that *maḥar* would mean "the great Tomorrow, the final consummation."[36] The difficulty is that this terminology is never used elsewhere in the teachings of Jesus, as

---

Marshall, Morgan & Scott, 1972), 138; P. B. Harner, *Understanding the Lord's Prayer*, 84–99; H. Benedict Green, *The Gospel according to Matthew* (London: Oxford Univ. Press, 1975), 90–91; and Ulrich Luz, *Das Evangelium nach Matthäus: l. Teilband, Mt 1–7*, EKK I/1 (Zürich: Benziger Verlag; Neukirchen-Vluyn: Neukirchener Verlag, 1985), 345–46. A survey of still other works, and critique, is provided by Anton Vögtle, "Der 'eschatologische' Bezug der Wir-Bitten des Vaterunser," in *Jesus und Paulus: Festschrift für Werner Georg Kümmel zum 70. Geburtstag*, ed. E. Earle Ellis and Erich Grässer (Göttingen: Vandenhoeck & Ruprecht, 1975), 348–53; cf. also J. Carmignac, *Recherches sur le 'Notre Père,'* 132–36.

[29] J. Jeremias, "The Lord's Prayer in the Light of Recent Research," 100.

[30] Appian, *The Civil Wars* 1.13.110; Josephus, *Life* 293.

[31] Longus, *Daphne and Chloe* 1.13; Libanius, *Orations* 18.268; 19.56; 22.21; Gregory of Nazianzus, *Oratio* 16.300 (PG 35:937).

[32] Josephus, *Life* 161; 290; idem, *Jewish Antiquities* 3.30; 3.249.

[33] See note 20 above.

[34] Cf. W. Foerster, "ἐπιούσιος," TDNT 2:596.

[35] Philipp Vielhauer, "Jewish-Christian Gospels," in *New Testament Apocrypha*, ed. E. Hennecke and W. Schneemelcher, 1:142. Cf. also E. Lohmeyer, *The Lord's Prayer*, 143, and G. Strecker, *The Sermon on the Mount*, 118.

[36] J. Jeremias, "The Lord's Prayer in the Light of Recent Research," 100.

transmitted in our sources, to refer to the age or kingdom to come.[37] On one occasion a table companion speaks of eating bread in the kingdom of God (Luke 14:15), but it is questionable whether Jesus would teach his disciples to pray for "our bread of the Tomorrow." To be sure, the latter interpretation is found in certain patristic sources,[38] but it cannot likely be traced back to Jesus of Nazareth. Whether it was current in Greek-speaking Christianity and at the time of the writing of the gospels in particular, so that the evangelists held such a view, is another matter. But it is fitting to look at another possibility.

III. Epiousios Artos

There is another possibility that seems not to have been considered but which merits a hearing. That is a proposal that builds upon the substantial and widely held view that ἐπιούσιος is derived etymologically from a participial form of ἐπιέναι ("to come upon") but which does not propose and introduce ἡμέρα as the implied word that the adjective modifies. The phrase τὸν ἄρτον . . . τὸν ἐπιούσιον is grammatically equivalent to τὸν ἐπιούσιον ἄρτον, i.e., the adjective modifies ἄρτον. This was recognized in antiquity, for in commenting on the fourth petition various writers wrote the expression τὸν ἐπιούσιον ἄρτον.[39] The phrase, when set this way, can mean simply "the coming bread" or "the bread which comes upon [us]." The words τὸν ἄρτον ἡμῶν τὸν ἐπιούσιον would thus be equivalent to τὸν ἄρτον ἡμῶν τὸν ἐπιόντα. The entire petition would then be translated as "Give us today our coming bread," i.e., the bread which comes to us from God. In a more ample clause, one could put it this way: "Give us today, Father, our bread which comes upon us from you." There are several points that can be made in favor of this proposal.

1. Certain ancient versions translate τὸν ἄρτον ἡμῶν τὸν ἐπιούσιον into words which mean "our bread which comes." These include the Palestinian Syriac and the (Coptic) Sahidic texts at Matthew 6:11[40] and the (Coptic) Sahidic and Bohairic texts at Luke 11:3.[41] One need not claim

---

[37] Cf. Matt. 6:30//Luke 12:28; and Luke 13:32–33 for the use of "tomorrow." In these cases the term has an ordinary, temporal sense.

[38] Cf. note 27 above.

[39] Cf. Origen, *Excerpta in Psalmos* on Ps. 77 (PG 17:145); Athanasius, *De incarnatione Verbi Dei et contra Arianos* 16 (PG 26:1012); Basil, *Epistola 361* (PG 32:1101); idem, *Regulae breviorum tractate* 252 (PG 31:1252); and Gregory of Nyssa, *In suam ordinationem* (PG 46:548).

[40] Here I rely on the textual variants cited by S. C. E. Legg, *Novum Testamentum Graece: Evangelium secundum Matthaeum* (Oxford: Clarendon Press, 1940) *ad loc* for Matt. 6:11.

[41] Here I rely on three sources of information. First, there are the textual variants cited in *The New Testament in Greek: The Gospel according to St. Luke, Part One: Chapters*

that these versions reflect a pre-literary prayer tradition that is older than our written, canonical gospels in Greek—although that is possible—for they may simply be early attempts at translation from Greek into Syriac and Coptic. Nevertheless, they are significant as early interpretations of ἐπιούσιος ἄρτος as "bread which comes" to those who pray.[42]

Besides the readings of these versions, there is a significant comment by Ambrose at one place where he says that, although Latin-speaking persons speak of "daily" (quotidianum) bread in this petition of the Lord's Prayer, Greek-speaking people say ἐπιούσιος, by which they mean "coming" (advenientem) bread.[43] Here there appears to be evidence that, at least in some circles known to Ambrose, the term ἐπιούσιος was interpreted as "coming." Moreover, Peter of Laodicea, although rather late (seventh century), has written that the term could have been derived from the verb ἐπιέναι ("to come upon") and could be equivalent to τὸν ἐπιόντα ("that which comes").[44] He finally does not settle the matter, for he also grants that the term could have been derived from οὐσία. Yet the fact that he, a learned Greek-speaking person, considers the possibility that τὸν ἐπιούσιον is equivalent to τὸν ἐπιόντα in his exposition of the Lord's Prayer indicates that it does not fall out of the bounds of linguistic possibilities. It may also reflect an interpretation current in his time, although that is not a certainty.

2. There is also an ancient tradition of rendering ἐπιούσιος ἄρτος as "constant" or "continual bread." In the apocryphal (Syriac) Acts of Thomas at 144 this petition of the Lord's Prayer reads, "Give us the constant bread of the day."[45] The Curetonian Syriac, Sinaitic Syriac, and

---

1–12, ed. The American and British Committees on the International Greek New Testament Project (Oxford: Clarendon Press, 1984), 244. The textual evidence (with literal translations into English) is also provided in the following two sources: *The Coptic Version of the New Testament in the Southern Dialect, Otherwise Called Sahidic and Thebaic*, ed. and trans. George Horner, 7 vols. (Oxford: Clarendon Press, 1911–24), 2:213: "Our bread which cometh give it to us daily"; and *The Coptic Version of the New Testament in the Northern Dialect, Otherwise Called Memphitic and Bohairic*, ed. and trans. George Horner, 4 vols. (Oxford: Clarendon Press, 1898–1905), 2:155: "Give to us daily our bread which cometh."

[42]   Some modern commentators have come close to this as a possible interpretation. I. H. Marshall, *The Gospel of Luke*, 459, has written that one possibility would be, "'Give us today the bread *that comes to it*', i.e., 'the bread *that we need* for today.'" But his explanatory clause seems to complicate the meaning, and in the final analysis he rejects this possible meaning anyway. Bernhard Orchard, "The Meaning of *ton epiousion*. (Mt 6:11 = Lk 11:3)," *BTB* 3 (1973): 279, has suggested that in this petition "we are told to pray for the bread 'that comes on the scene', for the 'bread that turns up', and 'that we come upon' when we go for it." There is some confusion here concerning the subject of the implied action: Is it the bread, or is it the petitioner that does the "coming"?

[43]   Ambrose, *De sacramentis* 5.24 (PL 16:452).

[44]   Petrus Laodicenus, *Expositio in orationem dominicam* (PL 86:3333A).

[45]   This is the translation by Robert McL. Wilson, "The Acts of the Holy Apostle Thomas," in *New Testament Apocrypha*, ed. E. Hennecke and W. Schneemelcher, 2:519.

Armenian versions have "continual bread."[46] It is plausible that these renderings are based on an understanding that the bread for which one prays "continues" from the hand of God.[47] The term ἐπιούσιος (as "coming upon [us]") suggests such an understanding.

3. The language concerning bread as "coming" from God recalls familiar biblical idioms in which the Lord "gives" to his people "bread from heaven." At Exodus 16:4, in the story of the manna from heaven, the Lord says to Moses, "I will rain bread from heaven (LXX, ἄρτους ἐκ τοῦ οὐρανοῦ) for you," and at 16:15 the manna is called "the bread which the Lord has given you to eat (ὁ ἄρτος, ὃν ἔδωκεν κύριος ὑμῖν φαγεῖν)." The several allusions to this story in later biblical literature illustrate its significance for Israel's memory and, above all, how familiar the term "bread from heaven" was: at Psalm 78:24 (LXX, Ps. 77:24) the psalmist refers to the giving of the manna as bread of heaven (ἄρτον οὐρανοῦ) which the Lord gave to the people; at Psalm 105:40 (LXX, 104:40) the psalmist refers to the event, saying that God "gave them bread from heaven in abundance (ἄρτον οὐρανοῦ ἐνέπλησεν αὐτούς)"; at Nehemiah 9:15 (LXX, 2 Esdras 19:15) the writer addresses God, "Thou didst give them bread from heaven (ἄρτον ἐξ οὐρανοῦ ἔδωκας αὐτοῖς)"; and at the Wisdom of Solomon 16:20 God is addressed, "Thou didst furnish them bread from heaven (ἄρτον ἀπ᾽ οὐρανοῦ)." The petitioner who prays, "Give us today our bread that comes from you," would not simply ask for bread but would also in the same breath make a confessional statement, reflecting the centuries' old conviction that everything needful for life has been given "from heaven" (= God).

4. The motif of bread from heaven not only predates this petition but is echoed in the Fourth Gospel. In reply to those who speak of the manna in the wilderness, Jesus says, "It was not Moses who gave you the bread from heaven (τὸν ἄρτον ἐκ τοῦ οὐρανοῦ); my Father gives you the true bread from heaven (τὸν ἄρτον ἐκ τοῦ οὐρανοῦ τὸν ἀληθινόν). For the bread of God is that which comes down from heaven (ὁ καταβαίνων ἐκ τοῦ οὐρανοῦ) and gives life to the world" (6:32–33). Jesus goes on in this discourse to speak of himself as the bread of life (6:35) who has come down from heaven (6:38); the two statements are combined in the saying of 6:41: "I am the bread of life which came down from heaven (ὁ καταβὰς ἐκ τοῦ οὐρανοῦ)." In Johannine thought the bread from God is Jesus himself. But behind this way of thinking is the motif of bread which comes from God. The motif is rooted in Exodus 16 and repeated in the frequent allusions

---

[46] Cf. D. Y. Hadidian, "The Meaning of ἐπιούσιος and the Codices Sergii," *NTS* 5 (1958): 77, 80–81.

[47] The term "continual bread" (RSV) or "bread of continuity" appears at Num. 4:7 (*leḥem hattāmîd*; LXX, οἱ ἄρτοι οἱ διὰ παντός), but it does not seem to be the basis for the expression in the Syriac texts cited.

to it in Jewish literature and in the larger compass of John 6 after the feeding of the multitude.[48] Yet it has been shown that the Lord's Prayer was almost certainly known and prayed in the Johannine community.[49] In that community the bread petition could well have been understood as a petition for bread which comes down from heaven to give life to the world. Through the repetition of this petition and the christological reflection characteristic of the community, including the theme of the descent and ascent of the Son of man (3:13–14; 6:62), the language of the petition would then be the basis for the imagery of Jesus as the bread which comes down from heaven to give life to the world. Admittedly there is conjecture here, but clearly the extent of "spiritualizing" that has taken place in John 6 concerning the bread shows eucharistic symbolism and enactment, which alerts us that reflection on Exodus 16 is not sufficient by itself to account for the meanings attached to bread in John 6. We suggest here that the bread petition of the Lord's Prayer— understood as a petition for bread from heaven, and prayed in eucharistic and other gatherings—also stimulated the spiritualizing of bread in John 6.

5. The proposal made here coheres well with aspects peculiar to both forms of the petition in the gospels. This is obvious especially in the case of Luke's version. Here one prays that God will keep on giving the bread in question "every day" (τὸ καθ᾽ ἡμέραν).[50] It seems fitting that the bread in question be understood by Luke and his readers as the ordinary bread of everyday existence "which comes" from God. An eschatological interpretation ("Keep giving to us the bread of the future kingdom day by day"), while by no means impossible, seems strained. What kind of bread would this be? Presumably the word "bread" would have to be a metaphor for spiritual gifts. But elsewhere Luke's concern for the feeding of the body is so eloquent (6:21; 4:13–14; 16:19–31) that one hears "bread" in his version of the Lord's Prayer to signify food, drink, and other things needful for life. In Matthew's version of the prayer matters are more ambiguous, to be sure. Here one prays that God will give the bread in question "today" (σήμερον). Again, it is fitting that the bread in question be understood by Matthew and his readers as ordinary bread "which comes" from God. God knows the needs of his children (6:32) and "makes his sun rise on the evil and on the good, and sends rain on the just and the unjust" (5:45). The petition expresses the dependence of Jesus'

---

[48]   The major work on this is by Peder Borgen, *Bread from Heaven: An Exegetical Study of the Concept of Manna in the Gospel of John and the Writings of Philo*, NovTSup 10 (Leiden: E. J. Brill, 1965; reprinted, 1981).

[49]   Cf. William O. Walker, Jr., "The Lord's Prayer in Matthew and in John," *NTS* 28 (1982): 237–56. Walker cites other scholars who share in this judgment.

[50]   The article τό is meaningless; cf. BAGD 346 (#2); BDF 88 (#160).

disciples in the Matthean community upon God, and it expresses the piety of the psalm, "The eyes of all look to thee, and thou givest them their food (σὺ δίδως τὴν τροφὴν αὐτῶν) in due season" (Ps. 145:15; LXX, 144:15). Again, although an eschatological interpretation ("Give us the bread of the future kingdom today") is not impossible, it is certainly not required, and Matthew's emphasis on God's provision for all, even for those of "little faith" who should not be anxious about tomorrow (6:30), favors the interpretation proposed here.

6. Although the eschatological character of the petitions in the Lord's Prayer has been emphasized in recent scholarship, one should not overlook the shift that takes place with the fourth petition. Günther Bornkamm has made the observation: "[The] first three petitions pray . . . for the revelation of God and his kingdom, while the following petitions pray for the deliverance from the troubles which beset and threaten the petitioner now: our bodily concerns, guilt, temptation and the power of evil."[51] Similarly Eduard Schweizer has written that, since the next two petitions after this one "refer unambiguously to this world," so the bread petition does as well.[52] And if this is so with Matthew's version, it is even more clear in Luke that the petition has to do with the present condition of those who pray.[53] The view that the petition concerns ordinary, indeed "daily," bread "that comes" from God continuously coheres with the non-eschatological interpretation. Yet it does not undercut the eschato-logical emphases of the gospel tradition in other respects.

7. Finally, the meaning of the term proposed here would have been capable of giving rise to the other interpretations. No other interpretation is equally capable. Three other interpretations are close at hand: (1) as suggested already, it is but a small step from praying for our bread "which comes" (or "proceeds to" us) from God to pray in another language for our "continual" bread, as in certain Syriac and Armenian texts; (2) the bread "which comes" from God comes "daily," which is not only an article of faith but is taught by the well known story in Exodus about the bread from heaven, in which it is said that the Lord provided "a day's portion" (*debar yôm b^eyômô*; LXX, τὸ τῆς ἡμέρας εἰς ἡμέραν, Exod. 16:4); and (3) the bread "which comes" from God is of course "necessary for existence," and the easy association of ἐπιούσιος with ἐπί and οὐσία helps to establish that interpretation.

But does the interpretation proposed here account also for the view that ἐπιούσιος refers to bread "for the coming day"? The word ἐπιούσιος, as we have maintained, modifies the noun "bread." But given the

---

[51] Günther Bornkamm, *Jesus of Nazareth* (New York: Harper & Brothers, 1960), 137. Cf. also W. Foerster, "ἐπιούσιος," *TDNT* 2:597.

[52] E. Schweizer, *The Good News according to Matthew*, 154.

[53] Cf. J. A. Fitzmyer, *The Gospel according to Luke*, 899–900, 904.

similarity of the unusual ἐπιούσιος to the familiar ἐπιοῦσα [ἡμέρα], it would have been easy in time for interpreters to take the adjective as referring to "the coming day." We see this happen in the passage quoted from Ambrose earlier. The ἐπιούσιος bread, he says, is the "coming" (*advenientem*) bread, according to the Greeks, but he also says that Latin-speaking people call it "daily" (*quotidianum*) bread "because the Greeks speak of τὴν ἐπιοῦσαν ἡμέραν, the coming day (*advenientem diem*)."[54] The logic of Ambrose in moving from (1) "coming bread" to (2) "coming day" to (3) "daily" is of course not compelling. But our point that an original "coming bread" (or "bread which comes") can give rise to "bread for the coming day" is illustrated in this passage. Once the shift to "coming day" was made, the latter term could also take on an eschatological reference so that the petition could be understood to refer to the bread of the coming age.

It must be admitted finally that the word ἐπιούσιος remains a puzzle. Regardless of what meaning is proposed, including this one, the question still lurks: Why didn't the evangelists use a commonly understood term? If ἐπιούσιος means "coming," why didn't the evangelists, and even traditions before them, render the phrase with comprehensible participles, e.g., τὸν ἐπερχόμενον or τὸν ἐπιόντα? But the same kind of question can be raised concerning alternatives. If ἐπιούσιος means "necessary," "daily," or "of tomorrow" (in either its temporal or eschatological nuances), why do we not have a familiar Greek term which would translate into one of these? The meaning proposed in this essay may finally be judged inadequate, but it seems to open up linguistic and exegetical possibilities that should be tested more thoroughly than here. In the meantime, the word "daily" is perhaps so embedded in the English tradition that no matter how strongly one might propose an alternative to it as linguistically or exegetically superior, it is likely to stay. The members of the International Consultation on English Texts, for example, have written:

The translation "daily bread" is notoriously uncertain. It may mean "bread for tomorrow," referring not only to the next day but also the "great tomorrow," or the final consummation. The petition would then be for the food of the heavenly banquet, and this would fit well with the eschatological perspective which seems to control the whole of the prayer. On the other hand it could mean simply "the bread which is necessary," without any particular temporal reference. There would seem to be no sufficient reason for substantially varying the familiar

---

[54]   Ambrose, *De sacramentis* 5.24 (PL 16:452).

translation. In a world where so many are hungry, there may seem especial reason to maintain it.[55]

One can hardly resist the conclusion that familiar usage is the canon being employed in this instance. Regardless of what the word might mean, the familiar is endorsed for use.

Although the familiar cannot be a criterion, it should be pointed out that the use of "our daily bread" in the petition can stand more readily on the basis of our proposal than the eschatological proposal ("our bread for the coming age," etc.) that is so widely championed. We pray then for "our bread which comes" from the Giver and Sustainer of all life, asking that it be given "today" (as in Matthew) or "every day" (as in Luke). We confess in our prayer that God does indeed open his hand and satisfy the desire of every living thing (Ps. 145:16), and we ask that God continue to do so. So understood, there is probably no other expression in English that serves as well as "our daily bread," and there is no compelling reason to supplant it . . . even if we could.

---

[55] *Prayers We Have in Common: Agreed Liturgical Texts Prepared by the International Consultation on English Texts*, 2d ed. (Philadelphia: Fortress Press, 1975), 2–3.

What Q Could Have Learned
from Reginald Fuller

EDUARD SCHWEIZER*

In the same year that I finished my monograph on *Erniedrigung und Erhöhung bei Jesus und seinen Nachfolgern*,[1] Reginald Fuller published his first christological book.[2] I have learned much from it, and I used it when I rewrote my monograph in a shortened version for the English translation,[3] and for the second German edition. Fuller did not simply rewrite his book, but published a new one in 1965,[4] in which he kindly referred several times to my work. Later on, he and Mrs. Fuller even spent (and lost) quite an amount of their time and strength by translating my book *Heiliger Geist*.[5] Thus, it might be a good idea to continue this almost life-long dialogue. It might even give Reginald some pleasure, perhaps even more so, because Philo, of whom we shall have to speak below (5.1,3), is, as all his friends know, a name very dear to him, since it has not merely belonged to a philosopher of the first, but also to a very good dog of the twentieth century.

1. The Christology of Q

I agree with Fuller in his evaluation of the existence of Q: that it is a very probable hypothesis, though we cannot reach absolute certainty.[6] Like me, the (end-)redactor of Q could have learned a lot from Fuller, if he could have read his books and essays. He certainly had a strong interest in Christology.[7] However, this interest is only implicitly

---

* Eduard Schweizer is retired Professor of New Testament, University of Zurich, Zurich, Switzerland.

[1] E. Schweizer, *Erniedrigung und Erhöhung bei Jesus und seinen Nachfolgern*, ATANT 28 (Zurich: Zwingli Verlag, 1955; 2d ed., 1962).

[2] Reginald H. Fuller, *The Mission and Achievement of Jesus*, SBT 12 (London: SCM Press, 1954).

[3] E. Schweizer, *Lordship and Discipleship*, SBT 28 (London: SCM Press, 1960).

[4] Reginald H. Fuller, *The Foundations of New Testament Christology* (New York: Charles Scribner's Sons, 1965).

[5] E. Schweizer, *The Holy Spirit* (Philadelphia: Fortress Press, 1960); trans. of *Heiliger Geist* (Stuttgart: Kreuz Verlag, 1978).

[6] Reginald H. Fuller, *A Critical Introduction to the New Testament* (London: G. Duckworth, 1966), 72.

[7] Reginald H. Fuller, *Interpreting the Miracles* (London: SCM Press, 1963), 47–48; cf. also his *Introduction*, 74: "Q also contains a christological kerygma." This kerygma would

expressed.[8] As a psychotherapist helps us to detect and to express explicitly what we really think and want to say, Fuller could have shown him what a challenging and, in many ways, modern Christology he actually proclaimed.

In *Mission* Fuller ranges the "raw materials of Christology" according to the titles Son of God, Servant of God, Son of man, Christ, and Lord. In *Foundations* he deals, first, with the background in Palestinian and Hellenistic Judaism and in paganism, then with the historical Jesus, the earliest church, the Hellenistic-Jewish, and the Hellenistic-Gentile mission, so that the lists of christological titles appear within the respective areas. We may, therefore, follow to some degree the list in *Mission* and speak first of the "Son of God" (section 2 below). "Servant" does not appear as christological title anywhere in the gospels (except in an Old Testament quotation at Matt. 12:18), but the Jewish figure of the Servant is certainly of influence also in Q (section 3). "Son of man" designates in Q the earthly Jesus and the coming Lord (section 4). "Christ" is missing in Q, and "Lord" is merely the address to the earthly and the coming Jesus. However, his specific relation to the Wisdom of God distinguishes him from all other men and describes his status in a way comparable to what the titles "Christ" and "Lord" mean (section 5).

2. The Son of God

2.1 Jesus enters the picture of Q, as far as we can reconstruct it, in the story of his temptations. It is certainly possible that his baptism was also reported by Q, since the tempter starts from the statement, "If you are the Son of God."[9] The location of the temptations in the desert seems to belong to Q and is not merely taken over from Mark.[10] The answers of Jesus repeat God's directions to Israel in Deuteronomy. Thus, the pattern in the background is that of Israel in the desert, faced both by God's call to become and act as his own people in obedience to his word, and by the temptation to disobey on that long journey through the desert. Jesus is no longer the new Adam (as in Mark 1:13b), who overcomes the temptations to which Adam succumbed. He is the one who overcomes the temptations of Israel, the only obedient one, the new Israel. Fuller suggests that this is the conception of sonship that shapes the Christology of Q: as Israel is the son of God, but lost this status in its disobedience, so Jesus, the only

---

not be the same as that of, e.g., 1 Cor. 15:3–5, but perhaps like that of the church of Caesarea (*Introduction*, 73–75).

[8] Cf. R. Fuller, *Foundations*, 254.

[9] If there had been a "paidology" in the background, as Fuller suggests (*Mission*, 81, 86–95; *Foundations*, 115–16, 170, 194), it would have been so in both stories.

[10] Cf., e.g., Siegfried Schulz, *Q: Die Spruchquelle der Evangelisten* (Zurich: Theologischer Verlag, 1972), 177–78.

obedient Israelite, becomes the son who really listens to God and lives according to his directions.[11]

2.2 The quotations of Matthew 4:1–11 par. follow, more or less literally, the LXX. The story belongs to a LXX-milieu.[12] The call "to worship the Lord" (Matt. 4:10 par.)[13] is not to be found in Deuteronomy 6:13. It may stem from 5:9, where προσκυνεῖν and λατρεύειν are used together (in a negative way), and/or 32:43 LXX (not in the Hebrew text); here, "the sons of God" are both the angels, who worship God (in a positive way), and the Israelites, whose blood is vindicated. In the context of his discussion of the Son of man, Fuller thinks that Jesus himself had "individualized" the corporate conception (with regard to Israel) of the Son of man and Servant to describe his own status[14] and speaks, in the context of Wisdom 2:13, of an "individualization of Israel's corporate sonship of God in the OT,"[15] which influenced New Testament Christology, including probably the temptation story of Q.[16]

2.3 In John 1:51 the Son of man is presented in the image of Jacob-Israel (Gen. 28:12; cf. 32:28).[17] Jesus proclaims himself as "the true vine," which is a frequent metaphor for Israel.[18] In Psalm 79:16 (LXX) the vine (Israel) and the son of man are "equivalent concepts" for the people of God.[19] Even if the identification of the son of man with Jacob-Israel and of the vine with the people of Israel were not in the pre-Johannine background,[20] some influence of Genesis 28 and passages like Psalm 79

---

[11] R. Fuller, *Mission*, 84–85 (cf. p. 95); expressed more cautiously (including discussion) in his *Foundations*, 115–19.

[12] Cf. Krister Stendahl, *The School of St. Matthew and Its Use of the Old Testament*, 2d ed. (Philadelphia: Fortress Press, 1968), 150.

[13] In Q it was probably the final answer of Jesus (as in Matthew, contra Luke).

[14] R. Fuller, *Mission*, 102.

[15] R. Fuller, *Foundations*, 71.

[16] Cf. ibid., 193–94. Note 34 on p. 83 refers to Wis. 16:26 where the Israelites are the sons of God. It may be added that the answer of Jesus in Matt. 4:3 reflects the same word as that very verse: that a person lives not by bread alone, but by every word . . . of God.

[17] "Ascending and descending" appear in the same sequence (though the logic would ask for the reverse order), and Jewish rabbis (of the third century A.D.) understood the text as saying that the angels did so "on him" (Jacob), not "on it" (the ladder). Cf. Eduard Schweizer, "Die Kirche als Leib Christi in den paulinischen Homologumena," *TLZ* 86 (1961): 166–67; reprinted in E. Schweizer, *Neotestamentica* (Zurich: Zwingli Verlag, 1963), 283–84 (Jacob as a divine figure in Philo, etc.); Rudolf Schnackenburg, *Das Johannesevangelium*, 3 vols.; HTKNT 4 (Freiburg: Herder & Herder, 1965–75), 1:319–20; Fritzleo Lentzen-Deis, *Die Taufe Jesu nach den Synoptikern*, FTS 4 (Frankfurt: Josef Knecht, 1970), 214–27, 233, 242–43, and esp. 225–26.

[18] C. H. Dodd, *The Interpretation of the Fourth Gospel* (Cambridge: Cambridge Univ. Press, 1953), 136–37; R. Schnackenburg, *Johannesevangelium*, 3:118–21. *Lib. Ant.* 12.8 can be added, because there the vine (Israel) is rooted in the abyss, and its branches reach up to the throne of God.

[19] C. H. Dodd, *Interpretation*, 411.

[20] R. Schnackenburg, *Johannesevangelium*, 4:3, while skeptical with regard to 1:51, is positive in regard to 15:1.

(80) and/or their Jewish interpretations is highly probable. Personally, I still think that even the Pauline "body of Christ" embracing all its members is basically the same concept as the Johannine "vine" embracing all its branches.[21] The shift from an original thinking in the (temporal) pattern of *Heilsgeschichte* within Israel to thinking in spatial terms, no longer limited to Israel, but open to universal salvation, is clearly to be seen in the New Testament.[22] There are, at least, some strong hints to a development (or perhaps, to independent different ideas that were simultaneously in the wind), in which the vague idea of Jesus replacing, eschatologically, the old Israel, as the one obedient son of God, became clearer in a pre-Johannine equation of the Son of man Jesus with Jacob-Israel and/or the *true* vine in contrast to the unfruitful vine Israel. In the same way, he is the *good* shepherd in contrast to the blind leaders of Israel (John 9:40–41; 10:11–15), the bread *of life* in contrast to the manna of Israel (6:32–35), etc.

2.4 If the divine sonship of Jesus was, already in Q, understood in the pattern of the corporate sonship of Israel[23] and, therefore, from the very beginning totally different from any idea of a "divine man,"[24] because the one obedient Son of God, the new Jacob-Israel, rejects exactly this suggestion of the tempter, it would mean very much for our understanding of the early Christology. If the Q-redactor could have read Fuller's book he would have marveled at what decisive steps he had taken towards a clearly cut image for Jesus' importance to his church, just by reporting and, perhaps, slightly interpreting that story of the temptations of Jesus. He could have told us whether or not we are barking up the wrong tree, whether or not Israel's corporate sonship of God (or even the individual sonship of the Israelite; cf. below 5.1), which he certainly knew from the Old Testament, was really important to him. If so, he could have explained to us in which way he considered the status of Jesus as the son of God unique or, at least, different from that of Israel or the righteous Israelite. Unfortunately, he did not have the privilege we have to read Fuller's books. Hence he did not realize how much he contributed to the early Christology in the making, and we can still not be sure how much

---

[21]   E. Schweizer, "σῶμα," *TDNT* 7:1068–71.

[22]   Cf. R. Fuller, *Foundations*, 254–55, who speaks of the preexistence of Christ in Israel's history becoming universal in an ontic preexistence (as an "ontic identity-in-distinction"), e.g., in Phil. 2:6–11, without basically changing the earlier view.

[23]   Cf. n. 11 above, and for the Son of man as a kind of "corporate" image of the people of God, see below at 4.3.

[24]   R. Fuller, *Mission*, 80–85, and *Foundations*, 181, n. 93. I am very skeptical about the presupposition that the concept of a "divine man" existed at all in the Hellenism of the time of Jesus and Paul. Cf. my essay, "Towards a Christology of Mark," in *God's Christ and His People: Studies in Honour of Nils Alstrup Dahl*, ed. Jacob Jervell and Wayne A. Meeks (Oslo: Universitetsforlaget, 1977), 30–31, and Fuller's reticence, *Foundations*, 72 ("we need not deny . . . "; cf. 227–29, 232).

the concept of Jesus as the new Israel was in the wind in the time and area of Q, and therefore also in that of the pre-Johannine community.

3. The Servant of God

3.1 In the second paragraph of chapter 4 in *Mission* Fuller deals with Jesus as the Servant of God or, as he specifies in *Foundations* (pp. 167–73), as the Mosaic prophet-servant. Since the title is not to be found in Q and the hypothesis of an underlying "paidology" is uncertain and, at any rate, no longer relevant for the last redactor of Q, we shall concentrate, first, on the sayings about the rejection, the suffering, and the death of Jesus, and then in paragraph 4 we shall focus on those about his vindication or exaltation.

Fuller has, of course, realized that the passion of Jesus is not mentioned in Q and certainly not an expiating death. He emphasizes, however, that Matthew 8:20 is not simply a literal statement of the fact that Jesus has no bed for the coming night; it is a sign of rejection and criticism, which, as Q knows full well, have culminated in the cross.[25] Matthew 11:19 par. expresses clearly the rejection of Jesus by the people "in the light of his subsequent vindication."[26] Between Jesus and the coming Son of man there is still the cross, just as in Daniel 7, it is the suffering Israel that will be vindicated like the Son of man in the vision of the prophet.[27] The rejection of Jesus and his disciples is, in Q, certainly seen in an eschatological context. It is the last chance given to Israel, and "the blood of all the prophets . . . may be required of this generation" (Luke 11:49–51 par.; cf. below 5.2,3).[28] The explicit expectation of Jesus that he will die in Jerusalem the death of all the prophets (Luke 13:33) may have been included in Q, at least in the copy Luke possessed.[29]

3.2 In this context, Fuller refers to Isaiah 53 and Wisdom 2, where the suffering righteous one is both servant and son of God, and will be vindicated by God.[30] Thus, servantship includes both election by God to a unique status and humiliation, even rejection by the world. In Isaiah 53:11 as well as in Wisdom 2:13, the "knowledge (γνῶσις) of God" plays an important role in the task of the Servant of God.[31] Interestingly

---

[25]   R. Fuller, *Mission*, 104–105, and *Foundations*, 148; cf. also below at 5.2.

[26]   R. Fuller, *Foundations*, 148–49; cf. 128.

[27]   R. Fuller, *Mission*, 103–104; cf. *Introduction*, 74: "The cross and resurrection are the indispensable presuppositions of Q."

[28]   R. Fuller, *Mission*, 63, n. 1; *Foundations*, 151 (and n. 35).

[29]   According to Fuller, *The New Testament in Current Study* (New York: Charles Scribner's Sons, 1962), 44, Luke 13:31–33 may well be an authentic word of Jesus. It is the only word in which Jesus speaks, in an understatement, of himself explicitly as a prophet (*Mission*, 78, n. 1).

[30]   R. Fuller, *Mission*, 94 (cf. 108); *Foundations*, 66.

[31]   R. Fuller, *Mission*, 91–92; *Foundations*, 70–71.

enough, the same keyword dominates also the saying of Jesus that "no one knows the Son except the Father, and no one the Father except the Son and any one to whom the Son chooses to reveal him" (Matt. 11:27 par.).[32] As in Isaiah 53 and Wisdom 2, God entrusts his servant (his "son": Wis. 2:16, 18) with the revelation of his name to Israel. In Q, the preceding verses[33] show that it is exactly the "babes" that will understand him, whereas "the wise and understanding" reject his message.

3.3 Again, what a fascinating Christology! If the Q-redactor had been able to read Fuller's books, he would have realized that he presented us with a rather modern approach to understanding the death of Jesus. This is certainly not all that can be said. Isaiah 53:5, 10 speaks of the servant "wounded for our transgressions" and of his "offering for sin." Mark 10:45 and the kerygma of 1 Corinthians 15:3, etc.,[34] take this up with reference to Jesus' crucifixion. The hymn in Philippians 2:6–11, however, stresses Christ's humiliation and sees his death (on the cross, if this is not a Pauline gloss) as the culmination of his solidarity with mankind.[35]

In a different way, 1 Timothy 3:16 uses the concept of epiphany in order to include "a positive evaluation of the historical life of Jesus."[36] Finally, John 1:1–18 describes the incarnation of the Logos as the culmination of God's salvation-history, though the earthly life of Jesus is the revelation of God's *glory,* and the evangelist proceeds from there and includes the death on the cross even in the topic of the "exaltation" of the incarnate Christ.[37]

What an avenue has Q opened towards a Christology that is true and, at the same time, an understandable formulation of the mystery that surpasses all understanding, so that, though the mystery still remains mystery, modern men may get help to realize what it means for them and their lives. It would be fascinating to listen to the response of the Q-redactor to Fuller's thoughts and to see how much of the later

---

[32] R. Fuller, *Mission,* 94–95, and *Foundations,* 136 (n. 54), considers this a word of Jesus in its content, though not in its present form.

[33] These may not have been originally connected with the saying in Matt. 11:27; cf. S. Schulz, *Q: Die Spruchquelle,* 215.

[34] T. W. Manson, *The Sayings of Jesus* (London: SCM Press, 1949), 16, claimed that Q knew "the kerygma." This is certainly true, but the decisive question is *what* kerygma Q knew. Cf. R. Fuller, *New Testament in Current Study,* 141: "While . . . the kerygma is basic to all of the New Testament writings, it is less clear than it was that the kerygma is identical throughout." Since Fuller, *Foundations,* 161, even dates the interpretation of the death of Jesus as "for our sins" at Passover of A.D. 31, and the formula of 1 Cor. 15:3b between A.D. 31 and 33, he would probably include this phrase in the kerygma known to Q. He reckons with the usual date of A.D. 30 for the crucifixion. It may interest some that a date of May 4, 28, has been suggested by Walther Hinz, "Chronologie des Lebens Jesu," *ZDMG* 139 (1989): 301–309.

[35] Cf. R. Fuller, *Foundations,* 209–12.

[36] Ibid., 217.

[37] Ibid., 222–27. According to p. 227, "the *anabasis* is presumed" even in the prologue.

development was already lying in his thinking. He might often have recognized his own ideas in later formulations, and he might, sometimes, not have done so.

4. The Son of Man

4.1 Since the death of Jesus is not or, at the best, only marginally reflected in Q, any treatment of his resurrection is equally missing in Q. Whether the earthly Jesus identified himself with the Son of man that will come at the parousia, as I think, or expected an apocalyptic figure yet to come, as Fuller views it,[38] Q certainly identified (at least, in the last redaction) both figures. We may, therefore, deal in this section with Jesus in his exalted status, whatever this may mean, and with the influence of this coming event to his earthly ministry. In Luke 12:8–9 "it is Jesus who is the coming Son of man, and who will appear at the End to vindicate his word and work openly as he had already appeared in his resurrection appearances to his disciples."[39] Of course, whether (and if so, how much) Q knew of these appearances we do not know. But what is important here is that the function of the Son of man's appearance in the parousia is the vindication of his earthly life. This means that Easter is not so much the victory over death, but rather the exaltation of the humiliated and rejected Jesus to his true dignity in the coming world of God.[40] Fuller even thinks that all Q-sayings about the coming Son of man are authentic words of Jesus, although they may have been moderated secondarily and, in his view, understood in a new way when the earliest church (before Q in its definitive form) identified the Son of man with Jesus.[41]

4.2 In Q, without any doubt, Jesus himself will be the Son of man who will come at the End. Fuller even suggests that a "demythologized

---

[38]   In *Mission*, 102–104, R. Fuller still identifies cautiously the present and the coming Son of man. The suffering Jesus will be vindicated *as* the Son of man, parallel to the destiny of the one like a son of man (Israel) in Dan. 7. Jesus is "destined to be the triumphant Son of Man" (p. 108); thus, the functions of the Servant and of the Son of man refer to two periods (p. 107). In *Foundations*, 130, he corrects this view. As I see it, Fuller himself gave the best arguments against this self-correction: Jesus never numbers himself among those who wait for the coming Son of man (*Mission*, 103). According to Matt. 11:3 par. (Q), Jesus is "the coming One"; there is no waiting for another one (*Miracles*, 47; Fuller considers this to be a tradition prior to Q, but not an authentic word of John the Baptist). However, this question may remain open between him and me.

[39]   R. Fuller, *Foundations*, 144.

[40]   Cf. ibid., 184–86, and *New Testament and Current Study*, 140–41. In *The Formation of the Resurrection Narratives* (New York: Macmillan, 1971; reprinted, Philadelphia: Fortress Press, 1980), 82–83, he suggests that in Matt. 11:27 par. (Q) it is, as in Matt. 28:18; John 3:35, actually the exalted Jesus that speaks. Would this mean that even Q understood exaltation from the beginning as installation to a lordship over the church and its mission between Easter and the parousia?

[41]   R. Fuller, *Foundations*, 145.

trinity"[42] may be at the root of these visions. The apocalyptic triad of Angels, the elect One, and the Lord of the Spirits (1 Enoch 39:5–7; 51:3–4; 61:8–10) may have led to the early Christian triad of the Son of man, the Father, and the angels, then to that of Father, Son, and angels, and finally to Father, Son, and Holy Spirit.[43] This is, and was for my research, a challenging suggestion. We should, probably, restrict it in a more cautious way to a statement about some ideas that were in the wind, without drawing a developing line. On the one hand, the chapters of 1 Enoch referred to cannot be dated with security. On the other hand, Luke 9:26 combines Son of man, Father, and angels, but of course this is a redactional change of Mark 8:38, where the angels are merely accompanying the Son of man ("with the holy angels") and are not equal to him. The same is true for 1 Thessalonians 3:13, *if* "all the saints" are really angels. 1 Timothy 5:21 is the best reference; it puts God, Christ Jesus, and the elect angels side by side. Revelation 3:5 (Jesus Christ "confessing before my Father and before his angels") is not so good, but 1:4–5 ranges God, the seven spirits (who are actually angels),[44] and Jesus Christ together. Thus, there are some traces of such a triad in the New Testament, and Revelation 1:4–5 even shows how exchangeable the concept of angels and that of spirits was and how the seven spirits are indeed the one Spirit as distributed to the seven churches.[45] Whether Q knew of such a triad, we cannot be sure. It may lie in the background of Luke 12:8 par., but this is no convincing example, since when "the Son of man acknowledges (his follower) before the angels of God," God and the angels are not separately listed, and the phrase simply describes the judgment scene.[46] Moreover, in the parallel of Matthew 10:32 "Son of man" is replaced by "I," and "the angels of God" by "my Father in heaven." Though both differences show, probably, the redactional hand of Matthew,[47] there is no certainty about that.

4.3 As we have seen, Luke 12:8–9 speaks of the Son of man at the scene of the last judgment, not of his lordship over the church between Easter and the parousia. This is the focus in all Q-sayings. Yet, the distinction of the two views is not an absolute one. The future action of the Son of man is decisive for the attitude of the church on her way from Easter to the End. In the parables of Matthew 24:45–51 par. and 25:14–30 par.,[48] the Son of man is the coming "Lord," but as such also the

---

[42]   Reginald H. Fuller, "On Demythologizing the Trinity," *ATR* 43 (1961): 121–31.

[43]   R. Fuller, *Mission*, 83, with n. 3; elaborated in *Formation*, 87.

[44]   Cf. Tob. 12:15 and my remarks in E. Schweizer, "πνεῦμα," *TDNT* 6:450–51.

[45]   Cf. my essay, "Die sieben Geister in der Apokalypse," *EvT* 11 (1952): 502–12; reprinted in *Neotestamentica*, 190–202.

[46]   R. Fuller, *Foundations*, 175, n. 8.

[47]   Ibid., similarly S. Schulz, *Q: Die Spruchquelle*, 83 (with some hesitation).

[48]   According to Fuller, *Introduction*, 72, neither passage belongs to Q.

Lord who rules the lives of his servants in the times before his return. Therefore, he is, also in Q, already addressed "Lord, Lord" (κύριε, κύριε), as he will be on the last day (Matt. 7:21–22//Luke 6:46; 13:25).[49] Also the word of the Son of man eating and drinking with the outcast (Matt. 11:19 par.) presupposes his subsequent vindication; thus, "'Son of man' expresses the vindicated *exousia* of Jesus on earth."[50]

Matthew 19:28 par. expects the final triumph of the Son of man, and the disciples, "who have left everything" and "continued with him in his trials," will share it.[51] The picture of twelve judges over the twelve tribes of Israel includes a view of the final, eternal life that does not primarily think of bliss, but rather of responsibility for others, of guidance and care, as it is portrayed in the judges of the Old Testament.[52]

4.4 This means that Q represents a Christology that, strictly speaking, does not center on death and resurrection, but on rejection and vindication, which is closely related to the contrast of humiliation and exaltation. Again, this was a very fruitful beginning of a trend that we also find elsewhere. Resurrection is, usually, understood in terms of a victory over death, which grants us the guaranty of eternal life. This is certainly also true; yet, the resurrection of Jesus was, first of all, a new beginning of discipleship in the service of the living Lord. In all the gospels and in Acts nothing is said in the reports of the resurrection about the hope for eternal life, but very much is said about the mission of the disciples as witnesses of the resurrection. In some way or other, Easter is the beginning of the "lordship" of Jesus.

4.5 Here again, the distinction between a future lordship in and after the parousia and a present lordship over the church on earth is not a clear cut either-or. In Philippians 2:10–11, Paul doubtless thinks of the adoration of the "Lord" at the parousia (cf. Rom. 14:11; 1 Cor. 15:25–28), which is, in my view, also the original understanding of the hymn (in parallel to the eschatological theophany in the Old Testament, in which God reveals himself in his glory). However, we cannot be sure how the first hearers of this hymn interpreted it. The very fact that it could have been understood, from the very beginning, in both ways, of Christ's triumph over all his enemies since Easter morning and/or his final triumph in and after the parousia, shows how easy the transit from one understanding to the other was.

Contrariwise, in the hymn of 1 Timothy 3:16 the Easter event is also

---

[49]   R. Fuller, *Mission*, 30, 112, and *Foundations*, 158; he points to the close relationship of the term "Lord" to that of "Son of man" in Mark 13:35//Matt. 24:42 (Lord) and Matt. 24:44//Luke 12:40, Q (Son of man).

[50]   R. Fuller, *Foundations*, 148–49.

[51]   Here again Jesus and his disciples form the new people of God; cf. 2.4 above.

[52]   Should we even be allowed to expect that earthly suffering, as with the disciples, may be an avenue to specific responsibility and service in eternity?

the "vindication" (literally now) of the one who was manifested in the
flesh, but here it is the mission to the nations and the faith in all the world
which proves this. It is paralleled by Christ's triumph before the angels
and his entry in the heavenly glory. This is parousia language; however,
it is not clear at all at what time this happened, and one would normally
assume that it took place in his ascension to heaven on or shortly after
Easter. Again, the distinction of both views is not sharp. For many
believers, the hymn might have included, again from the very beginning,
the final triumph of Christ or even reminded them primarily of it.

4.6 Again, Q's focus does, of course, not imply all the angles of the
truth of the Easter event. Yet, it is again a central contribution to New
Testament Christology. If the Q-redactor had read Fuller's writings, he
could have explained to us whether, and if so in what way, the presently
exalted Lord was, in his view, decisive for the life of the church between
Easter and the parousia. Is this so merely through his words and acts
during his earthly ministry and through the expectation of his final coming
and his role in the last judgment? Or is he normative for the life of the
church today by his present guidance and blessing, challenging it,
sending teachers and prophets, giving new ideas and tasks, and granting
strength and courage to do his will?

5. The Preexistent Wisdom of God

5.1 As we have said, the title "Christ" does not appear in Q,[53] and
"Lord" is the address to the Son of man (cf. above 4.3), but not actually
a title. The dignity that both titles attribute to Jesus is, in Q, rather
expressed in terms of Wisdom-theology, as we find it in the Old
Testament and in Judaism. Differently from his first monograph, Fuller
emphasizes in *Foundations* the influence of the picture of the wise man
as the suffering servant and son of God, condemned to shameful death
and exalted to heaven, as we find it in Wisdom 2–5,[54] and of the myth of
Sophia descending to earth, rejected by the nations, fleeing to Israel, or
returning to heaven[55] upon New Testament Christology. In this context,

---

[53]   Matthew adds it in 11:2 (cf. 5.3 below); he takes it over from Mark in 24:23, whereas
Luke 17:33–34 (Q) speaks only of the Son of man.
[54]   R. Fuller, *Foundations*, 70–71, 193–94; cf. E. Schweizer, *Lordship*, 29–30.
[55]   R. Fuller, *Foundations*, 72–75, 208, 211, 225–27; E. Schweizer, *Lordship*, 102, with
n. 2; idem, "Zur Herkunft der Präexistenzvorstellung bei Paulus," *EvT* 19 (1959): 65–70;
reprinted in *Neotestamentica*, 105–109; and idem, "Die Kirche als Leib Christi in den
paulinischen Antilegomena," *TLZ* 86 (1961): 243–44; reprinted in *Neotestamentica*, 295–96,
nn. 6–9.

Philo becomes important as witness to intertestamental Hellenistic-Jewish thinking.[56]

5.2 "The identification of the *person* of Jesus" with the "poetic *personification* of the Wisdom and of the creative Word of God"[57] has not yet been made by Q.[58] Jesus is the messenger of Wisdom like John the Baptist, though the last and definitive one; in him the Wisdom of God is present, speaking through his words, manifest in his acts, rejected by the majority, vindicated by those who are "the children of wisdom" (Luke 7:35, Q). Jesus is, together with his disciples, the one who fulfills the task of Wisdom in the last generation on earth; through him, the Wisdom of God calls Israel to its last chance of penitence (Luke 11:49–51, Q). The combination of apocalypticism and wisdom-theology, typical already for the book of Wisdom, is also to be found in the praise of the Father by the Son in Luke 10:22 (Q),[59] and in the great commandment.[60] Whether the experience of Wisdom, rejected by all nations, forms also the background of the word about the Son of man who has nowhere to lay his head (Matt. 8:20 par.) remains uncertain.[61]

5.3 This is a Christology in which Jesus is, basically, the last prophet. Whether or not his voice is heard and he is himself "acknowledged before men" will decide a person's fate in the last judgment "before the angels of God" (Luke 12:8–9).[62] Thus, it is only one more step to say that in Jesus the Wisdom of God has become not merely manifest, but incarnate.[63] This is what Matthew states explicitly in 11:2, 19; in 23:34; and by his addition of 11:28–30, a saying very similar to that of Sirach 51:23–27.[64]

---

[56]   R. Fuller, *Foundations*, 74–76, 208, 215, 221, 241, n. 76; E. Schweizer, *Neotestamentica*, 295–96, nn. 6–7; idem, "Aufnahme und Korrektur jüdischer Sophiatheologie im Neuen Testament," in *Hören und Handeln: Festschrift für Ernst Wolf*, ed. H. Gollwitzer and H. Traub (Munich: Kaiser Verlag, 1962), 334; reprinted in *Neotestamentica*, 115, nn. 12–14, with reference to C. H. Dodd, *Interpretation*, 274–75 (also 276–77).

[57]   Hartwig Thyen, "Johannesevangelium," *TRE* 17:220–21 (my translation).

[58]   Q belongs to the two-foci, in some parts the two-stage, Christology, not yet to the three-stage Christology. Cf. R. Fuller, *Foundations*, 144–151, 155, 158, 170–71, 193–94. Cf. also Fuller's criticism of the monograph of Felix Christ in "Das Doppelgebot der Liebe: Ein Testfall für die Echtheitskriterien der Worte Jesu," in *Jesus Christus in Historie und Theologie: Neutestamentliche Festschrift für Hans Conzelmann*, ed. Georg Strecker (Tübingen: J. C. B. Mohr [Paul Siebeck], 1975), 329, n. 23. The same view was expressed recently by Dieter Lührmann, "The Gospel of Mark and the Sayings Collection Q," *JBL* 108 (1989): 66.

[59]   S. Schulz, *Q: Die Spruchquelle*, 224–28; D. Lührmann, "The Gospel of Mark and the Sayings Collection Q," 66.

[60]   R. Fuller, "Das Doppelgebot," 329.

[61]   I. Howard Marshall, *The Gospel of Luke*, NIGTC (Grand Rapids: Wm. B. Eerdmans, 2978), 410.

[62]   Cf. above at 4.2.

[63]   M. Jack Suggs, *Wisdom, Christology and Law in Matthew's Gospel* (London: Macmillan, 1970), 30–97.

[64]   Details in Eduard Schweizer, *Theologische Einleitung in das Neue Testament*, GNT

Matthew even omits the short pericope of the widow's mite in order to emphasize that the judgment over Jerusalem and its temple is performed by the exit of Jesus (in whom Wisdom speaks, 23:34), leaving "the house forsaken and desolate" (23:38; 24:1–2). Since the (female) Wisdom and the (male) Logos are interchangeable,[65] Matthew could even have written John 1:14: "and the Logos became flesh," though he would have understood: in the words and deeds of Jesus, rather than in his "person" as a whole. However, he could have said that wherever the Wisdom of God was at work calling the nations and especially Israel to God and even helping by miracles like the water coming out of the rock,[66] it was basically the same manifestation of the presence of God as it happened definitively (or eschatolgically) in Jesus. In this sense, what happened through him was already "pre-existent" in God's history with Israel, in his Wisdom speaking and acting there.

5.4 The next step has been taken by the hymn in Philippians 2:6–11 and by the prologue to John. If the Q-redactor could have read what Fuller wrote, he would have realized that Jesus himself was in his preaching well rooted in both the apocalyptic hope and the wisdom theology of contemporary Judaism and that he, the Q-redactor, had only made explicit this wisdom theology of Jesus, which found its culmination in the Johannine prologue.[67] It would be most interesting to hear whether he could have seen John 1:1–18 as such a culmination. After some discussion, he might have understood why Fuller drew this line from Jesus to the prologue of John with him, Q, somewhere in between. Nonetheless he might also have uttered some warning against the danger of weakening monotheism, though he might not have protested directly to a concept that would be near to that of the Wisdom figure.

6. Q's Answer to Fuller's Approach as a Whole

6.1 When confronted with all of Fuller's suggestions, what would the Q-redactor have answered? He would not have known what the difference between functional and ontological Christology was, which Fuller emphasizes in order to show the fundamental unity of both.[68] Fuller

---

2 (Gottingen: Vandenhoeck & Ruprecht, 1989), parts 7.8–10; cf. also idem, "Jesus Christus," *TRE* 16:697 (6.2); 701 (6.4.1).

[65] Wis. 9:1–2; Philo, *All.* 1.1.65; cf. 1.43; *Fug.* 50–52; *Conf.* 146; *Som.* 1.215; R. Fuller, *Foundations*, 75–76; details in Eduard Schweizer, "Zum religionsgeschichtlichen Hintergrund der 'Sendungsformel,'" *ZNW* 57 (1966): 204–206; reprinted in idem, *Beiträge zur Theologie des Neuen Testaments* (Zurich: Zwingli Verlag, 1970), 89–90.

[66] Exod. 17:6; Num. 20:7–11; 1 Cor. 10:4; Philo, *All.* 2.86 (Wisdom); *Det.* 115–18; cf. Wis. 10:17.

[67] R. Fuller, "Das Doppelgebot," 329.

[68] R. Fuller, *Foundations*, 247–57.

would have explained it to him, taking all his time, in his kindness so often experienced by all his friends. His partner would finally have realized that this was the same difference that arose wherever Jewish and Hellenistic Christians met, or where a teacher open to the Hellenistic world like Paul quoted a Jewish-Christian creed as in Romans 1:3–4. He would not have denied that Jesus was the Son of God, though he might still have understood this, more or less, in the way Israel was the son of God (cf. 2 above). He might, at first, not have grasped why Fuller made so much of Jesus' death and resurrection; he might, however, have detected how much they were the fundament of his own understanding (cf. above n.7). Be this as it may, he would have been open to Fuller's argument that the wise man, the suffering righteous, was, according to Isaiah 53, the one who was rejected and dying "for our sins," and that the same was true of Jesus' whole "pre-existence,"[69] his teaching and healing and his final rejection by Israel (cf. 3 above). He would, of course, have agreed that it was Jesus' resurrection by which he was exalted to the status of the coming Son of man (cf. 4 above). He would not have known the term "pre-existence," but he would have shared with Fuller the conviction that whatever of the Wisdom and the Word of God became manifest in Jesus, it had already been at work in Israel and even universally since the creation of the world (cf. 5 above).

6.2 When that long talk of the two would have ended, the Q-redactor might have added: Are not Jesus' words and deeds rather marginal with you? I think that they are really central. And I suppose that Fuller would have responded in a very friendly manner, admitting that neglecting this side of Christology might be a danger of the church today.[70] Well, my fantasy has been concluded; this discussion has not taken place. Or, should we not say that it has taken place in the theological research of the last decades, in which Fuller's contributions play an important role? With Fuller, at least, it is not so much that he only tried to interpret and even to correct Q, but that he, time and again, listened very carefully to what Q (besides all the other New Testament authors) had to tell him and the church of today.

---

[69]   The term is used by Heinz Schürmann, for example, in his "Jesu Todesverständnis im Verstehenshorizont seiner Umwelt," *TGI* 70 (1980): 156.

[70]   R. Fuller, *New Testament in Current Study*, 136, stresses the importance of the historical Jesus (cf. his cautious remarks on pp. 138–40). In *Miracles*, 122–23, he refers to the deeds of Jesus as an important part of our faith. Finally he chooses the great commandment as the topic of his contribution to the Conzelmann *Festschrift* and reinforces the arguments for its place in Q ("Das Doppelbegot," 317–18).

John's Gospel and Gnostic Christologies: The Nag Hammadi Evidence

PHEME PERKINS*

I. Patterns of Influence

Several distinctive elements of Johannine Christology have led scholars to wonder whether or not the understanding of Jesus in the Fourth Gospel was intended as an appropriation of or correction to the various myths of the divine savior emerging in the heterodox Jewish circles which gave rise to gnostic mythological systems.[1] Or, if not a direct response to such developments, it has been suggested that the Johannine perspective provided the symbolic resources out of which gnosticizing Christianity might develop.[2] The Johannine emphasis on the sending of the divine Son from the Father into a world which proves hostile and more enamoured of darkness than the light associated with the one from God (e.g., John 12:44–50)[3] sets the stage for a mythological account of the origins, descent, and return of the revealer, which the gospel itself never supplies.[4]

Lest the gnosticizing trajectory of Johannine materials undermine the traditional understanding that it provides the canonical foundation for the later development of incarnational Christology, scholars like Professor Fuller point out that Jewish traditions of "sending" and divine agency can

---

* Pheme Perkins is Professor of Theology, Boston College, Chestnut Hill, Massachusetts.

[1] See the summary of this position in K. Rudolph, *Gnosis* (San Francisco: Harper & Row, 1983), 305–308. Its most forceful articulation remains Rudolf Bultmann's commentary on the gospel, *The Gospel of John* (Philadelphia: Westminster Press, 1971 [Ger., 1964]).

[2] Wayne Meeks, "The Man from Heaven in Johannine Sectarianism," *JBL* 91 (1972): 44–72, has argued this position from the perspective of a sociological approach to the function of religious symbols. The alienation in the gospel between Jesus who is "from heaven" and the believers who ultimately share Jesus' destiny provides the foundation for the emergence of full blown gnostic sectarianism.

[3] This sudden, fragmentary piece of discourse, which commentators frequently associate with the final editing of the gospel materials (cf. Rudolf Schnackenburg, *The Gospel According to St. John*, 3 vols. [New York: Crossroad, 1968–82], 2:419–25) exhibits the form of "disembodied" address by the revealer which becomes a frequent form of speech in gnostic writings.

[4] Cf. Marinus de Jonge, *Jesus: Stranger from Heaven and Son of God* (Missoula, MT: Scholars Press, 1977), 141–61. The gospel cannot be reduced to "functional Christology," since the divine origin of Jesus is crucial to his mission. Yet the evangelist gives no hint of mythic speculation about those origins in the divine world.

account for the christological perspective of the gospel as we have it.[5] Another unique element in the Fourth Gospel, its opening Logos hymn, owes little to cosmological speculation about the role of the Logos.[6] Just as orthodox Logos speculation is not primarily cosmological but takes on Spirit terminology to describe Christ as an agent of revelation,[7] so the Johannine prologue centers upon a soteriological claim: believers become children of God (vv. 12–13).[8] Cosmological speculation about the functions of the divine Logos already developed in Philo are less important for the Fourth Gospel than they are for second century cosmological speculation such as one finds in gnostic writings.[9]

The Johannine tradition correlates belief in Jesus as the only revelation of God with rebirth as "children of God" and eternal life (e.g., 1:12–13; 3:3–15). Jesus' unique position as revealer depends upon the fact that no one else has descended from or returned to heaven (1:18; 3:13). At the same time, belief/disbelief indicate that persons are either "from above" or "of God" or else "from below."[10] When this dualism, which is characteristic of the discourse material in the gospel,[11] is embedded in narratives about Jesus' conflict with "the Jews," then the symbolism can be taken to reflect the conflict between Johannine Christians and a Jewish religious world from which they were expelled (e.g., John 9:22) and which now serves as a symbol for continuing experiences of perse-

---

[5]   See Fuller's treatment of Johannine Christology in Reginald H. Fuller and Pheme Perkins, *Who Is This Christ?* (Philadelphia: Fortress Press, 1983), 96–108. Detailed studies of the Jewish materials on this theme can be found in J. B. Mirada, *Der Vater mich gesandt hat* (Bern: Lang, 1972) and J. A. Buhner, *Der Gesandte und sein Weg im vierten Evangelium* (Tübingen: J.C.B. Mohr, 1977).

[6]   Its affirmations are easily accounted for by traditional formulae and allusions to Genesis. Many exegetes note that the insertion of the first reference to the Baptist at John 1:6 suggests that the evangelist considers the cosmological section concluded at v. 5. See the discussion in R. Schnackenburg, *John*, 1:221–81. Schnackenburg links the middle section of the hymn with revelatory activity prior to the incarnation such as that attributed to Wisdom (pp. 256f.).

[7]   See the discussion of the emergence of Logos Christology in the second and third centuries by Jaroslav Pelikan, *The Emergence of the Catholic Tradition, 100–600* (Chicago: Univ. of Chicago Press. 1971), 187–89.

[8]   See R. A. Culpepper, "The Pivot of John's Prologue," *NTS* 27 (1980):1–31. J. Ashton, "The Transformation of Wisdom: A Study of the Prologue of John's Gospel," *NTS* 32 (1986):161–86, has insisted that the wisdom background to the Logos material in the Fourth Gospel presumes the on-going activity of Wisdom in revelation and salvation history. Therefore, the prologue should not be read as cosmology followed by incarnation.

[9]   The cosmological functions of the Logos include emphasis on its ties to the intelligible world, which makes the Logos the source of knowledge of the otherwise unknowable and transcendent God. See the detailed presentation of this material in J. D. G. Dunn, *Christology in the Making* (Philadelphia: Westminster Press, 1980), 220–41. Dunn insists that this cosmological speculation does not depend upon any earlier myth or inherently lead to such speculation (p. 240).

[10]   De Jonge, *Jesus*, 144–46.

[11]   So ibid., 150.

cution (16:1–4a).[12] The symbolic correlation between the believers who
are also "not of this world" (15:19) and their divine savior who has
returned to his place in heavenly glory, which they will share (17:1–26),
suggests a correlation between the gospel's Christology and the true
identity of believers, which supports what one exegete has called "an
ideology of revolt."[13] Divorced from the narrative context that recalls a
concrete history of religious division, this "revolt" might easily adopt the
revolutionary posture characteristic of gnosticism as a religious
phenomenon.[14]

Rather than propose yet another variant of the relationship between
Johannine traditions and emerging gnosticism, we shall put the question
of influence in the other direction. What have Johannine traditions
contributed to gnostic mythologizing or to Christian gnostic speculation
about the mythological traditions that they have inherited?[15] Patristic
attacks on the exegesis of the Johannine prologue by gnostic teachers, as
well as Origen's refutation of Heracleon's commentary on John in his own
work,[16] might suggest that Johannine texts played a formative role in
gnostic systems. In the Nag Hammadi texts, however, Johannine themes
such as the sending of the Son by the Father from above, the activity of
the Logos, or the begetting of believers as "children" of the Father appear

---

[12]   See the development of this perspective into an hypothesis about the history of the
Johannine community by Raymond E. Brown, *The Community of the Beloved Disciple*
(New York: Paulist Press, 1979). Brown takes great pains to avoid the apparent conclusion
that such a communal history would create deeply rooted sectarianism (pp. 89–91).

[13]   Jerome Neyrey, *An Ideology of Revolt* (Philadelphia: Fortress Press, 1988), 115–49.
Neyrey concludes that the revolt against "the world" which attends the development of the
gospel's high christology included "apostolic" churches as well as unbelieving Jews (p. 143).

[14]   See the classic description of *gnosis* as revolt in Hans Jonas, *The Gnostic Religion*, 2d
ed. (Boston: Beacon Press, 1963), 91–94. Jonas emphasizes the paradoxical elements of
gnostic allegorizing as evidence that gnostics did not seek to accomodate earlier traditions
but to subvert them (p. 94).

[15]   Both the existence of writings which are superficially Christianized among the Nag
Hammadi codices and our ability to trace fundamental stories and elements of gnostic
mythologies back to heterodox Jewish traditions (as in G. A. G. Stroumsa, *Another Seed:
Studies in Gnostic Mythology*, NHS XXIV [Leiden: E. J. Brill, 1984]) strengthen the case
for the development of gnostic sects concurrently with Christianity. Their development and
subsequent mythologizing may have been significantly altered by the speculative and
communal strength of Christian gnostic teachers in the mid-second century C.E. and the
subsequent conflict with ecclesial Christianity.

[16]   See the catalogue of false claims about the Johannine prologue in Irenaeus, *Adv.
Haer*. III.11,1–9, as well as his insistence on the reality of incarnation against Valentinian
accounts of the Savior descending into Jesus as a vessel, *Adv. Haer*. I.9,3; II.16,1–8.
Irenaeus argues that had John intended to reveal the emanations of the Valentinian pleroma
in the prologue as Ptolemy claimed, he would have given the entites in their proper order
and not mixed masculine and female names. "Light" and "life" are not separate entities but
attributes of the one divine Son (*Adv. Haer*. I.8,5–9,2). Also see Epiphanius, *Pan*.
XXXI.5,1–7,5; *Exc. Theod*. 6,1–7,5; 21,1–3; 26,1, and Hippolytus, *Ref*. VI.29,2–36,4. For
an exegetical study of Heracleon and Origen as exegetes, see J.-M. Poffet, *La Méthode
Exégétique d'Héracléon et d'Origène* (Fribourg: Éditions Universitaires, 1985).

as secondary developments in material which is clearly dependent upon other sources for its structural or symbolic coherence.

II. Sending the Divine Son

In the Fourth Gospel, identification of God as the "Father" who is known only through the revelation of the Son, who has been sent from above and returns to the glory he had enjoyed with the Father, provides such a close parallel to gnostic emphasis on the transcendence of God and the necessity of revelation that exegetes often assume that the evangelist intended to refute the claims of gnostic revealers as well.[17] *Gos. Truth* is particularly rich in allusions to Johannine language. In an extended meditation on the "living book" of revelation, we learn that the Word of the Father brings about knowledge of God throughout the aeons which had been searching for him:

> In this way the Word of the Father goes forth in the totality, as the fruit [of] his heart and an impression of his will. . . . The Father reveals his bosom.—Now his bosom is the Holy Spirit.—He reveals what is hidden of him—what is hidden of him is his Son—so that through the mercies of the Father the aeons may know him and cease laboring in search of the Father. (23,33–24,18)[18]

Since *Gos. Truth* is unusual among gnostic systems in identifying the Son and the Word, this passage may be an example of gnostic conformity to the style of "orthodox" or canonical Christian expression.[19]

Continuing its allusive style, *Gos. Truth* associates this act of revelation with the gnostic mythologizing of the enlightenment of Adam after his creation by the "in-breathing" of light or the Spirit:

> Having extended his hand to him who lay upon the ground, he set him up on his feet, for he had not yet risen. He gave them the means of knowing the knowledge of the Father and the revelation of his Son. For when they had seen him and had heard him, he granted them to taste him and to smell him and to touch the beloved Son. (30,19–31)[20]

---

[17] So R. Schnackenburg, *John*, 2:180–84.

[18] Translation from J. M. Robinson, ed., *The Nag Hammadi Library in English*, 3d ed. (San Francisco: Harper & Row, 1988), 43. See the discussion of this section by H. Attridge and G. MacRae, *Nag Hammadi Codex I—Notes*, ed. H. Attridge; NHS XXIII (Leiden: E. J. Brill, 1985), 69–72.

[19] The Son is usually distinguished from the Word, which is frequently a lower being in the aeons, as is the case in *Tri. Trac.* (57,8–67,37) where the Word operates in the realms of reality which come into being outside the Pleroma (cf. Attridge and MacRae, *Codex I*, 69f.).

[20] Cf. *Hyp. Arch.* 88,10–16; 89,11–17; as a deceitful plot to get the demonic creator to

Gos. Truth apparently intends that the reader associate this primal coming of revelation with the enlightenment experienced by the recipient of gnosis.[21]

The mythological development of the primordial enlightenment of Adam in gnostic sources included a "salvation history" in which the primal seed of the future gnostic race had to be rescued from the hostility of the lower powers. The *epinoia* of light comes to the newly created Adam, but she takes on a "docetic" image which prevents the lustful archons from defiling her (*Ap. John*, *CG* II 20,9–28).[22] Attacks against gnostic ancestors are frequently warded off by the descent of angelic figures. When Eleleth rescues Norea from the archons, he also brings her knowledge of her true origins and the eschatological destruction of the powers at the coming of the Immortal Man and the revelation of her descendants (*Hyp. Arch.* 96,17–97,20).[23]

Christianizing this pattern, gnostic writers merely identified the definitive appearance of the revealer which brought about both the manifestation of the gnostic seed in this world and the destruction of the authorities with the gnostic Christ. *Gos. Eg.* and *Treat. Seth* have identified Christ with the heavenly Seth, whose interventions in the lower world preserve and establish the "seed" of the gnostic race. Typically, Seth or his counterpart has been "sent" by the will of the Pleroma as a whole. In *Gos. Eg.*, he takes on a "Logos-begotten" body:

> The great Seth was sent by the four lights, by the will of the Autogenes and the whole pleroma through the gift and good pleasure of the great, invisible Spirit. . . . He passed through the three parousias . . . to save her (the race) who went astray through the reconciliation of the world, and the baptism through a Logos-begotten body which the great Seth prepared for himself secretly through the virgin, in order that the saints may be begotten by the Holy Spirit through invisible secret symbols, . . . through the incorruptible, Logos-begotten one, even Jesus the living one, even he whom the great Seth has put on. And through him he nailed the powers of the thirteen aeons, and established those who are brought forth and taken away. He armed them with an armor of knowledge of this truth, with an unconquerable power of incorruptibility. (*CG* III 62,24–64,8)

Treat. Seth echoes the indwelling language of the Fourth Gospel, "It is I who am in you [plural] and you are in me, just as the Father is in you in innocence" (49,32–50,1). The destruction of the "powers" associated with the final descent of the revealer becomes the task to be accomplished

---

blow the power he has received from the Mother into Adam to cause him to rise in *Ap. John*, *CG* II 19,15–33.

[21]   H. Attridge and G. MacRae, *Codex I—Notes*, 87.

[22]   See the extensive discussion of this mytheme in G. Stroumsa, *Another Seed*, 35–70.

[23]   For other examples of this pattern, see ibid., 82–112.

through the apostolic preaching of the knowledge brought by Christ as the "Immortal Man"/revealer in *Soph. Jes. Chr.*:

> I have come here that they may be joined with that Spirit, . . . and might from the two become one just as from the first, that you might yield much fruit and go up to Him Who Is from the beginning. . . . And I came to remove them from their blindness that I might tell everyone about the God who is above the universe. Therefore tread upon their graves. . . . I have given you authority as Sons of Light, that you might tread upon their power with your feet. (*CG* III 117,1–5; 118,23–119,8)

After being gathered to receive such a revelation from the exalted, heavenly Christ, that he was the pleroma, sent into the appearance of a mortal body (136,16–25), the apostles wage war against the powers by preaching this message of salvation (137,20–30) in *Ep. Pet. Phil.* They are exhorted to prayer and are promised the Father's assistance and the abiding presence of Jesus.[24]

III. Conclusion: The Gospel in Gnostic Polemic

Echoes of Johannine language in writings which have identified the "Son" of the gospel with one of the savior figures in the gnostic pleroma may serve one of two functions. In writings like *Ap. John, Gos. Eg.*, and *Soph. Jes. Chr.*, the Christianized revealer who promises a heavenly, immortal destiny to his "seed" assures the reader that Jesus brought the salvation promised in gnostic myths and gnostic rituals such as the baptisms referred to by *Gos. Eg.* The deliberately allusive language of *Gos. Truth*, which can often be read as easily within a framework of second century orthodoxy as within that of a gnostic Sophia myth, may well have sought to persuade non-gnostic Christians of the truth of gnostic teaching.[25] There is no indication that these writers depend upon a fixed tradition of sectarian exegesis of the Johannine text.[26]

Unlike the Logos in the prologue to the Fourth Gospel, the gnostic

---

[24] See K. Koschorke, "Eine gnostische Pfinstpredigt: Zur Auseinandersetzung zwischen gnostischem und kirchlichem Christentum am Beispiel der 'Epistula Petri and Philippum' (NHC VIII,2)," *ZTK* 74 (1977): 323–43.

[25] See H. Attridge, "The Gospel of Truth as an Exoteric Text," *Nag Hammadi, Gnosticism and Early Christianity*, ed. Charles Hedrick and Robert Hodgson (Peabody, MA: Hendrickson, 1986), 241–55.

[26] Even the Valentinian evidence is so variable that it is difficult to be certain that authors have a set text which they are expounding. For a contrary view, see J. A. Williams, *Biblical Interpretation in the Gnostic Gospel of Truth from Nag Hammadi*, SBLDS 79 (Atlanta: Scholars Press, 1989), 23–26, who presumes that Valentinus is the author of *Gos. Truth* and has interpreted passages such as John 14:1–7 in *Gos. Truth* 18,16–24 so as to resolve textual ambiguities.

Logos is rarely said to "incarnate" or dwell among human beings. Most gnostic texts remain closer to the speculative cosmological traditions reflected in Philo. The Word is a power or entity operative in the Pleroma. It is not identified with the highest God, the "unknown Father." In *Gos. Truth*, the Logos represents that creative activity which enables the Pleroma to come to knowledge of the Father. The Logos is usually a divine power distinct from the revealer.[27]

The Nag Hammadi material does preserve two examples in which gnostic authors have apparently revised the structure of a gnostic presentation in order to provide a more foundational role for the Logos, *Trim. Prot.* and *Tri. Trac.* The theology of the latter presents a completely monistic system in which the weakness of the Logos results in the formation of the intermediate and material worlds. All the androgenous aeons and the tales of higher and lower Sophia figures so commonly found in Valentinian texts are missing from this system. Yet its understanding of spiritual and psychic Christians in the church as well as the process of conversion and such cosmological principles as the heavenly "church" which the earthly reality only mirrors, the partial revelation in the Hebrew prophets, the positive activity of the demiurge and the like lead exegetes to presume that *Tri. Trac.* is a radical development of Valentinian thought.[28] However, the speculative theology of *Tri. Trac.* owes little to the Fourth Gospel. It safeguards the transcendence of God by separating the Logos from the eternally begotten Son.[29] The author's revisionism may represent accomodation to an emerging tradition of Christian Platonism, since it apparently meets many of the objections that such authors had to Valentinian thought.

Trim. Prot. proceeds from the hints supplied in the Johannine prologue to incorporate the Word as the "Son" and third member of the divine triad, Father, Mother, and Son.[30] The work contains a revelation speech by each member of the triad, which includes the descent of each entity to bring salvific revelation into the darkness of the lower world (41,20–42,2; 45,12–46,3; 47,14–49,30). In the last instance, the Word puts on Jesus and takes him from the cross to "establish him in the dwelling places of his Father" (50,13–15). This conclusion may allude to

---

[27] See my "Logos Christologies in the Nag Hammadi Codices," *VC* 35 (1981):380–84.
[28] E.g., H. Attridge and E. Pagels, *Codex I*, vol. 1, 177–90.
[29] See P. Perkins, "Logos Christologies," 387–93.
[30] Y. Janssens, "The Trimorphic Protennoia and the Fourth Gospel," *The New Testament and Gnosis: Essays in Honour of R. McL. Wilson*, ed. A. H. B. Logan and A. J. M. Wedderburn (Edinburgh: T. & T. Clark, 1983), 229–44; C. A. Evans, "On the Prologue and the Trimorphic Protennoia," *NTS* 27 (1981): 395–401. Evans observes that while *Tri. Prot.* apparently depends upon Johannine language, it maintains the emphasis of gnosticized wisdom traditions on cosmology and has not followed the gospel's incarnational Christology (p. 399).

John 14:3, but it also leaves open the possibility that the "dwelling places" to which Jesus is taken differ from the highest divine being. Some gnostic texts have Jesus at the right hand of the lower demiurge (e.g., *Adv. Haer.* I.30,13). Explicit polemic against orthodox belief and the divisiveness of the orthodox churches contrasted with the unity and friendship of the gnostics such as that found in *Treat. Seth* points the finger at belief in a "dead man" (60,13–61,14).

Sometimes a docetic account of the crucifixion scene supports gnostic rejection of orthodox belief (*Treat. Seth* 54,4–19; *Apoc. Pet.*). In other examples the extent to which the revealer actually descends into the lower world remains unclear, especially if the revelation is cast as the speech or rescue of an angelic figure from above. A hymnic formulation in *2 Apoc. Jas.* (58,2–23) summarizes the Christology of that text:[31]

He was the one whom he who created heaven and earth, and dwelled in it, did not see. He was [this one who] is the life. He was the light. He was that one who will come to be. . . . He was the Holy Spirit and the Invisible One, who did not descend upon the earth. He was the virgin and that which he wishes happens to him. I saw that he was naked and there was no garment clothing him.

Identifying Christ with the "Invisible One" implies such a complete separation from the created, material world that no realistic meaning can be given to traditions which implicate the divine Savior in the lower world. Perhaps the inability of James and Peter to follow the Savior's ascent at the conclusion of *Ap. Jas.* (15,13–28) is to be read by the gnostic as an attack upon orthodox traditions about the ascent of Jesus into the heavens. Certainly those described in the narrative represent only the "heavens" of the lower creator god or of his offspring (as in *Hyp. Arch.* 95,17–96,3; *Orig. World* 104,26–106,11).

The Nag Hammadi texts suggest that gnostic teachers had difficulty assimilating both the realistic narratives about Jesus as Son of the Father who returned to his Father from the cross and the theological identification of the Word incarnate in Jesus with the highest divine Triad. Stroumsa has suggested that *Apoc. Adam* had such Christianizing gnostic teachers in mind when it rejects those who say about the Illuminator, "every birth of their ruler is a word. And his word received a mandate there. He received glory and power" (82,13–16).[32] Though the Fourth Gospel provides an opening for a gnostic understanding of revelation of the "unknown Father" as the key to salvation as well as the description of

---

[31] Armand Veilleux, *Les Deux Apocalypses de Jacques* (Quebec: Les Presses de l'Université Laval, 1986), 176–77.

[32] G. Stroumsa, *Another Seed*, 90–91. Since *Apoc. Adam* castigates opponents for defiling baptism in the voice of the guardian angels of baptism from *Gos. Eg.*, the circles from which the latter derives may have developed the opinion that is rejected here.

the origin and destiny of the revealer and his "fellow spirits" in terms of descent and ascent, the gospel's commitment to depicting Jesus' activity within the confines of the created world could never be incorporated as part of the "sending" of the gnostic Illuminator. Whether or not the evangelist sought to shape in image of Jesus to refute or compete with gnosticizing developments, the ambiguity of Johannine materials in the formation of gnostic Christologies suggests that the gospel of itself would not generate such mythic interpretations of Jesus. It only becomes "gnosticizing" within the context of a powerful mythic impulse that has been shaped from other materials. Some gnostic readers might even agree that the gospel as it stands shows a dangerous proclivity toward the materialist, incarnationalism that would be strengthened by the orthodox developments which led to Chalcedon.

Romans 3:1–8: Structure and Argument

PAUL J. ACHTEMEIER*

It seems altogether appropriate, in a volume dedicated to Professor Reginald Fuller, that an essay on the benefits of formal analysis of New Testament literature be included. Professor Fuller has contributed richly to the analysis of formal elements within the gospels, and so has helped his colleagues understand more clearly the meaning of the New Testament writings to which he has devoted his attention. This essay is an expression of gratitude to my friend and colleague, from whom I have learned so much, and from whose friendship I have derived such satisfaction.

The person who undertakes an analysis of Romans 3:1–8, in an effort to unravel its rhetorical structure, soon becomes aware that the passage is responsible for a variety of confusions on the part of others who have made a similar attempt. The reaction of at least some of the scholars who have undertaken the analysis, whether or not they confessed to their perplexity, has been stated in rather trenchant form by C. H. Dodd, who found Paul muddled here and who concluded that, since Paul had obviously gotten badly off the track of his argument, Romans would have been better off had these verses been omitted altogether.[1]

There are several reasons for such perplexity. It is not clear, for example, from whom the questions come. Are they questions from an objector, with whom Paul is here arguing, and hence are they an attempt to head off questions which Paul knows from experience will be raised against him?[2] Or are they questions which grow out of the internal logic

---

* Paul J. Achtemeier is Herbert Worth and Annie H. Jackson Professor of Biblical Interpretation, Union Theological Seminary, Richmond, Virginia.

[1] C. H. Dodd, *The Epistle of Paul to the Romans* (New York: Harper & Row, 1932), 46. Ernst Käsemann takes a different view in his *Commentary on Romans* (Grand Rapids: Wm. B. Eerdmans, 1980), 78. John Calvin also felt that vv. 5–8 were a digression which, he said, was nevertheless necessary; see his *Commentaries on the Epistle of Paul the Apostle to the Romans* (Grand Rapids: Wm. B. Eerdmans, 1948; reprinted, Grand Rapids: Baker Book House, 1979), 118. In what follows I shall cite a limited number of commentaries simply to illustrate possible reactions to these verses. It lies beyond the scope of this essay to attempt an exhaustive account of the ways these verses have been explained.

[2] So C. K. Barrett, *A Commentary on the Epistle to the Romans,* HNTC (New York: Harper & Row, 1957), 63; cf. also John Chrysostom, "Homilies on the Acts of the Apostles and the Epistle to the Romans," *A Select Library of the Nicene and Post-Nicene Fathers of the Christian Church: First Series,* ed. Philip Schaff, 11 vols. (New York: Christian Literature Company, 1886–90), 11:372.

of Paul's argument, and hence are raised by Paul himself in diatribe style in order in this way to advance his argument?[3] Or do we have to do with some questions that grow out of the logic of Paul's argument, with some others, say, vv. 5–8, reflecting actual objections raised against Paul?[4]

A further perplexity grows out of reflection on the nature of Paul's questions, and that is the nature of the answers. This is particularly true of v. 8, where Paul says that "the condemnation of such people (or, such things) is deserved." Is that a curse on his opponents, which they have earned because of their slanderous misinterpretation of the intention of his apostolic proclamation of God's grace in Christ?[5] Is that the reason for the apparent tangled construction of v. 8, namely, that Paul has gotten so worked up about the inaccuracy and bad faith of that particular objection (i.e., one could infer one ought to do evil to increase good) that he has lost the grammatical thread of his argument?

Resolution of such perplexities determines in its turns how further problems will be resolved. How one answers the question of the source of the objections contained in 3:1–8, for example, will determine how one judges the adequacy of Paul's linguistic formulations. Commenting on v. 5, C. K. Barrett suggests that while the second question in that verse is phrased so that the appropriate answer can only be "no" (it is introduced with μή, which expects a negative answer), logically a sentence expecting the answer "yes" would have been more appropriate, since Paul's objector is speaking, and from the objector's perspective, a "yes" would be the expected answer.[6] In that case Paul has got a bit mixed up in his language.

The nature of the questions raises yet further problems in relation to the structure of this passage. Was it Paul's intention, for example, as Chrysostom had already argued, to answer an absurdity (v. 5) with another absurdity (v. 6), and then, because Paul felt his rhetorical question in v. 6 was "indistinct," to restate it in v. 7? Are these verses thus to be understood as making the same point in different language, with no advance in the argument?[7] Again, would Paul, as Calvin suggested, have completed his elucidation of v. 6 in vv. 7–8 had he not broken off his sentence in the middle, so moved was he with indignation at the nature of the objection?[8] Or is it the case that vv. 7 and 8 are really not to be

---

[3] E. Käsemann, *Romans*, 78–79; he senses a shift in the nature of the argument after v. 4 (p. 83).

[4] Ibid., 84. I have not extended my consideration here to 3:9. For an illuminating and useful proposal regarding that verse, see Nils A. Dahl, "Romans 3:9: Text and Meaning," in *Paul and Paulinism: Essays in Honour of C. K. Barrett*, ed. M. D. Hooker and S. G. Wilson (London: SPCK, 1982), 184–204.

[5] So E. Käsemann, *Romans*, 84; C. K. Barrett, *Romans*, 65; J. Calvin, *Romans*, 121.

[6] C. K. Barrett, *Romans*, 64.

[7] J. Chrysostom, "Homilies," 11:373.

[8] J. Calvin, *Romans*, 121.

construed as in any way parallel, lest we end up with the "monstrous structure of a double question in a single sentence,"[9] provided of course that we are dealing in vv. 7–8 with a single sentence! All of this indicates that a, if not the, central problem in 3:1–8 has to do with the structure of this passage. If we could find the rhetorical pattern Paul employed, it would perhaps aid us in resolving some, at least, of these perplexities.

Given the dialogical nature of this passage, an obvious place to start would be to inquire if Paul is here employing the structure of the diatribe. There has been a good deal of discussion of this formal structure in the recent past, ranging from Karl Donfried, who has questioned the existence of such a genre—he feels what Bultmann identified as diatribe is better understood as "philosophical dialogue"[10]—to the dissertation of Stanley K. Stowers, in which he seeks to subject the kind of dialogical format Paul used, particularly in Romans, to a more careful and critical analysis than it has hitherto received.[11]

The earlier work to which both these authors refer in the course of their discussions is of course the doctoral dissertation of Rudolf Bultmann.[12] Whether or not Bultmann's "Jugendarbeit" was adequate to the topic I do not wish to debate here. Both Donfried and Stowers have done it, and I have nothing of value to add. What is noteworthy, I think, is the fact that Bultmann all but ignored our passage. In the whole of his book, if I have counted correctly, he refers only three times to any of the verses comprising Romans 3:1–8, twice on p. 67 (vv. 1, 3, and 1–3) and once on p. 95 (v. 4). In none of these instances is the reference more than passing, and there is no attempt to relate the whole passage to the diatribal form.

Such an analysis had to await the work of Stowers, who noted the uniquely dialogical structure of Romans,[13] and who has analyzed numerous parts of it, among them 3:1–8. As I will show below, his analysis of 3:1–8 has much to commend it, but more careful attention to the rhetorical pattern of those verses will allow us not only to reconstruct the rhetorical form Paul is using, but also resolve the issue of the nature of Paul's affirmation at the end of 3:8—"Their condemnation is just." Nevertheless, there is much we can learn about Romans as a whole, and the form of 3:1–8 in particular, from Stowers' analyses, and a brief review of some aspects of his conclusions is appropriate here.

---

[9]   E. Käsemann, *Romans*, 84.

[10]   Karl Donfried, "False Presuppositions in the Study of Romans," in *The Romans Debate*, ed. K. P. Donfried (Minneapolis: Augsburg Publishing House, 1977), 140.

[11]   Stanley K. Stowers, *The Diatribe and Paul's Letter to the Romans*, SBLDS 57 (Chico, CA: Scholars Press, 1981).

[12]   Rudolf Bultmann, *Der Stil der paulinischen Predigt und die kynisch-stoische Diatribe*, FRLANT 13 (Göttingen: Vandenhoeck und Ruprecht, 1910).

[13]   S. Stowers, *The Diatribe*, 179.

One of the elements which Stowers has analyzed, and which belongs to the genre, is the appearance of an imaginary interlocutor. The function of this dialogue partner is a basic issue in understanding the origin and intention of the diatribal form, and it is a topic which we will need to examine carefully below. It can for the moment suffice to suggest that the interlocutor may not in fact, as Bultmann and others following him had suggested, represent objections raised by opponents of Paul, similar to those Paul would have encountered in his "street preaching" as an evangelist, i.e., when he evangelized an area for the first time.[14]

Be that as it may, it is clear that the way the imaginary interlocutor functioned in Paul's letter to the Romans is similar to the function the interlocutor exercised in secular diatribes. As an example of Paul's use of an imaginary interlocutor Stowers points to Romans 2:1–5, where the sudden turning in 2:1 to an interlocutor is familiar enough in the diatribe. The indicting rhetoric characteristic of the genre can be found in vv. 3–4, and the allusion to Psalm 62:13 in v. 6 is in keeping with the use of quotation and allusion in the diatribe.[15] Similarly, the use of second person singular pronouns, the sudden turning to address the opponent, the use of indicting questions, and the list of vices all point to Romans 2:17–24 as conforming to the diatribal use of the imaginary interlocutor as well.[16]

The imaginary interlocutor is thus intended to represent a certain type of person whose moral shortcomings and contradictions are indicted, but apparently more with the idea of improvement than condemnation. The censure of the interlocutor appears to be pedagogic, not hostile, and seeks to expose to the interlocutor himself, and to others who recognize themselves in him, those shortcomings so that improvement can be made.[17] To argue therefore that the presence of diatribal elements precludes acquaintance of Paul with the addressees is to overlook the nature and purpose of the imaginary interlocutor, as though the interlocutor functioned purely as an outsider.[18]

As is clear from all of this, the purpose of the imaginary interlocutor is to introduce a false conclusion, which is deduced from the author's own position.[19] It is just at this point that misunderstanding has been introduced into the discussion of Paul's use of the diatribal form, a misunderstanding which has had some adverse consequences for the

---

[14] Ibid., 117.

[15] For Stowers' analysis, see ibid., 93–96.

[16] Ibid., 98. See pp. 99–100 for similar analyses of 9:19–21 and 11:17–24.

[17] Ibid., 110; cf. also p. 180. The model for such pedagogical indictment of the pretentious and arrogant person is found in Socrates (so p. 109).

[18] Cf. ibid., 180, where Stower cites G. Bornkamm as one who holds this erroneous view.

[19] Ibid., 119.

understanding of Rom 3:1–8. Most importantly, it has led some scholars to the assumption that Paul is in dialogue with Jewish opponents and Jewish positions, and the style, particularly the frequent use of μὴ γένοιτο, is supposed to show that Paul is arguing with them on an emotional and intuitive, rather than on a rational level.[20] An analysis of the structure of the diatribe which involves the objections and false conclusions of the imaginary interlocutor, however, leads to different conclusions.

Stowers' examination of the role of the fictitious interlocutor has led him to the conclusion that far from voicing the objections raised by opponents of a given author's position, the interlocutor far more often raises questions that grow out of, and set forward, the argument being propounded. For that reason, the interlocutor is frequently "colorless and almost without any identity."[21] Far from being an opponent who seeks to discredit the line of argument, then, the interlocutor represents rather a device whereby to introduce, and thus counteract, false inferences and mistaken deductions which could be drawn from the author's line of argumentation. For that reason also interlocutors frequently appear at a point in the argument where a major thesis or basic proposition has been proposed.[22]

An examination of Paul's letters shows that many of these characteristics are also to be found where he uses fictitious interlocutors. Careful examination of Pauline argument indicates that such questions often follow the introduction of a thesis, and that they serve not so much to represent the position of foes of the Christian message Paul is expounding as to present false inferences Christians might be tempted to draw.[23]

Such an examination also reveals that Paul in fact makes far more use of this kind of format—false inferences enunciated by a fictitious interlocutor which are then refuted—than do other Hellenistic authors who use this form. They occur in Paul more frequently, for example, than in Epictetus, a point that is particularly noteworthy with respect to Romans.[24] While Paul also uses an "exemplum" in his response to an objection (e.g., Rom 11:1), he tends to use quotations from Scripture in a way different from the employment of literary quotations in secular Hellenistic authors.[25] The most common pattern into which all of these

---

[20]   For a convenient survey of such views, see ibid., 122–24.
[21]   Ibid., 129; see the whole discussion, pp. 128–133.
[22]   Ibid., 144, 146.
[23]   Stowers (ibid., 148) cites as examples 3:1; 6:1; 7:7; 9:14 and 11:1.
[24]   Ibid., 148. For a careful study of the use of μὴ γένοιτο in the writings of Epictetus and in those of Paul, see Abraham J. Malherbe, "*MH GENOITO* in the Diatribe and Paul," *HTR* 73 (1980): 231–240; the correct p. 236, which in vol. 73 wrongly repeated p. 238, was printed as frontispiece in *HTR* 74 (1981).
[25]   S. Stowers, *The Diatribe*, 136, 151.

rhetorical devices are fitted tends to be an objection or false conclusion which is rejected, followed by a reason for the rejection supported by examples or quotations.[26] As we shall see, perhaps typically, Paul makes use of a similar structure in Romans 3:1–8, but with enough modification to indicate his own rhetorical creativity. Diatribal influence has clearly passed through the screen of Paul's own considerable rhetorical skill.

What all of this means for the intention of the fictitious interlocutor is clear: the interlocutor functions not in a setting which is to be understood as polemic, but rather as pedagogic. That is, if the objections grow out of the flow of the argument, rather than being raised as objections from outside, then the objections serve more in the style of students' questions than of opponents' objections. The diatribe therefore represents not the situation of the street preacher meeting hostile objections to his position, but rather the situation of the class-room, with the interlocutor serving as replacement for the input of students. In the classical function of the diatribe—indictment and protreptic—the fictitious interlocutor raises points that give the author an opportunity to clarify further for his students key points in the argument.[27] That insight will be important for our consideration of the intention of Paul's statement at the end of Romans 3:8, as of course it would be for the consideration of the intent of many other passages in Romans.

In that light, it is clear that the diatribe is used more to educate than to confute, and more to enlighten than to defeat. The clear inference from that is that the diatribal form is thus intent upon uncovering in the student reservations which, upon being answered, allow him or her to make further progress in learning. Socrates as the originator of the dialogical model also provides the clue to the intention of the dialogical diatribe: the dialogue is carried on until a person's vices and inconsistencies have come to light, and the situation is thus created where progress can be made.[28] From this origin the common diatribal elements of indictment and protreptic have emerged, elements which enable the teacher/author to display for self-reflection the students' pretentions and arrogance.[29] The purpose is therefore not refutation of one who opposes the author, but rather the purpose is to reveal the student to himself or herself, so a deeper commitment to the teaching of the author is possible. The style is suited for those who already have a basic commitment, and who need further instruction, instruction which is possible only when internal impediments, whether of character or intellect, have been

---

[26] Ibid., 133.
[27] Ibid., 141, 152–53.
[28] Ibid., 106.
[29] Ibid., 109, 116, 175.

removed.[30] It is to the removal of such impediments that the diatribe is aimed.

In this respect as well, it is clear that much of Paul which reflects the dialogical style so characteristic of the diatribe is better understood in terms of a student–teacher relationship than in terms of a street preacher–opponent relationship. The purpose of the frequent dialogical episodes in Romans is thus not so much to refute outside opponents as it is to aid those who are already Christians to a deeper understanding and commitment of their lives to the gospel Paul preaches.

All of this obviously has a bearing on our analysis of Romans 3:1–8. If Stowers' analysis is correct, we should expect to find the objections of the fictitious interlocutor to be points that grow out of the logic of the argument itself,[31] rather than from objections on the part of outsiders or unbelievers. What we will find then in 3:3, 5, 7, and 8 are not so much objections as false conclusions, to be understood as pedagogical aids to the Roman readers, rather than as refutations of an opponent, Jewish or other.

What we have not found is a clue to the actual rhetorical pattern of Paul's argument in Romans 3:1–8. We have learned what we may expect from the dialogic-diatribal form into which Paul has cast that argument—pedagogy rather than refutation—but we have not yet found the key to the rhetorical pattern of that pedagogical argument. It is to that analysis that we must now turn.

That Paul is capable of aiding the impact of his argument in Romans with the skillful use of rhetorical patterns is evident to anyone who has paid careful attention to the structure of Paul's language in Romans. His three-fold use of παρέδωκεν αὐτοὺς ὁ θεός in 1:24, 26, 28, the double chiastic parallelism of 2:7–10,[32] his double use of ἀλλὰ λέγω, μή in 10:18, 19, his repeated λέγω οὖν, μή. . .μὴ γένοιτο in 11:1, 11, all attest his

---

[30]   Ibid., 164, 174, 176, 182. This represents a major conclusion of Stowers' work, as well as a major advance in the understanding of the style and intention of the diatribe.

[31]   Support for this supposition is provided, if only indirectly, by the fact that the questions with which these verses are introduced (3:1) grow directly out of Paul's immediately preceding discussion in 2:28–29. There Paul has argued that physical circumcision does not carry the kind of religious significance Jews had apparently attributed to it. That of course is immediately to raise the question of the value of such circumcision, and by inference therefore the value of the entire religious heritage of the Jews, and those of course are exactly the questions Paul raises in 3:1.

[32]   The double chiasm consists in one chiasm which concerns the order of reward (A) and punishment (B): the order in vv. 7 (A) and 8 (B) are reversed in vv. 9 (B) and 10 (A); and a second chiasm dealing with (1) what a person does and (2) what results from such action: the order in vv. 7 (1,2) and 8 (1,2) is reversed in vv. 9 (2,1) and 10 (2,1). This gives the structure A 1,2; B 1,2; B 2,1; A 2,1. Adding to the sophistication of the structure is the presence of an additional parallelism in vv. 9–10, namely, the presence of the phrase "to the Jew first, and also to the Greek." An author who can formulate so complex a construction is hardly one lacking in compositional skills.

skill in that regard. It would not therefore be beyond the bounds of imagination that Paul could be using a rhetorical pattern in these verses that would provide some clues, at least, to his intention.

It is evident from even a cursory glance at 3:1–8 that Paul is repeating some constructions: phrases begun with εἰ and with μή, and the phrase μὴ γένοιτο, for example. The εἰ and μή are each employed three times (εἰ vv. 3, 5, 7; μή, vv. 3, 5, 8). The μὴ γένοιτο is used twice (vv. 4, 6) but in each instance immediately following the question introduced with μή. That pattern would suggest that Paul is stating something he thinks is true (the statement introduced with εἰ), followed by an inference he thinks is false (the statement introduced with μή), followed by a vigorous denial of the false inference (μὴ γένοιτο). The second and third εἰ phrases introduced with εἰ do not follow immediately on the μὴ γένοιτο, however. In vv. 4 and 6, Paul gives what appear to be the reasons he thinks the inferences introduced by μή deserve an immediate denial: God will remian faithful and true (v. 4) no matter how perfidious human beings may be (v. 3); God cannot forego wrath (v. 5), since that would also mean foregoing eschatological judgment (v. 6). In vv. 5–6, the question τί ἐροῦμεν does not precede the phrase introduced with εἰ as it does in v. 3 (τί γάρ), but rather follows it. In both instances, however, it is clear that the response introduced with μή is an inference, and a false one, to the preceding and true statement introduced with εἰ. Whether the question introduces the εἰ statement, therefore, or follows it, the point is the same.

It is this pattern, I want to urge, that Stowers failed to see in his analysis of Romans 3:1–8. He saw perceptively enough that Paul has formed an *inclusio* in vv. 1 and 9 with the question τί οὖν but has attempted to treat 3:1 as the first objection, which in turn led him to fail to see the repeated structure we have just outlined. Because he failed to see that structure, he was then unable to see the way the assertion at the end of v. 8 fit into it, and he has classed it simply as an *ad hominem* retort. He has also failed to see the significance of the εἰ δέ in v. 5, which again in its turn, I suspect, kept him from discerning the structure we have outlined.

What we have, then, is a sequence of thought that asks what one's inference ought to be from statement "A." Ought it to be statement "B"? Decidedly not, for the following reason "C." The basic rhetorical pattern can thus be reconstructed in this way (recognizing that the question can either precede or follow the phrase introduced with εἰ):

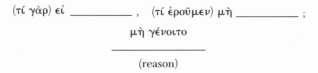

(τί γὰρ) εἰ _____ ,   (τί ἐροῦμεν) μὴ _____ ;

μὴ γένοιτο
_____

(reason)

That pattern is applied then by Paul in his argument in Romans 3:1–8 in the following way (for the sake of clarity, I have placed the question after the εἰ phrase in both instances):
vv. 3–4:

εἰ ἠπίστησάν τινες   τί γάρ;   μὴ ἡ ἀπιστία αὐτῶν τὴν
                                        πίστιν τοῦ θεοῦ καταργήσει
                        μὴ γένοιτο
                γινέσθω δὲ ὁ θεὸς ἀληθής

vv. 5–6:

εἰ δὲ ἡ ἀδικία ἡμῶν θεοῦ   τί ἐροῦμεν;   μὴ ἄδικος ὁ θεὸς ὁ
δικαιοσύνην συνίστησιν   ἐπιφέρων τὴν ὀργήν
                        μὴ γένοιτο
                ἐπεὶ πῶς κρινεῖ ὁ θεὸς τὸν κόσμον

If this pattern were then to be applied to the argument in vv. 7–8, the results would appear as follows:

εἰ δὲ ἡ ἀλήθεια τοῦ   (τί ἐροῦμεν;)   μὴ ποιήσωμεν τὰ κακά
θεοῦ ἐν τῷ ἐμῷ   ἵνα ἔλθῃ τὰ ἀγαθά
ψεύσματι ἐπερίσσευσεν
εἰς τὴν δόξαν αὐτοῦ
                        (μὴ γένοιτο)
                ὧν τὸ κρίμα ἔνδικόν ἐστιν

The fact that the pattern can be found in these last two verses as well suggests that Paul had the same general pattern in mind, but the material we have had to add (included within parentheses), and the material we have omitted, indicate that something has occured to distort the pattern. The distortion is occasioned in two ways: a first false inference, not introduced by μή is given (v. 7b: τί ἔτι κἀγὼ ὡς ἁμαρτωλὸς κρίνομαι;), and a personal denial by Paul that he is responsible for the second false inference, which is then introduced by μή (v. 8a: καθὼς βλασφη-μούμεθα καὶ καθώς φασίν τινες ἡμᾶς λέγειν ὅτι).

Of these two distortions, the second, which defends Paul against a charge which apparently was in fact leveled against him (he refers to it again in Rom. 6:1) is easy enough to understand. Paul simply wants to call attention to the fact that he regards this inference, apparently attributed to him, to be false. But the anticipation of defending himself against this false inference may have led him to put more emphasis on that false inference than on the first one given, namely, the inference that if sin contributes to God's glory, sin is good and not bad in its ultimate outcome, and ought therefore not be condemned by God who profits from it. It may therefore be the case that we ought to reconstruct the argument in vv. 7–8 in the following way:

εἰ δὲ ἡ ἀλήθεια τοῦ   (τί ἐροῦμεν;)   (μὴ) ἔτι τί κἀγὼ ὡς
θεοῦ ἐν τῷ ἐμῷ   ἁμαρτωλὸς κρίνομαι
ψεύσματι ἐπερίσσευσεν
εἰς τὴν δόξαν αὐτοῦ

                            (μὴ γένοιτο)
                    ὧν τὸ κρίμα ἔνδικόν ἐστιν

However we may want to decide the question of the false inference in vv. 7–8 (it may be that Paul wanted in fact to include them both), the basic pattern does enable us to isolate the parenthetical remark Paul includes in his own self-defense, and therefore to understand the final phrase not as a kind of vindictive curse on those who misunderstand Paul, but rather to understand it as the reason why God's overcoming grace does not legitimate playing fast and loose with his eschatological justice. Understood that way, namely, that the presence of grace does not make sin less odious, Paul's subsequent argument (3:9–20) makes good sense: he now emphasizes that very fact, i.e., that everyone is guilty of sin despite the goodness of a gracious and faithful God. It is also clear that these verses, far from being a digression, are the logical consequence of Paul's argument in 2:17–29, and especially vv. 28–29, namely, that performance, and not possession and/or appearance are what God requires. The set of three questions and answers which Paul includes in 3:1–8 shows that although the Jews are in fact the chosen people (3:1–2), they are not exempt from judgment on their performance (3:9; for the statement of this thesis, see 2:6).

Tracing out that pattern would also argue, I think, that Paul is dealing with an objection specifically directed against his own formulation of the gospel only in the final inference introduced with μή, which in turn led to the parenthetical denial. The absence of such denials to the earlier false inferences would suggest that those false inferences are Paul's way of drawing out the logic of his argument, and do not necessarily represent disputes he had with Jews, or for that matter Gentiles, in the course of his preaching.

Careful consideration of both the rhetorical pattern in which Paul has cast his argument in 3:1–8, therefore, as well as careful consideration of the literary form most similar to the kind of format Paul has chosen, enables us to understand the nature of Paul's argument (its intention is to educate, not refute) as well as the way it is structured (v. 8 constitutes a statement of theological fact, not an *ad hominem* retort to opponents).

Such an investigation has helped us see how these verses fit into their present context in Romans, and show that far from being a digression, they continue in logical and consequent form the argument Paul has been pursuing in the early chapters of his letter to the churches in Rome. It is precisely from such careful consideration of literary form and rhetorical pattern, I would suggest, that progress in understanding Paul's intentions in his letters will come.[33]

---

[33] Ibid., 119–20. Stowers presents the following outline:

3:1—Two objections and an answer
3:2—Reason for the answer
3:3—Objection (introduced with τί γάρ)
3:4—Rejection (μὴ γένοιτο) and reason
3:5—Objection (introduced with εἰ δέ)
3:5b—Objection (introduced with μή)
3:6—Rejection (μὴ γένοιτο), and Reason for rejection
3:7—Objection (introduced by εἰ δέ)
3:8—Objection (containing parenthetical remark), and Reply to accusers (ad hominem retort)
3:9—False conclusion (repeated from 3:1), and Rejection (οὐ πάντως), and Reason.

Despite the differences between our analyses of these verses, they are close enough to provide me with some assurance that I am on the right track with my analysis, which was reached independently of, and prior to, the work of Stowers.

The Law Courts in Corinth:
An Experiment in the Power of Baptism

LLOYD A. LEWIS, JR.*

One of the most fascinating aspects of Reginald Fuller's career as a scholar has been the delightful way he has crossed the borders of many areas of study. It was always a joy for me as a young teacher to watch him in a classroom as he related his study of the New Testament to the study of liturgics, inter-faith relations, and preaching. This was not, I think, so much his way of working out the eternal conflict between the generalist and the specialist in his scholarship as it was and is his way of showing that all of these disciplines have a common home in the church, in its life and faith.

Several years ago Professor Fuller contributed an essay to a volume on Christian initiation.[1] That particular essay inspired my own interest in the importance of baptism, not only as a sacrament of the church, but also as an important event by which the church defined its relationship to the world and its institutions. My contribution to this volume is offered in appreciation to Professor Fuller for sparking that interest.

I. Paul's Prescription to the Corinthians

One of the more intriguing aspects of Paul's writings is the apostle's suggestion in 1 Corinthians 6:1–11 that there should be a procedure for the judgment of legal cases among Christians which would remove such litigation from pagan law courts. This seems quite remarkable since Paul hardly appears as an isolationist in 1 Corinthians. He addresses the situation of marriages between believers and unbelievers in the congregation (7:12ff.). In issues of sharing meals with pagans, he sees no reason why Christians should withdraw from eating with unbelievers simply because of the fact that they do not belong to the church (10:27ff.). More often than not he suggests that members of the church, mindful of their

---

* Lloyd A. Lewis, Jr., is Associate Professor of New Testament, Virginia Theological Seminary, Alexandria, Virginia.

[1] Reginald H. Fuller, "Christian Initiation in the New Testament," in *Made, Not Born: New Perspectives on Christian Initiation and the Catechumenate* (Notre Dame: University of Notre Dame Press, 1976), 7–31.

baptism, should live in such a way in this world as if this world's
institutions did not have the final claim on them. Rather, in the light of
the crucifixion and resurrection of Jesus Christ people now live in a new
frame of reference. This frame of reference did not necessitate one's
abandoning life in this world.

Why then did Paul suggest that Christian courts should exist for law
cases among Christians? Although it is tempting to focus on the particular
nature of the cases to be tried, I would suggest that the most important
issue for Paul was the qualification of those who would stand as judges,
since that qualification, I believe, would determine the type of justice
which a Christian could expect in such a court.

II. The Unity of 1 Corinthians 6:1–11

It is necessary at the outset to establish the thematic unity of 1
Corinthians 6:1–11 within the context of chapter 6. The intrusion of the
vice list in 6:9ff. with its explicit mention of sexual irregularities may lead
us to connect verses 9–11 with the discussion of sexual immorality and
purity following in 6:12ff. On the other hand, one might assume that
6:9–11 is part of a loosely connected tradition added by Paul almost as an
afterthought. This, however, overlooks other evidence which points to
the unity of this passage.

In 6:1 Paul states that the scandal of the Corinthians' action is found
in the fact that they have brought their cases before the ἄδικοι. In 6:9 it
is this same word ἄδικοι which stands at the beginning of the vice list.
Lexically, the word ἄδικος may indicate that the outsiders are, literally,
unjust.[2] Thus Paul's statement in 6:1ff. would have to be a pragmatic one.
He warns Corinthian Christians to avoid pagan courts because the judges
are corrupt. But if we translate the word ἄδικοι "unjust" in 6:1, then what
are we to do with the word as it appears in context in 6:9? Here being
ἄδικος means that one cannot inherit the kingdom of God. The designation is further contrasted with the statement in 6:11 that one has been
washed, sanctified, and justified in the name of the Lord Jesus and in the
Spirit. The logical antithesis of ἄδικος is δίκαιος, but the explicit
antithesis in 6:1 is ἅγιοι. This causes us to look again at 6:1, for Paul
states that the ἄδικοι are the unbaptized. His main concern, then, is to
establish that the absence of justification, not of justice, is primarily at
issue in the scandal about litigation among the members of the Corinthian
church.[3]

---

[2] BAGD 17–18.

[3] Frederik W. Grosheide, *Commentary on the First Epistle to the Corinthians* (Grand
Rapids: Wm. B. Eerdmans, 1953), 133: "Paul calls the pagan judges unrighteous since they

At the same time we might say that the passage 6:1–11 is connected with a whole complex of ideas which begins with the discussion in chapter 5 and continues on to the end of chapter 6. We have already suggested that the vice list alludes to πορνεία and to other instances of sexual irregularity (6:9). Paul alludes to these matters outside of 6:1–11 in 5:1–13 and 6:13–20. Similarly, 6:1–11 is concerned with the practical matter of judgment, an issue which includes legal matters (6:1, 4–6) and eschatological judgment (6:2–3). In the wider context of chapters 5 and 6 the verb κρίνω appears in 5:3, 12. Is it legitimate, then, to isolate 6:1–11 as a self-contained argument, or must it be read as part of one argument which begins with 5:1 and continues through the end of chapter 6?

Paul's style in 1 Corinthians suggests an answer. There are several instances within the letter where Paul makes an excursus to particularize or to explain his argument. When we consider the three-chapter section beginning at 8:1, we see that Paul seems to leave behind his concern with the consumption of idol meat in order to speak in chapter 9 about the ἐξουσία he has since he is a legitimate apostle.[4] The word ἐξουσία, however, is also the key word used by Paul in the issue of idol meat both in chapters 8 and 10. His autobiographical excursus helps to strengthen his argument that the Corinthians should be willing to give up their ἐξουσία, even as Paul had, for the sake of others. Similarly, chapters 12–14 contain a discussion of love as "the more excellent way." Chapter 13, as a unit, presents this more excellent way. It draws into it the gifts of tongues, knowledge, and prophecy. Thus it is linked with the themes of 12 and 14, while at the same time remaining a unified excursus.

The existence of such thematically-linked excursuses in 1 Corinthians justifies our taking 6:1–11 as such an excursus. It is thematically and lexically linked to its context. At the same time it is self-contained and focuses on the issue of judicial procedures in the Corinthian church. Clarification of this issue was necessary before the exegesis began, for we will argue that though the passage seems to switch its concern from law courts, judges, and litigation to issues concerning baptism, Paul is drawing the importance of baptism into the qualifications for a judge over Christian law cases. With this in mind we can now move to the exegesis.

---

are not members of the church, who are the saints. . . . Unrighteous, in contrast with 'holy in Christ,' means: not righteous before God and therefore not truly righteous." But Grosheide, in speaking about 6:9 specifically, identifies the word ἄδικοι with the Gentiles (pp. 139–140). One wonders whether or not he would include the unbaptized people of Israel, who are also outside of the Christian community.

[4] In 1 Cor. 9:3ff. It is possible to agree with Hans Conzelmann, *First Corinthians*, Hermeneia Commentary (Philadelphia: Fortress Press, 1975), 151, that a different type of freedom is spoken of in 1 Cor. 9 from that which is found in 1 Cor. 8 and 10, but what seems to be more at issue is the attitude which both apostle and the strong among the Corinthians take to the freedom which they have. In both cases ἐξουσία is something which the Christian should be free to forgo.

III. Exegesis

The particular πρᾶγμα which had caused the grievance in 1 Corinthians 6:1ff. is not mentioned by Paul, though common speculation is that it was a suit in which money was involved.[5] Paul commonly begins with a concrete incident in order to state a general rule for the congregation. In 1 Corinthians 5:1, for example, Paul pointed to the case of sexual immorality in Corinth. Yet even as he condemned the actions of the offender, Paul more vehemently condemned the inappropriate tolerance of the Corinthians in letting the offending brother remain in the congregation. In much the same way, Paul shifts his concern from the particular lawsuit to the twin matters of who is fit to judge another member of the church and whether members of the church should engage in judicial proceedings at all.

Paul's response to the "inability" of the Corinthians to find judges among themselves is found in the two rhetorical questions in 6:2 and 3:

οὐκ οἴδατε ὅτι οἱ ἅγιοι τὸν κόσμον κρινοῦσιν;
οὐκ οἴδατε ὅτι ἀγγέλους κρινοῦμεν, μήτι γε βιωτικά;

In form, these questions are devices regularly used by Paul, and they are particularly prominent in 1 Corinthians 6. They indicate what was considered general knowledge, and as such they were a way of shaming the Corinthians.[6]

In both verses members of the church (ἅγιοι in 6:2; the understood ἡμεῖς in 6:3) are pictured as participating in acts of judgment. The tense of both verbs, however, is future. In the first case the judgment of the world is mentioned. Conzelmann has suggested that the background for this might be found in Daniel 7:22 and Wisdom 3:8 where it is said that in the final days the righteous will join in the inauguration of the new age. Part of their function will be to participate with God in his reign. The function of the saints as the judges of angels is more difficult to explain, but as in the case of the judgment of this world, the image remains an eschatological one.[7]

---

[5] J. H. Moulton and George Milligan, *The Vocabulary of the Greek New Testament Illustrated from the Papyri and other Non-Literary Sources* (London: Hodder and Stoughton, 1914–1930), 532, indicates that the word πρᾶγμα was used in Hellenistic legal papyri for fiscal matters (BGU I22, P Ryl II 76[14], P Ryl II 113[13], P Strass I 41[38]).

[6] This diatribal pattern which starts with the verb and negative occurs at 6:3, 9, 15, and 19 in this chapter and at 3:6; 5:6; 9:13; and 9:24 in the rest of the letter.

[7] E. B. Allo, *Première Épître aux Corinthiens*, EBib (Paris: Gabalda, 1934) 133–134: "Le Christ avait annoncé à ses apôtres qu'ils jugeraient les Douze tribus d'Israel; ici la promesse s'étend à tous les fidèles, à l'égard du monde entier, c'est-à-dire de toutes les créatures intelligentes, Anges et hommes. Elle est essentiellement eschatologique, et cette

On what basis would baptized Christians participate with God in this eschatological judgment? It is found in the eschatological nature of what it means to be adopted as children of God. In Romans 8:14–30 membership in the Christian community has both present and future components. Thus Christians have already been given υἰοθεσία (Rom. 8:15–16) while they await the revelation of that υἰοθεσία in its fullness (Rom. 8:23). Those who are the children of God can expect that in the eschaton they will be qualified to stand as judge over all things. This will not be the right or duty of those who are not of the family of God. Paul's initial concern, however, is to contrast the qualifications of those outside of the church with those who are within. Since those who belong to the Christian family will judge the world and angels, certainly they can be fit judges for trivial matters. By placing lawsuits before those esteemed least by the church, that is before outsiders, those who are "not members of the brotherhood" (6:5), members of the Corinthian congregations show ironically that they have totally misunderstood the last days and their part in them. The Corinthians' much vaunted eschatological understanding is flawed.

Paul insists that there must be someone within the Christian community, based on the qualifications he has mentioned in 6:3–4, who can act as judge. His description of a judge is expanded in the complete phrase, οὕτως οὐκ ἔνι ἐν ὑμῖν οὐδεὶς σοφός; (6:5). As in the statement about the events of the eschaton, Paul is again being quite ironic. Wisdom and knowledge were the proud possessions of the Corinthians. In 3:18 false wisdom had led to their boasting in themselves, rather than in the Lord. We know that in Romans 1:22 Paul understands misguided wisdom as the seed of idolatry.

Paul, however, conceded the fact that another type of wisdom was available to members of the church. This wisdom was given to those who were mature (1 Cor. 2:6). It was a gift of the Spirit, and therefore it provided for the upbuilding of the church (12:7). As with all such gifts it was granted or quickened at baptism (12:13,11), the moment when one became a part of the church.

This particular wisdom is linked to the cross. Eloquence and wisdom, Paul states in 1:7, rob the cross of its power, for it is precisely in the paradox of the cross that true wisdom is revealed through weakness and suffering. Again we remember Paul's statement about sonship in Romans 8 where one is son, heir, and joint heir precisely because one participates in weakness and suffering in the present.

This study on the meaning of wisdom in 1 Corinthians helps to

mention, jetée comme en passant, révèle déjà la place que tenait l'eschatologie, même à Corinthe, dans l' enseignement de Paul." Allo notes that there is significant division over the matter of the judgment of the angels, whether Paul had in mind the angels which were fallen, or all angelic beings. In any case it is an eschatological act.

remind us of the connection of Paul's sayings about judgment and these motifs connected with baptism. Thus far Paul has stated that the passing of judgment is guaranteed to the church as an eschatological privilege. Being a member of the church through baptism equips a person for this task. Non-eschatological matters of judgment, however, confront the church in its life in the present.

At the same time Paul states that among the Corinthians there are those who do have wisdom. This wisdom is a gift of the Spirit, bestowed with other gifts through baptism. Yet this wisdom is connected to the cross and suffering of Jesus Christ. If the wisdom which Christian judges possess is imparted through baptism, then it shares with the granting of sonship the concept that Christians suffer with one another in the present, even as they suffer together with Christ.

In 6:6b Paul restates his thesis, and he does so using more language of baptism. The scandal is described in the fact that "brother goes to law against brother, and that before unbelievers." To switch the description of membership in the church to the relationship between brothers is to remind the Corinthians of their baptism again. Certainly the word ἀδελφός meant more to Paul than familial relationship in a physical sense. The word had become a part of Christian argot,[8] borrowed from the vocabulary of Israel, which indicated membership in the church. It stated in a way the reality which Christians affirmed when they called themselves God's children. Those who were baptized were God's adopted. They shared a common father, and thus they were equally brothers and sisters of one another. Thus Paul could recast the issue of the lawsuits as a family squabble among siblings, carried out before strangers.

In 6:7 Paul upbraids the Corinthians because they have engaged in judging one another, but even more so for having lawsuits at all. Verse 7b–c provides the preferable alternative for the Christian community:

διὰ τί οὐχὶ μᾶλλον ἀδικεῖσθε;
διὰ τί οὐχὶ μᾶλλον ἀποστερεῖσθε;

Paul has stated the same sentiments in 1 Thessalonians 5:15. There he applied it generally as the duty of Christians to all. One should not harm others. By using the parallel passive verbs in 6:7 Paul shifts the

---

[8]   When the Christian community uses this figurative familial language it is certainly following what had been done by Judaism. Christine Mohrmann, "Linguistic Problems in the Early Christian Church," VC 11 (1957): 11–36, identifies use of the term ἀδελφός as one example of the use of argot by the Christian community, one borrowed from Old Testament antecedents. "'Ἀδελφός in the Septuagint means 'brother Jew,' and ἀδελφός becomes thus the term for fellow Christian. This linguistic custom was so noticeable that the pagans made scornful remarks about it. The choice of a particular terminus technicus in Early Christian Greek, is often determined by the example of the Septuagint" (p. 22).

focus of his argument from what Christians do to what they should be willing to bear. Paul states that it is better for a Christian to accept being wronged than to act wrongly against a fellow Christian, to be defrauded rather than to defraud one's fellow Christian. Is Paul now saying that the Christians should not act as judges of one another?

Chapter 6:1–6 is concerned with the question of placing law cases before pagan judges, an issue which Paul seems to resolve in the negative: there should be members of the Christian community who will stand as judges whenever there are lawsuits, and fellow Christians are the only appropriate judges in such cases. Chapter 6:7–8 asks if brothers in the church should judge one another at all. The two questions are distinct, though they are connected in that they pose the question of when the church or its members should assume the role of being judge.

We might contrast the situation in chapter 6 with the one we find in chapter 5. In chapter 5 Paul shows his anger against the Corinthians because they refused to judge a fellow member of the congregation. Paul's reaction to the situation is quite clear: it is a matter which should have been handled swiftly by the church. Paul sees this issue to be a religious one rather than one which is purely legal.

Paul's choice of words in describing the situation in chapter 5 helps to make this clear, for the language he uses is cultic language from Israel's passover (5:6–8). The retention of the offending individual threatened the purity of the congregation. Therefore extraordinary action had to be taken, including an assembly of the church and a solemn act of expulsion of the individual from the community.[9] The act of expulsion itself was guaranteed both by the presence of the apostle and by the fact that the church met and acted in the name of the Lord.

The act of judging, however, is not indiscriminate in this case. Paul is not concerned with passing judgment on immorality in general, but on immorality within the church. Those religious assemblies met to judge an ἀδελφὸς ὀνομαζόμενος (5:11), not the pagans. It is the misbehaving brother who is to be shunned and judged by the church. The judgment of the pagans would come at the end of time (6:2–3), and only then would the members of the church participate in that act.

When we return to the situation in chapter 6:1–11 we see that Paul did not think that civil lawsuits demanded the same type of response from the church. There is no hint at all that Paul expected that the issue would be settled by a solemn gathering of the church: a wise individual within the congregation was needed to arbitrate (6:5) between the contending brothers. Nor is there any hint that settling πράγματα would result in the

---

[9]   So Göran Forkmann, *The Limits of Religious Community*, ConBNT 5 (Lund: Student-litteratur Lund, 1972), who lists situations in which expulsion from the community should occur.

defaming of the church. Paul only introduced a permissive[10] procedure to be followed if it were not possible to get the individuals to settle out of court or, more preferably, to abandon litigation altogether.

In 6:6 Paul states that it is scandalous for members of the church to place their cases before pagan judges. By virtue of their participation in the final judgment of the world (6:2), the members of the church will stand as judge over pagan judges. This undercuts any appeal to superiority which pagan judges might make.

In verse 8 Paul introduces a condemnation of litigation among Christians. The preferable way would be to bear wrong and fraud. Thus a member of the church, a brother, would suffer injustice, rather than to pursue the suit. The final τοῦτο ἀδελφούς particularizes the issue.

Verse 9 begins a diatribal reminder of things known well by the Corinthians: οἱ ἄδικοι cannot be inheritors of the kingdom of God. We know that inheritance is one metaphor used to describe the estate of those who had received membership in the church (Gal. 3:29). Paul therefore defines the borders of the Christian community with these words, for those outside of the kingdom in both actuality and in potentiality are those who neither possess sonship by baptism (as do the Christians, both Jewish and Gentile) nor by eschatological promise (as do the Jews). The vice list which follows points to the actions of those who are pagans, and therefore of those who are outsiders to God's family.

Lists of virtues and vices such as the one found in 6:9f. are part of catechetical teaching. They present an ordered description of the life of an individual in society. Such lists were often stock in nature and needed not to indicate the actual social and moral situation of those addressed.[11] They could be post-baptismal reminders, which marked off the old life which was to be abandoned when one became a baptized person. Paul indicates that this was an accurate description of the way of at least some of the Corinthians (6:11), but now the Corinthians were washed, sanctified, justified in the name of the Lord Jesus and in the Spirit.

When we looked at the case presented in chapter 5 we noted that language of purity was clustered about the status of the Corinthian church. Immorality threatened the church's purity. In 6:1–11 the lan-

---

[10]   H. Conzelmann, *First Corinthians*, 105.

[11]   With regard to the specificity of the catalogues of virtues and vices, see Anton Vögtle, *Die Tugend- und Lasterkataloge im Neuen Testament* (Munster: Aschendorff, 1936), 31f. James Moffatt, *The First Epistle of Paul to the Corinthians* (New York: Harper and Brothers, 1938), seems strongly partial to using the list to illustrate the moral horrors of Corinth on pp. 66–67. It is possible therefore to agree with one like Morton Enslin, *The Ethics of Paul* (New York: Harper and Brothers, 1930), 161–162, who warns against over-exegeting the vice lists while at the same time recognizing that the lists formed one way of articulating the type of life expected of those who belonged to the Christian church.

guage of purity and sanctification surrounded individual members of the
church, and it was closely connected with references to baptism.

Nils Dahl has shown that the contrast of the old life with the new life
was typical of one form of early Christian preaching.[12] This preaching
functioned to remind the congregation of its baptism. Insofar as the
church reminds members of their baptism, the time of their incorporation
into Christ, when the distinctions of class, sex, and race were made of no
ultimate importance, it returns them to that moment when they crossed
over into the church. The vice list in 6:9ff., the "once you were . . . now
you are" patterns in 6:11, the use of the terms "saints" and "brothers" to
refer to members of the church, all are reminders of baptism. Why has
Paul put these references to baptism here?

We need to return to our original decision concerning the division of
1 Corinthians 6. We suggested that the material explicitly concerning
baptism in 6:9–11 was a necessary part of Paul's argument about the
qualifications for judges in cases where Christians entered litigation with
one another. Through baptism one becomes a member of the church, as
Paul has stated, for baptism marks the transition into a new life and state.
Patterns of behavior which are antithetical to the new state must be
abandoned. Not only does one abandon sexual immorality; one also
abandons thievery, covetousness, and extortion in that transition (6:10).
Members of the church enter a situation of conformity to the commonly-
held preaching found in the kerygma.

We have also learned that adoption confers common status. Within
the brotherhood and sisterhood created through baptism only Christ
holds the status of first-born son by virtue of his resurrection. All other
Christians bear exactly the same relationship to one another by virtue of
the fact that they are all children of the same father through their
incorporation by adoption. Since the Corinthian Christians lived at the
same time in the church and in pagan society, they could expect that
others outside of the church were under no compulsion to abandon
distinctions and status when they were called upon to interact with the
church and its members. The stronger claim of fraternity made on the
Christian through baptism would override the claims of this world.

---

[12]   Nils A. Dahl, *Jesus in the Memory of the Early Church* (Minneapolis: Augsburg
Publishing House, 1976), 33–34. To emphasize the "in house" nature of this form of
teaching helps to show its application to the issue of judges even more clearly. Paul is setting
down rules. These rules are for members of the Christian group. Inasmuch as judges are to
be Christians, then they, like those whom they judge, should keep themselves from
non-Christian behavior and thus give witness to their baptism.

IV. Conclusions

Now let us return to our initial questions. Paul shows that entering litigation is not the preferable way for Christians. Christians are brothers and sisters of one another, and therefore they are related to one another as the children of God. To remind the Corinthians of their baptism as Paul did was to remove the importance of status among them. Also to remind individuals of their baptism was to remind them of the fact that they would have to endure suffering. Both of these parts of the baptismal reminder would give the ideal of "no litigation among Christians" the highest place. At the same time Paul was a realist. Cases do appear, and adjudication must be made. Threats to the integrity of the community such as those found in 1 Corinthians 5 had to be tried by the church, met in assembly in the Lord's name. Pagans were to have no jurisdiction over these matters—Paul does not even discuss this as a possibility. Nor would Christians in the present exercise religious judgment on the pagans. That would be one of the duties of the church at the end of time.

In Roman society civil courts had jurisdiction. But Christians, by virtue of their baptism, bear a different relationship to the unbaptized than that which they bear to one another. In the case where there would be Christian litigants before Christian judges, judge and litigants would, by virtue of their baptism, be peers of one another. In purely pragmatic terms, this would be the one guarantee that the litigants would be tried impartially.

Only by a judge from within the group could a case be settled equitably—one child of God who arbitrates between two other Christians must render a judgment which is worthy of the equal relationship which he or she shares with both of the litigants. One can understand why pagan judges would not be considered truly objective: the common basis for the needed objectivity (the status of being the adopted of God) would be lacking—as would be the Spirit, the common gift found in all who were baptized.

The same factors might explain Paul's decision to forgo acting as judge over the pagans. Only at the eschaton, when one's adoption is truly revealed and one participates in judgment of the world with God, could a Christian legitimately judge an outsider.

What can we say about this particular use of baptismal language by Paul? In this case we have an example of how Christians lived in the wider society. Since the Christian community was not separated from the world by its own choice, contact with non-Christians and with the institutions of non-Christians was to be expected. Some things, however, were reserved for members of the family.

This case, as Wayne Meeks has rightly stated,[13] shows that the church did set up, in certain instances, parallel institutions to handle its own affairs. Here we see that internal settlement of legal matters between Christians fell into this lot. One aspect of baptismal language guaranteed that members of the family would treat their peers with love, self-sacrifice, and justice. At the same time the norms of "family" concern could be used to justify a "hands off" attitude towards outsiders, at least until such time as they would enter the family or until the end of time arrived.

---

[13]   Wayne A. Meeks, *The First Urban Christians* (New Haven: Yale Univ. Press, 1983), 103–105, suggests that the establishment of Christian law-courts was one way of establishing the autonomy of the Christian community. As such it would be one way of marking the difference between Christians and outsiders. The internal focus of these institutions is equally important.

Christ and the Hierarchies in First Corinthians

John Koenig*

It may seem inappropriate to use the word "hierarchy" in a study of Paul's views on the role of Christ in the ordering of power. After all, the originator of this Greek term, assumed by medieval theologians to be the Dionysius of Acts 17:34, who was converted to Christ by Paul's speech on the Areopagus, has now been identified as a fifth or sixth century C.E. writer who drew heavily on the thought of Plotinus and other Neo-Platonists. In modern scholarly circles this writer is usually referred to as Pseudo-Dionysius.[1] If Paul had been asked, in the first century, to explain his position on hierarchy, he would have first needed to inquire about what the questioner meant by this new word.

On the other hand, even a quick reading of Pseudo-Dionysius shows that this creative theologian wrestled with many of the same issues Paul did.[2] Above all, he took seriously the consequences of rankings among the heavenly and earthly powers. Paul had blazed this trail by devoting considerable attention to diverse authorities and principalities as they exerted influence upon human life in Christ, and vice versa. Moreover, at one crucial point Paul and Pseudo-Dionysius agree wholeheartedly. For both, questions about the ordering of power fall into the larger category of questions about how God effects the salvation of humanity. Soteriology furnishes the key to rank. It may be, then, that anachronistic as it is, the concept of hierarchy developed by Pseudo-Dionysius will provide a useful re-entry into Pauline thinking about inequalities in the various relationships between Christ, the corporate powers, and believers—a set of issues that could hardly be more contemporary. I have chosen the letter we now call 1 Corinthians as the Pauline data base for our experiment, first, because in it the apostle refers so frequently to differences of status within that new world situation which he terms "the end of the ages" (10:11); and second, because he reflects upon these

---

* John Koenig is Professor of New Testament, The General Theological Seminary, New York, New York.

[1] Paul Rorem in *Pseudo-Dionysius: The Complete Works*, trans. Colm Luibheid with collaboration by Paul Rorem (New York-Mahwah: Paulist Press, 1987), 1–3. Henceforth, page references to this volume will appear as *PS-D*, plus the page number.

[2] Our pseudonymous author clearly thinks of himself as standing in a line of succession beginning with Paul. He refers to the apostle as "that guide in divine illumination, that light of the world by whom I and my teacher are led, the one great in divine things." See *The Divine Names* 649D; *PS-D* 67.

differences quite intentionally in the light of his convictions about how God and Christ relate to each other in the plan of salvation.

Before examining 1 Corinthians itself, we need to set forth a few of Pseudo-Dionysius' major ideas. In a treatise entitled *The Celestial Hierarchy* our author offers several definitions of his neologism; but the most comprehensive is probably this one: "a hierarchy is a sacred order, a state of understanding, and an activity approximating as closely as possible to the divine" (Ἐστι μὲν ἱεραρχία κατ' ἐμὲ τάξις ἱερὰ καὶ ἐπιστήμη καὶ ἐνέργεια πρὸς τὸ θεοειδὲς ὡς ἐφικτὸν ἀφομοιουμένη; 164D). For its members, the goal of a hierarchy is "to be as like as possible to God and to be at one with him. A hierarchy has God as its leader of all understanding and action" (165A). By means of hierarchy God reaches out, through a chain of intermediaries, to draw all sentient beings back to himself. Here Pseudo-Dionysus almost certainly bases his thinking on the Neo-Platonic philosophy of divine emanation. But his explicit claim is that the notion of hierarchy derives from the biblical teaching on angels. Pseudo-Dionysius understands these celestial servants of God to be divided into three descending ranks.[3] Each rank is the purveyor of sacred truth, and thus of divine essence, to the group just below it on the scale and then, finally, to humans. This constellation enables the lower members to rise toward the Divine by means of enlightenment. The angelic ranking has its threefold counterpart in what Pseudo-Dionysius calls the ecclesiastical hierarchy. This consists of none other than the holy orders of bishop, priest, and deacon, through which the work of the angels is extended on earth. Because Pseudo-Dionysius speaks of these orders as "fixed and unconfused" and organized according to "sacred norms" laid down in the Scriptures (*Ecclesiastical Hierarchy*, 377A), we should probably think of them as possessing an ontological character.

It is important to notice that for Pseudo-Dionysius ἱεραρχία always refers not to individuals *per se*, whether angels or humans, but to individuals placed by God into an energized order so that the goods of salvation can descend and beings who are lower in the order can ascend to their proper position in the divine reality. As parts of this system individuals are called members or, at the upper reaches, hierarchs (*EH* 373C). Hierarchy itself does not exist apart from the ordering action of God for the sake of human divinization (θέωσις; *Divine Names* 649C; *EH* 376A,B)

Unlike Pseudo-Dionysius, Paul does not describe human destiny in terms of divinization. Although precisely in 1 Corinthians he looks

---

[3]   *Celestial Hierarchy* 177D-261D. Pseudo-Dionysius "admits that the triadic arrangement of the nine biblical names [for angels] is not itself scriptural but is taken from Hierotheus" [his teacher]. See *PS-D* 160, n. 68.

forward to the eschatological moment when God will be πάντα ἐν πᾶσιν, he also asserts that Christ will remain distinguishable from the Father and even become subordinate to him in a new way (15:28). In contrast to God, Christ will continue to have a body, and so will those who bear his image at the end (15:42–54). Similarly, when Paul anticipates the coming of the perfect, with the disappearance of all partial knowledge, this means for him not the loss of human individuality but a vision of God "face to face" (13:8–12).

On the other hand, Paul does exhibit a form of what Pseudo-Dionysius calls "procession," that is, an ordered reaching out by God, through intermediaries, to accomplish the salvation of humans. Indeed, to describe what he means by procession, Pseudo-Dionysius cites 1 Corinthians 8:6, where the apostle confesses: ". . . for us there is one God, the Father, from whom are all things and for whom we exist, and one Lord, Jesus Christ, through whom are all things and through whom we exist" (*DN* 649B–652A). Moreover, to the degree noted above, Paul also assumes a type of return to the Divine on the part of humans. Already the bodies of the baptized can be termed a "temple of the Holy Spirit" (6:19). At the resurrection, with bodies transformed from flesh and blood into spirit, believers will "bear the image of the man of heaven" (15:42–50). In addition, while Paul does not typically equate progress in faith with illumination (but see 2 Cor. 3:18), he does link maturity with a proper understanding of the word of the cross and the gifts of the Spirit (2:6–16; 12:1ff.; 14:20). Those who cannot receive this wisdom because of their contentious behavior are labeled "babes in Christ" (3:1–3). The apostle can discern the difference between infant and adult believers, presumably because he is their father in Christ (4:15) whom God has made "first" in the church (12:28). Moreover, he can enjoin the congregation as a whole to subject itself to certain fellow believers who are not apostles (16:15f.). And, in a passage which has now become notorious, he can argue from the proposition that as Christ is the head (κεφαλή) of every male, so the male is the head of the female (11:3).

Can we say, then, that Paul conceives of hierarchies in something resembling the Pseudo-Dionysian sense? And if so, are these hierarchies vital to his understanding of life in Christ? The answer to both questions would seem to be yes, which means that we shall want to try the word "hierarchy" on for size in examining the apostle's thought about the ordering of power. Obviously, careful exploration is required to determine whether the hierarchies identified in 1 Corinthians are all of the same character, whether they are ontological or situational, permanent or temporary, imposed from above or initiated from below, etc.

Before proceeding with our study of the relevant texts, however, we shall do well to remind ourselves once again of the eschatological framework within which Paul thinks and acts. Unlike Pseudo-Dionysius, Paul sees radical shifts occurring in the power structures of his day. The rulers of this age, which probably include both angelic and human forces,[4] are being set aside (2:6), with the result that the form of this world is passing away (7:31). Not only is the crucified and risen Christ currently subduing "every rule and every authority and power" (15:24). In Paul's view, he will bring this work to completion within the present generation by altogether eliminating the sting of death (15:26ff. in the light of 15:51–54). The interim time in which Paul believes himself and his contemporaries to be living is one of tremendous flux. It is characterized by the danger that believers may be confused and deceived and tempted to fall away from Christ by the declining powers of the present order (7:29–35; 9:26–10:13). At the same time—and this is the greater reality— there exist among believers expanding possibilities for the love of neighbors, mutual upbuilding in the church (see esp. chapters 13–14), and abounding in the work of the Lord (15:58). It is from this perception of the new world situation that Paul's thinking about hierarchy develops.

For purposes of analysis, the pertinent texts in 1 Corinthians may be classified according to four categories. These depict orderings of power which involve (1) God, Christ, and the hostile world-forces; (2) God, Christ, and human beings; (3) the apostle and the congregation; and (4) various groups within the congregation.

I. God, Christ, and the Hostile World-Forces

As in Paul's other letters, the sovereign actor in the creation and salvation of the world is God. All things flow from him (ἐξ οὗ τὰ πάντα, 8:6a; τὰ δὲ πάντα ἐκ τοῦ θεοῦ, 11:12), and he presently energizes τὰ πάντα ἐν πᾶσιν (12:6). Yet because of human sin a restoration of the cosmos is required before God can become fully πάντα ἐν παῶιν (15:28). Believers know this and confess themselves to be on the way toward such a relationship with God (ἡμεῖς εἰς αὐτόν; 8:6a). God reigns even now over the current world order, but his βασιλεία has not come to completion (6:9–10). This will happen at the end of a cosmic process punctuated by the visible return of Christ to earth (15:24).

Along with other first century believers, Paul experiences Jesus Christ as God's supreme mediator in the world's creation and redemption. Christ is the one figure "through whom" τὰ πάντα come into being and "through whom" believers find their way back to God (8:6d). Christ

---

[4] Walter Wink, *Naming the Powers: The Language of Power in the New Testament* (Philadelphia: Fortress Press, 1984), 40–45.

is "of God" (3:23) and God is the "head (κεφαλή) of Christ" (11:3). As risen κύριος, Christ reigns over the end of the ages for God. He is God's viceroy-son who will eventually return the βασιλεία to his Father (15:24). Until that τέλος he reigns in the face of opposition from "the rulers of this age" (2:6). The chief of these powers, "the last enemy," is death (15:26). Death receives this title because its continuing reality demonstrates the persistence of sin in the cosmos despite Christ's resurrection (15:56), and probably also because the other powers which oppose God and Christ derive their authority from death.[5] Paul does not speculate about sub-rankings among the hostile powers and in fact does not always draw clear distinctions between human and super-human powers.[6]

But something is happening to these powers during the interim reign of Christ. They are being subjected to Christ and deprived of their actual effectiveness in the world order. Paul uses two verbs to describe this process: καταργέω and ὑποτάσσω. These terms appear together in 15:24–27:

(24) Then comes the end when [Christ] delivers the kingdom to God the Father after destroying (ὅταν καταργήσῃ) every rule and every authority and power. (25) For he must reign until he has put all his enemies under his feet. (26) The last enemy to be destroyed (καταργεῖται) is death. (27) "For [God] has put all things in subjection (ὑπέταξεν) under his feet." But when it says, "All things are put in subjection (ὑποτέτακται) under him," it is plain that he is excepted who put all things under him (ἐκτὸς τοῦ ὑποτάξαντος).

The division of labor here between God and Christ is not altogether clear. Since the first "he" of 15:25 refers to Christ, we are easily led to the conclusion that the second one does so as well. On the other hand, the psalm verse alluded to (110:1) has God as its subject, and so does Psalm 8:6, quoted in 15:27. On either interpretation one must acknowledge that Christ is unable to accomplish his mission apart from decisive action by his Father (15:27). He is dependent upon God's power even as he reigns. And indeed, when the Son surrenders the βασιλεία, he will become subject to the Father (ὑποταγήσεται) in a new way (15:28).

The RSV translation of καταργέω in this passage needs to be challenged. Elsewhere in 1 Corinthians in reference to the powers, it is more properly rendered "bring to nothing" (1:28) or "pass away" (2:6). Although it seems that death especially requires absolute destruction for

---

[5] In an instructive chapter on "The Moral Reality Named Death" William Stringfellow spells out connections between *thanatos* and the world powers which seem to me to follow the grain of Paul's thinking. See *An Ethic for Christians and Other Aliens in a Strange Land* (Waco, TX: Word Books, 1974), 67–94.

[6] See Wink on 1 Cor.2:6–8 and 15:24–27 in *Naming the Powers*, 40–45; 50–55.

the fulfillment of God's purposes, three pieces of data tell against this view. First, when Paul notes in 15:24 that Christ will bring the present age to an end by rendering every rule and authority and power of no effect (καταργήσῃ), this is unlikely to mean obliteration, simply because of God's respect for all created beings. And what happens to death is the same as what happens to the powers as a whole (15:26).[7] Second, the present passive in v. 26 indicates that death is gradually or periodically losing its sting even in the time prior to the τέλος (see also the present tense in 15:57). Perhaps Paul has healings in mind; perhaps he refers to those who die in Christ, who sleep in him and are not really under death's power (1 Thess. 4:13–16). Finally, in 15:24–28 the ruling word is ὑποτάσσω. Καταργέω should probably be understood as a synonym of this (note the parallelism between vss. 24 and 25), as a right ordering under Christ and God. The most adequate translation of καταργέω, in reference to cosmic forces as a whole, would therefore be "deprive of hostile power".

In summary, we can say that the process of world salvation in 1 Corinthians is understood by Paul as a right ordering of power. God is the goal toward which all things rightly tend as subjects and dependents of the divine reign. Christ, the paradigmatic subject-dependent, wields the power of God for salvation like no one else. His particular task with regard to the hostile powers is to bring them into subjection. This is happening already, even as Paul writes (2:6; 15:26), although he presents no timetable that will enable his readers to discern stages of progress. In Pseudo-Dionysian terms, God and Christ relate to each other as Source and Chief Member of a hierarchy. The hostile powers, though arranged in a σχῆμα (7:31), do not comprise a separate hierarchy of their own because they have their origin and destiny in God, even though they are not properly ranked under God at the present time. Paul offers barely a hint as to how the angels of God function with Christ in the divine hierarchy (4:9; 6:3; 11:10; 13:1).[8]

---

[7]   Pointing to Rom.6:9 ("death no longer has any dominion over him"), Wink argues, convincingly I think, that Paul conceives of death as being neutralized at the end; it is not utterly destroyed but brought into a grand restitution of all things. *Naming the Powers*, 50–53.

[8]   Angels rank below Christ (though some have not yet been brought into full submission) and above humans. Yet Paul says little about their activity. In 4:9 they simply watch (from heaven?) as apostles struggle. At least some angels, presumably those disobedient to God and Christ in the present world order, will be judged by believers at the end of time (6:3). Paul implies in 13:1 that angels speak in heavenly dialects, probably in praise of God. See Gordon D. Fee, *The First Epistle to the Corinthians* (Grand Rapids: Wm. B. Eerdmans, 1987), 630f. The angels, because of whom women need to "veil" their heads (11:10), are treated in note 16 below. Except for Gal. 1:8, where Paul hypothesizes an angel from heaven preaching a false gospel, and Gal. 4:14, where he says his readers once received him as though he were an angel of God, the apostle never treats ἄγγελοι as messengers or ministering spirits, working among humans on behalf of God or Christ. On

II. God, Christ, and Human Beings

God's purpose is to become πάντα ἐν πᾶσιν, and believers are on their way to this consummate relationship (8:6b). Presently they participate in the divine hierarchy by entering, through faith and baptism, into Christ's body. To live in Christ is to dwell in a sphere of power distinct from the powers of this age.[9] The core of faith in Christ is to name Jesus as κύριος (the title is used some 48 times in 1 Cor., with υἱός, the next most frequent christological designation, occurring only twice). This means acknowledging that God has given Christ the rule over all cosmic forces and pledging one's loyalty to him as God's only viceroy. The Holy Spirit, who enters believers and resides within them, leads them, repeatedly, to make this confession (12:3).[10]

Yet it is possible to fall away from Christ's lordship (7:29–35; 9:23–10:12) or to live in Christ as a mere infant (3:1–3) because of one's submission, intentional or otherwise, to the influence of the hostile powers. Paul stresses this point in 1 Corinthians because he believes that a number of his readers consider themselves beyond the reach of the powers (4:8ff.). Thus the picture of Christ's activity with believers which emerges in this epistle is double-edged. On the one hand, Christ bestows benefits. He animates believers as a life-giving spirit (15:45) and sustains them until the day of his coming (1:8). He is experienced as the very power and wisdom of God for salvation (1:24) who grants his Spirit-filled mind (νοῦς) to the baptized (2:16). Through him they receive God's righteousness, sanctification, and redemption (1:30f.). By virtue of their membership in Christ's body, believers are joined with him and one another in a unique relationship of mutual caring called *koinonia* (1:9), which manifests itself most visibly in the Lord's Supper (10:16ff.).

On the other hand, it is precisely within this special *koinonia* that Christ reveals himself as absolute claimant upon the lives of believers, even to the point of jealousy:

---

the whole, Paul's references to angels carry a negative cast. See, in addition to the passages above, Rom.8:38; 2 Cor. 11:14; 12:7; Gal. 3:19; and the sub-apostolic references in Col. 2:18; 2 Thess. 1:7.

[9] See above all Ernst Käsemann, "The Pauline Doctrine of the Lord's Supper," in his *Essays on New Testament Themes*, SBT 41 (London: SCM Press, 1964), 108–135.

[10] It is beyond the scope of this essay to explore the important question of the relationship between Christ and the Holy Spirit in 1 Cor., but the following observations ought to be noted: (1) the Holy Spirit does not have a Father-Son relationship to God and is never named as Lord; (2) the Spirit supports Christ's lordship (6:11; 12:3, 13); (3) unlike Christ, the Spirit does not have a special vocation for subduing the hostile powers; and (4) explicitly hierarchical passages in 1 Cor. like 3:23; 8:6; and 15:24–28 mention only God and Christ, never the Holy Spirit.

The body is not meant for immorality, but for the Lord, and the Lord for the body (6:13). We must not put the Lord to the test as some of [the Israelites] did and were destroyed by serpents (10:9). You cannot partake of the table of the Lord and the table of demons. Shall we provoke the Lord to jealousy? Are we stronger than he? (10:21).

If anyone eats and drinks the Lord's Supper in an unworthy manner (which means, in context, despising or dishonoring one's neighbors through cliquishness), that person is met by Christ not as gracious host but as judge. To be sure, the Lord's judgment takes the form of παιδεία, designed to correct and ultimately to save. But it can actually result in weakness, illness, or even death (11:27–32; note also the comparable case of a judgment pronounced in the Lord's name against the church member who persists in living with his father's wife, 5:4f.).

As depicted in 1 Corinthians, the Lord Jesus Christ is committed to battle with hostile powers over the fate of the world and takes harsh measures to insure that those who live in him will not fall prey to the enemy. Indeed, he becomes almost ferocious in encounters with believers who are less than devoted to him and his ways. One thinks appropriately of Francis Thompson's Hound of Heaven and C. S. Lewis's Aslan in the *The Chronicles of Narnia*. It is no light thing to fall into the hands of the crucified and risen Lord. Conventional thinking about freedom and slavery gets reversed, as when Paul argues that "he who was called in the Lord as a slave is a freedman of the Lord. Likewise he who was free when called is a slave of Christ" (7:22). The same holds true for normal conceptions of wisdom and folly, strength and weakness. By belonging exclusively to Christ and submitting one's decisions to his will (4:19; 7:32–35; 16:7), one shares in his victorious rule. Even as Paul reprimands the Corinthians for excessive loyalty to their favorite leaders, he launches into a declaration of cosmic assurance:

So let no one boast of men. For all things are yours, whether Paul or Apollos or Cephas or the world or life or death or the present or the future, all are yours; and you are Christ's and Christ is God's. (3:21–23)

This is how God's hierarchy works: those who are owned by Christ and therefore on their way to God come into possession of individuals and forces which may seem to rule them.

III. The Apostle and the Congregation

But how seriously can we take statements about the Corinthians' ownership of Paul in the light of his frequent claims to apostolic power within the congregation? Does he not believe himself to be "over" the Corinthians in some fundamental way? There is material in 1 Corinthians to suggest that the apostle considers himself an extension of the divine hierarchy, much like the ecclesiastical hierarchs described by Pseudo-Dionysius.

For example, Paul addresses his readers as one "called by the will of God to be an apostle" (1:1) and notes that God has appointed apostles "first" in the church (12:28). Unlike his readers, Paul has seen the risen Lord (9:1; 15:8) and received from him a personal commissioning (1:17). Paul is the founder and father in Christ of the Corinthian church (2:1ff.; 4:15) who enjoins his readers, like children, to imitate his "ways in Christ" (4:17; see also 11:1). He threatens certain members of the congregation with the use of a "rod," a disciplinary power based on nothing less than God's kingdom (4:19–21). Indeed, writing from Ephesus, he pronounces judgment upon a member of the Corinthian congregation in the name of Jesus and expects to be present in spirit "with the power of the Lord Jesus" as the sentence is carried out (5:3–5).

To twentieth-century readers, schooled in contemporary theories of democracy and teamwork, Paul's language sounds altogether authoritarian. Is it the case then that the apostle believed himself to be a necessary intermediary in God's plan of salvation, ontologically superior to those he was sent to evangelize?

One suspects at the outset that such a picture is too simple and that ontology is not the best category for understanding the various inequalities which surface in relationships between apostle and congregation. For one thing, Paul does not think of his apostolic power as descending to him through ranks of angels (or through an ordination process). He receives his commission directly from Christ, the same Christ who is intimately known by the Corinthians. They can tell from their own new life in Christ whether Paul is really his apostle (9:1–2). Paul states emphatically that his readers must not think of him or other leaders of the church as mystagogues through whose personal touch and esoteric guidance at baptism they are initiated into Christ (1:12–17). The Spirit who dwells within them does not come directly from the hands of Paul (contrast Pseudo-Dionysus' description of the bishop's role in baptism in *EH* 393A–397A).

Moreover, Paul does not consider his apostolic call to be irrevocable; it is always possible for him to relax his self-discipline and suffer disqualification from the eschatological race (9:26–27). If the apostle thinks of himself as an imitator of Christ more skilled than some of his readers, he does not imply by this that he is essentially more Christ-like or God-like than they are. Rather, his claim is that he models for them the humble behavior of Christ in "not seeking my own advantage but that of the many, that they might be saved" (10:32–11:1; see also 4:8–17). As for Paul's bold use of judgment language, this would carry weight with the Corinthians only to the degree that they held Paul's other interpretations of Christ's power in their lives to be trustworthy.[11] He can rely on no ecclesiastical structure to back up his authority.

In what, finally, does Paul's primacy consist, and is it accurately described as hierarchical? Obviously his call and commissioning by Christ are foundational to his apostleship, but only as long as he remains faithful to them (4:2). This he does above all by steadfastly preaching the gospel (1:17; 9:16), and especially its core message, Christ crucified (2:2). Believers are not "being saved" by submission to other humans but by adhering to the gospel:

For the word of the cross is folly to those who are perishing, but to us who are being saved (τοῖς δὲ σωζομένοις ἡμῖν) it is the power of God (1:18; see also 1:21). . . . Now I would remind you, brethren, in what terms I preached to you the gospel, which you received, in which you stand, by which you are being saved (δι' οὗ καὶ σώζεσθε) if you hold it fast (15:1f.; my translation).

Taken together, these passages show that the gospel is something more than and "over" the apostle. Like his readers, he has had to receive the content of the gospel in ordinary words from other human agents (15:3).[12] Paul chooses his words carefully when he writes: "I became your father in Christ Jesus *through the gospel*" (4:14; emphasis mine). Only as he speaks and acts in accordance with this power of God can he continue to exercise parental authority.

By highlighting the gospel as a middle term between himself and Christ and between himself and the congregation, the apostle puts a significant check on his own authority.[13] He may wish to sound commanding as he writes to the Corinthians, but his very assertions invite a testing by his readers on the basis of their life in Christ and knowledge of the

---

[11] This point is well made by John H. Schütz, who shows that that the apostle wishes to help his readers perceive and experience the same charismatic power he enjoys and that in this effort he "must appeal—not to office, but to the familiar experience he shares with all Christians . . . which demands obedience from them like his own." See *Paul and the Anatomy of Apostolic Authority*, SNTSMS 26 (Cambridge: Cambridge Univ. Press, 1975), 278.

[12] Paul claims for himself no constant, unmediated access to the risen Christ. Although mysteries and words of the Lord are revealed to him (1 Cor. 15:51; Rom. 11:25; 1 Thess. 4:15), these also come to other believers (13:2; 14:2, 26). The apostle's role as steward of God's mysteries (4:1) has to do with his interpretive task (as in 2:12f.).

[13] In a way, the gospel takes the place of angels in Paul's conception of hierarchy. It is the supreme quasi-personal (9:23) message-intermediary between Christ, apostle, and congregation. Through it Christ and the Holy Spirit convey the goods of salvation to humanity (1:17f.; 2:1–5; 4:15; 15:1f.).

gospel.[14] Indeed, the bulk of his teaching in 1 Corinthians is characterized not by commands at all but by reasoned arguments and attempts to persuade that emerge from a body of experience common to him and his readers.[15]

We might state Paul's overall goal in 1 Corinthians as follows: he wishes to make known to his readers the gospel (in which they already stand!) so as to promote their "undivided devotion to the Lord" at the end of the ages (15:1f.; 7:35). That is, he wants to secure the Corinthians' continuing participation in the divine hierarchy so that they will not fall victim to the powers of this age. But authoritative as he is, Paul cannot present himself as a direct extension of the divine hierarchy. If we apply the term hierarchy to his apostleship at all, we must understand it as a hierarchy "once-removed," a hierarchy constituted and limited by the gospel. In principle, those who rank "below" Paul in calling and gifts can judge him according to the saving message he preaches. By belonging to Christ through the gospel, they do exercise a certain ownership of their apostle (3:22).

IV. Groups within the Congregation

The inequalities among believers alluded to in 1 Corinthians are numerous and seem to fall into two broad categories: (A) those which concern church members as they relate to the world in general; and (B) those which apply mostly or exclusively to relationships with other believers. In the first category are distinctions of wealth, social-political status, and learning. According to Paul, only a few of the Corinthians inhabit the upper echelons of these groups, as measured by "worldly standards" (1:26ff.). The congregation included heads of households and their dependents (1:11; 16:15), married and single people, Jews and Gentiles, slaves, former slaves (all in chapter 7), and presumably some who were free-born like Paul. Some owned houses, and some were quite poor (11:22).

To category B belong differences between mature believers and "babes in Christ" (2:6–3:4; 14:20ff.), those who are approved by God (δόκιμοι) and those being sifted in divine judgment (5:1–5; 11:19–32), those who are strong and weak of conscience (8:7–13), those who practice

---

[14]   This implicit invitation to test the apostle's authority on the basis of experience and the gospel becomes quite explicit (to the point of sarcasm!) in 2 Cor. 10–13.

[15]   See the various appeals to reason and tradition employed in chapters 7, 12–15, plus Paul's favorite word of exhortation παρακαλέω (1:10; 4:13, 16; 14:31; 16:12, 15), which ranges in meaning from "encourage" to "implore" but is always less than "command." See also note 11 above.

the higher *charismata*, especially prophecy, and those lacking such gifts (12:24–31; 14:1ff.). Apparently Paul thinks that men rank above women in the order of creation but that "in the Lord" this inequality is being offset by a new mutuality between the sexes (11:3–12).[16] At the head of the congregation stand apostles, prophets, and teachers, in that order (12:28). Finally, the household of Stephanas is singled out by Paul as a sub-group of believers to whom all members of the congregation should subject themselves (ὑποτάσσησθε, 16:15f.).

Given the limitations of space, we cannot examine these inequalities in depth. But we can identify the central dynamics at work in them and attempt to determine the ways in which they ought or ought not be understood as hierarchies. Paul offers the key to these issues when he reminds his readers that God's call to them as (mostly) lowly people has as its purpose to shame (καταισχύνη) the strong and wise of the world and bring to nothing the things that are (τὰ ὄντα καταργήσῃ) so that humans will no longer boast in themselves but only in the Lord (1:26–30). I take the aorist καταργήσῃ as gnomic,[17] which means that in Paul's view it is God's *characteristic act* at the end of the ages to relativize the power structures of this world by building up the body of Christ. Furthermore, Paul makes it clear at other points in 1 Corinthians that this divine nullifying of worldly pretensions also governs life inside the church, as believers relate to one another. God calls the slave as a freedman of the Lord (whether or not this person actually becomes free under the civil

---

[16] I agree with Elisabeth Schüssler Fiorenza that in 11:3–7 Paul argues from an assumed "descending hierarchy [I would place this word in quotation marks], God-Christ-Man-Woman, in which each preceding member, as 'head' or 'source', stands above the other in the sense that he established the other's being." Yet at the same time, as Schüssler Fiorenza also notes, the apostle does not deny to women the status of being in God's image; and in fact he affirms an equality between the sexes that allows for the right of women to prophesy. See *In Memory of Her: A Feminist Theological Reconstruction of Christian Origins* (New York: Crossroad, 1983), 229. But why "a veil [literally 'authority,' *exousia*] . . . because of the angels" (11:10)? Fee exposes the improbability of theories about an angelic lust for the Corinthian women. See his *Corinthians*, 521. Perhaps Schüssler Fiorenza is right that Paul and his readers thought of angels as mediating words of prophecy. See *In Memory of Her*, 228. But this view does not explain the note of caution inherent in Paul's words. The best position, I think, is that of Robin Scroggs, who argues that Paul is most interested in keeping clear the physical distinctions between the sexes which have pertained since creation. See his *Paul for a New Day* (Philadelphia: Fortress Press, 1977), 47. The angels act as guardians over these orders of creation (as at Qumran and in apocalyptic literature generally) and must be respected. But all of this means that Paul senses a tension between life in Christ and the orders of creation at the end of the ages. It is that which best accounts for his lack of clarity in 11:2–16. As for 14:33b–36 ("the women should keep silence in the churches"), I am convinced by Fee's careful discussion (*Corinthians*, 699–708) that we should regard this passage as an interpolation.

[17] That is, it carries a "timeless and almost futuristic" quality. See Nigel Turner, *Syntax*, vol. 3 of *Grammar of New Testament Greek* by J.H. Moulton, 4 vols. (Edinburgh: T. and T. Clark, 1908–76), 73. The nullifying of "the things that are" is thought by Paul to be constantly happening (2:6) until its conclusion at Christ's parousia (15:24–28).

law); but it is equally true that the freedman is called to be a slave of Christ (7:22). God works to bring the worldly and spiritual powers of individuals into a complementarity with those of their sisters and brothers in Christ so that none will be shamed, all will be honored, and the body of Christ will conform, more and more, to the Lord's mission of subduing the hostile powers.

Thus the Holy Spirit constantly inspires (ἐνεργεῖ) and distributes (διαιροῦν) spiritual gifts according to the divine will (12:11; see v. 6). And the principle guiding this distribution is not hard to articulate: "God has so composed the body, giving the greater honor to the inferior [or lacking; ὑστερουμένῳ] part, that there may be no discord in the body, but that the members may have the same care for one another" (12:24f.). No member may judge his or her neighbor to be dispensable (12:21). But neither may those who feel short-changed shrink from full participation in the body (12:14–18), for God will raise them up for ministry and recognition in his own way.

Because Paul takes this dynamic of equalization quite seriously, he denounces the selfish practices of the socially and financially privileged Corinthians at the Lord's Supper: "What, do you not have houses to eat and drink in? Or do you despise the church of God and humiliate those who have nothing?" (11:22).[18] While Paul does make allowances for changes in worldly status, he considers these to be of relatively small value given the short time remaining before the parousia (see chapter 7). His chief concern is to show the Corinthians that whatever their status, it has been sanctified by God's call (7:17–24) and offers great opportunities for spiritual abundance if they submit to the will of God in Christ. Some Corinthians may gain freedom from slavery and/or achieve material wealth; but the highest goal for everyone is to abound in the work of the Lord (15:58).

This gospel work carries with it an inherent tendency toward subordination to one's neighbor. Those who are privileged, either by the standards of the world (as males, free, wealthy, socially prominent, etc.) or by the call of God (as apostles, prophets, teachers, mature, strong of conscience, etc.), must spend their privilege in service so that honor will come to all. Paul holds up the household of Stephanas as an example of people who do it right, for "they have devoted themselves to the service of the saints" (εἰς διακονίαν τοῖς ἁγίοις ἔταξαν ἑαυτούς, 16:15). Only by ordering themselves (τάσσειν) to ministry do they earn submission (ὑποτάσσεσθαι) from the congregation (16:16). And clearly this is a submission which pertains only to their leadership as team workers and

---

18   For a fuller discussion of this situation see John Koenig, *New Testament Hospitality: Partnership with Strangers as Promise and Mission* (Philadelphia: Fortress Press, 1985), 65–71.

laborers (συνεργοῦντι καὶ κοπιῶντι). [19] If the privileged do not subordinate themselves to their brother and sister believers in this way, they can expect to be humbled and judged by the Lord (11:27ff.).

On the other hand, those who are lower in status, whether worldly or spiritual, can expect to be honored and empowered for ministry by God from within their lowliness, with eventual recognition by the church as a whole. The apostle considers himself to be part of this divinely willed process toward equity. In the eyes of the world and many of the Corinthians he and his colleagues are "fools for Christ's sake . . . weak . . . in disrepute . . . ill-clad . . . buffeted . . . homeless." Yet from these inferior circumstances they "bless . . . endure . . . conciliate" (4:10–13). And such people, Paul adds later, rank first in the church (12:28).

It should be evident then that all inequalities among believers are thought by Paul to be constantly changing in accord with God's plan of salvation, embodied in the Lord and proclaimed in the gospel. There is nothing approaching an ontological distinction between clergy and laypeople. Those who occupy the office-like positions of prophet and teacher in Corinth owe their status to a combination of *charismata* granted and loving service rendered (see especially chapters 13–14). But this is also true of priorities held by believers in general, e.g., the household of Stephanas. The only significant feature of a person's ranking is his or her practical recognition by the congregation (14:27; 16:10f., 18); and this must emerge as the result of persuasion (note the παρακαλῶ of 16:15) rather than coercion. Indeed, it is by no means clear what institutional form (if any) the subjection and recognition Paul calls for in his praise of Stephanas' people should take (16:16–18). He is certainly not asking for unqualified obedience.

The major force at work in all inequalities among believers is a divine intention to transform privilege into ministry and vice versa. This fits with Christ's own sacrifice of privilege in the crucifixion and with the apostle's distinctive proclamation of the gospel: no boasting, for God's saving power comes through weakness. If we want to use the word "hierarchy" to describe relationships among believers, we shall have to link it with modifiers. Given Paul's presuppositions, we may say that one should expect to find in the body of Christ nothing but evangelical hierarchies, [20] shifting hierarchies of cross and resurrection.

---

[19] Cf. G. Fee, *Corinthians*, 828–831. Fee calls attention to the word play on τάσσειν in vv. 15–16, paraphrasing the passage as follows: "They 'appointed themselves' . . . as your servants; you in your turn 'submit yourselves' . . . to them" (p. 830, n. 27).

[20] This term was suggested to me in conversation by Professor Sandra M. Schneiders.

V. Conclusion

In Pseudo-Dionysian terms, there is only one full-fledged hierarchy expounded by Paul in 1 Corinthians, namely, the relationship between God and Christ (with the Holy Spirit) which effects the world's salvation. At the heart of this salvation lie Christ's subjection to God and the ongoing subjection of the worldly powers to Christ. Within such a process, it is not surprising to find differences in status among members of Christ's body. Each individual's calling into Christ results in a unique combination of giftedness and devotion to the Lord, which in turn produces a kind of ranking for that person within the church. Apostles, for example, are those personally commissioned by Christ to preach the gospel. This is their peculiar mission and privilege, but it is also the standard by which their faithfulness is evaluated and their authority checked. The gospel, not the apostle, is the power of God by which humans are brought into Christ's dominion and through which they are "being saved" (1:18; 15:1f.). The gospel also interprets inequalities among believers so that these are always seen to be shifting in value and tending toward a complementarity within Christ's body where each member receives due honor. Egalitarianism itself is not the goal. Instead, one aims toward mutual subordination and equal caring for one another (12:24f.), as Christ and the apostle model them. Privilege in Christ becomes ministry, and ministry privilege. To persevere in this constant reformation is to retain a place in the one true hierarchy. And, though Paul does not spell it out clearly in 1 Corinthians, his thought surely implies that one's faithful use of inequality (which might be called an evangelical hierarchy) contributes to the progress of Christ's cosmic effort in subduing the hostile powers. This appears to be a fundamental part of what the apostle means by "abounding in the work of the Lord" (15:58; see also 16:10, 16).

First Corinthians 8–10:
Continuity or Contradiction?

Lamar Cope*

One of the characteristics of the scholar to whom this volume is dedicated is a healthy curiosity about the context and setting of the early Christian writings. Particularly in the area of New Testament Christology, he has helped us see how early Christian thought developed in the context of the ideas of Hellenistic culture. Sometimes attention to that important aspect of our study can cause surprises. One day, more than a year ago, at work on both a New Testament Introduction course and a course for lay adults, it occurred to me that what I had been saying about Paul's ethical strategy in 1 Corinthians 8 and 10 was deeply undercut by 1 Corinthians 10:1–22.

So I wrote to William O. Walker at Trinity University and asked him whether he had considered the possibility of interpolation in this section of the letter. His response was, "I have, in the past, assumed that the reference in 8:1–13; 10:23–11:1 is simply to *eating meat that has been offered to idols and then sold in the marketplace,* while that in 10:14–22 is to *participating in pagan festivals* (perhaps in the temples); Paul allows the former but forbids the latter. Noting, however, the words 'at table in an idol's temple' in 8:10, I am no longer so certain that the distinction I have made really holds. Perhaps there really is a conflict between the two passages."[1] And with that, he encouraged me to proceed.

Troubled by the logical inconsistency and by the odd shift in thought world in 1 Corinthians 10, I decided to investigate. Soon it became clear that the problems of chapters eight to ten are *the central ones* for the questions of the unity of the entire letter, *pivotal ones* for the question of the nature of Paul's audience, and that critical literature abounded, including Wendell Willis' new book on the topic.[2] Yet a preliminary investigation showed that the issue of the content of 10:1–22 and its authenticity to Paul had really not been carefully examined. So it seemed worthwhile to proceed.

The thesis of this essay is simple. Scholars have long noted that Paul's

---

* Lamar Cope is Professor of Religion, Carroll College, Waukesha, Wisconsin.
[1] Wm. O. Walker, Jr., unpublished private letter, March 12, 1988.
[2] Wendell L. Willis, *Idol Meat in Corinth,* SBLDS 68 (Chico, CA: Scholars Press, 1985).

advice about "idol meat" in 1 Corinthians 8 and 10 is problematic. In (A) 1:1–11 and (C) 10:23–11:1 he appears to hold that the idol meat is in itself neutral and one's only compunction about eating it is a concern for the other person. But in (B) 10:1–22, after an elaborate midrash on the Exodus generation, the eating of meat in an idol's temple is forbidden outright. Many solve the problem by saying that this material comes from two letters by Paul that were later combined in the editing/collecting process. In such a solution, Paul gives two different answers on two different occasions.[3] Others, however, argue that the text must be understood as it stands.[4] For the most part, however, none have challenged Pauline authorship of both parts. Yet the arguments for the unity of the section *always* read one of the two portions as the key for understanding the whole and *distort* the fairly clear sense of the other passage. But the arguments for partition generally leave the occasion of the second portion, 10:1–22, hanging in thin air. It is important to consider the further possibility that 1 Corinthians 8–10 cannot be made a united argument of Paul's, that it makes no better sense as two separate pieces of Pauline letters, and that the likelihood is strong that 10:1–22 is an interpolation by a later editor intended to bring Paul into line with the widely held views of subsequent Christianity.

To probe such a thesis in the space of this essay requires some setting of limits. One cannot focus on the issue of the nature of the Corinthian opponents, but can mention it only where it is absolutely necessary. Nor can one give more than passing mention to the problems associated with chapter 9 and with 11:2–16. And one must minimize treatment of the debate over which portions of chapter 8 are echoes of the Corinthians' own slogans. Any one of those topics is fuel for another essay, as the recent literature readily shows. This essay will focus upon the logical and literary problems created by Paul's comments about eating meat offered to idols.

The section in 1 Corinthians 8–11 is the first one in the letter which prompts the reader to puzzle over order and sequence.[5] Chapter 8 discusses the question about the eating of meat offered to idols that has presumably been posed by the Corinthians' letter referred to in 7:1. The

---

[3] John C. Hurd, *The Origin of I Corinthians*, 2d ed. (Macon, GA: Mercer Univ. Press, 1983). He deals with the partition theories in pages 42–47. To his list may be added, Jean Hering, *The First Epistle of Saint Paul to the Corinthians* (London: Epworth Press, 1962), xiii to xv; and Robert Jewett, "The Redaction of I Corinthians and the Trajectory of the Pauline School," *JAAR* 44/4, Supplement (December, 1978) B: 389–444, who adopts a revised Schmithals partition thesis.

[4] W. Willis, *Idol Meat;* J. Hurd, *I. Corinthians;* and Hans Conzelmann, *1 Corinthians,* Hermeneia (Philadelphia: Fortress Press, 1975), 2–4, can be cited as recent supporters of the unity of the letter.

[5] Problems do arise earlier for critics, notably between chs. 4 and 5, and in ch. 6. See R. Jewett, "The Redaction," 389 and 396ff.

basic stance here is that such meat is in itself neutral. So far so good. But chapter 9 presents an abrupt shift to the topic of the validity of Paul's apostleship and a defense of his refusal to accept aid from the Corinthians. If it is connected to 8 at all, it is by the theme of weakness found in both chapters. Then 10 resumes the discussion of Christian practice with regard to eating meat offered to idols. But here, as opposed to 8, the advice is a thorough-going prohibition of *eating meat offered to idols in an idol's temple because it involves fellowship with demons.* When that section ends, however, a new one resumes in 10:23 which goes back to the neutral stance of 8. Then 11:2–16 digresses about the role of women in worship, only to have the subject of eating resumed in 11:17 as Paul presents advice about the eucharist. No other section of 1 Corinthians is so disjointed as this. Whence the chaos?

Ever since Weiss, one answer to that question is that 1 Corinthians is an edited and compiled document. A number of theories of partition have surfaced and are helpfully enumerated by J.C. Hurd.[6] Such critics include Weiss, Loisy, Schmithals, Dinkler, Hering, and Jewett. Because almost all involve complicated theses dealing with numerous portions of 1 Corinthians and sometimes also 2 Corinthians, we may focus on the divisions of 8 and 10 for our problem. Virtually all such critics recognize that chapter 8 and 10:23–11:1 are of one piece. They also place 10:1–22 in another letter, usually earlier. The reasons are apparent even to the casual reader. Not only does 8 say that food itself is morally neutral, but it challenges eating in an idol's temple *only* on the grounds that it might harm a "weak brother" (8:10). And further, both 8 and 10:23–11:1 give no hint of any feeling that idols are dangerous "demons."

But 10:1–22 makes an elaborate midrashic case against participation in idolatry and on that basis condemns eating in an idol's temple. Proponents of division say that if Paul felt this way about the matter, he surely would have said so in 8. So they argue that the two sections come from different letters in which Paul was responding to different problems.

Of all the arguments for partition of 1 Corinthians, this is the most powerful (excluding what is widely recognized now as an interpolation in 14:33b-36). Consequently, proponents of the unity of the letter are most hard pressed to defend their position here. J. C. Hurd, and most recently Wendell Willis,[7] argue for unity. Hurd makes an intriguing case by pointing out that:

Concerning all these differences it should be noted first of all that the scholars who subdivide I Cor. consider the discrepancies between "AC" and "B" great enough

---

[6]   See footnote #3.

[7]   In addition to J. Hurd, *I Corinthians*, 43–47, see Wendell L. Willis, "An Apostolic Apologia? The Form and Function of I Corinthians 9," *JSNT* 24 (1985): 33–48.

to show that "B" was not written at the same time as "AC" but small enough to allow "B" to have been written by the same author, to the same group, and on the same topic as "AC". These scholars allow Paul to be inconsistent with himself concerning the Corinthians' use of idol meat from one letter to the next, but they do not allow the inconsistency in a single letter. This distinction is, therefore, possible but somewhat subtle.[8]

Hurd is basically correct. Almost all partition theories put this section with 2 Corinthians 6:14–7:1; 1 Corinthians 6:12–20; 11:2–34; and 9:24–27 in the earlier letter to the Corinthians. But what changed Paul so radically in the brief interim is not spelled out.

On the other hand, Hurd, Willis, et al. encounter the very same difficulty in showing that the present 8 and 10 sequence makes sense. Willis maintains that Paul is rhetorically dealing with the "strong" Corinthians' position in 8 and 10:23–11:1 but that his real position is expressed in 10:1–22.[9] He argues, however, that the coherence of the unit is demonstrated by the close parallel to 8 and 10 found in Romans 14–15.[10] Closer examination explodes this approach. The Romans passage does take up the argument of 1 Corinthians 8 and 10, just as Romans 12 and 13 take up the argument of 1 Corinthians 12–14. But there is no hint of any parallel to 1 Corinthians 10:1–22 in Romans. If 10:1–22 were Paul's primary position, its omission in Romans, on the same subject, is amazing.

The discussion has been deeply biased by a striking presupposition. Almost all writers have assumed that the material in 1 Corinthians should be taken at face value as from Paul, even though we have no data to support such a view. As Keck has reminded us, we do not have the autographs of these letters.[11] We have the letters at the end of a long editing and redacting process in the early church. Further, the growing consensus that in at least two cases there are non-Pauline insertions in the Corinthian correspondence (1 Cor. 14:33b-35 and 2 Cor. 6:14–7:1)[12] focuses the methodological issue which I wish to explore.

By and large we have treated the letters of Paul in terms of units. Intense effort has been made to establish whether they are Pauline or un-Pauline. Once the pedigree of the letters has been established, however, they have been treated as wholes. Even when the letter is

---

[8]   J. Hurd, *I Corinthians*, 132.

[9]   W. Willis, *Idol Meat*, 87, maintains that in 8 and 10 Paul is seeking to establish the reality of the pagan gods and especially their possible influence on Christians (esp. 10:19ff.), however he may regard them.

[10]   W. Willis, "Apostolic Apologia," 39, and *Idol Meat*, 271–274.

[11]   Leander E. Keck, *Paul and His Letters*, Proclamation Commentaries (Philadelphia: Fortress Press, 1979), 15.

[12]   William O. Walker, "The Burden of Proof in Identifying Interpolations in the Pauline Letters," *NTS* 33 (1987): 610–618, mentioned on p. 615.

partitioned this remains true, with the notable exception of Günther Bornkamm's treatment of 2 Corinthians 6:14–7:1. But we should be more careful. Not just the letters as whole units but no *section* of the letters may be assumed to be Pauline *a priori*. 1 Corinthians 10 is a classic case where the issue of a non-Pauline interpolation needs to be raised. Very few people, certainly not this writer, would challenge the Pauline authorship of the bulk of the material in this letter. (Though recent study *has challenged* the authenticity of both 1 Cor. 11:3–16 and 14:33b–35, and in my judgment has done so successfully.)

That raises the issue of methodological presuppositions. What constitutes evidence for interpolation? Or, as my colleagues at Carroll ask me, "If Paul didn't write it, how could you prove it?" Most of us have always taken this stance. But is it valid? In his recent article on this issue, Wm. O. Walker proposed that, "In the treatment of any particular passage in the Pauline letters, the burden of proof rests with the argument that the passage is an interpolation; in dealing with the letters as a corpus, however, or, indeed, in dealing with any particular letter in the corpus, the burden of proof rests with any argument that the corpus or, indeed, any particular letter within the corpus (with the possible exception of Philemon) contains no interpolations."[13]

That is a very cautious way of stating the issue. I believe it should be stated more strongly and in neutral fashion, as follows. "Given the collected and redacted character of the material we call the Pauline corpus, *every passage* needs to be subjected to scrutiny with regard to its origin, not just the letters as a whole. Moreover, the very same arguments which justify assigning a letter as a whole to Paul need to be marshaled in support of each passage, and vice versa." Furthermore, that principle works with respect to the pseudo-Pauline material as well. For example, Colossians 1–3 may be judged non-Pauline for good reason, but that does not allow us to render a judgment about the entire letter. Any part of the letters attributed to Paul may be a genuine fragment, and any part of the letters may be non-Pauline. Common sense tells us that is true, but its consequences are intimidating.

What evidence may be marshaled to judge a passage authentic or inauthentic? Clearly the case is different in the letters than in the Jesus tradition and different criteria are in order. At least the following considerations are in order. (1) Evidence from the manuscripts may suggest interpolation when there is confusion about placement of a passage, etc. But, since the earliest extant manuscripts are a century and a half after the writing of the letters, this will not very often be of help.[14]

---

13   Wm. Walker, Jr., "The Burden of Proof," 611.

14   Wm. Walker, "Interpolations," 615, says, "In short, it appears likely that the emerging Catholic leadership in the churches 'standardized' the text of the Pauline corpus

(2) Evidence of characteristic Pauline style and vocabulary, however difficult and subjective such judgments may be. (3) Coherence of thought with passages judged otherwise to be authentic. These are, after all, the standard tools for determining Pauline authorship in any respect.

In the case of 1 Corinthians 8 and 10, there is little or no manuscript help, so the question comes down to vocabulary, style, and content. To begin with the units (A) 1 Cor. 8 and (C) 1 Cor. 10:23–11:1, the evidence that this is Pauline material seems to be overwhelming. First, there are numerous connectors back and forward between these sections and the rest of the letter. To give an example, the "all things are lawful" quotation of 10:23 is an exact replica of 6:12. Or, again, the contrast of "knowledge" with "love" in 8:1 is echoed in chapter 13. Even more strikingly, the fundamental argument of these sections is echoed in abbreviated form in Romans 14–15 both in the advice about eating, and in specific references to "the weak" and "the strong." As a unit of thought, A and C, 1 Corinthians 12–14, and Romans 14–15 show as great a thematic and vocabulary coherence as could possibly be expected in genuine letters. There can be no doubt that this material is Pauline.

As soon as the question is raised, however, concerning 10:1–22, one notices a vast difference. The vocabulary has shifted radically, the style of argument has become midrashic, and the advice is in sharp contrast to units A and C. There are some phenomena of vocabulary and style which are strange here. Paul's other midrashim (Gal. 3:15–18; 4:21–31; 2 Cor. 3:7–10; and Rom. 4:1–15) are limited and precise. Only once, in the seed/seeds reading of Galatians 3:15, is the reader stretched beyond the range of simple application of the biblical text. But this interpretation is elaborate and strained. The reference to the people of Israel being "baptized" into Moses is, in fact, wrong (they were on *dry ground*), and one wonders if it is something the Pharisaic Paul would say.[15] Even if the Corinthians could grasp the meaning of *pneumatikos food* as the manna and *pneumatikos drink* as the water from the Rock, how could they be expected to be aware of the rather esoteric tradition of the Rock following the Exodus community?[16] And how could they make the equation that *the Rock* was Christ (since it provides only half of the *pneumatikos* meal)? This could be from Paul, but if so he has wandered far more technically into the arena of midrashic exegesis than at any other point in the letters.

Some other features of the section should be noted. The use of

---

in the light of orthodox views and practices, suppressing and even destroying all deviant texts and manuscripts. Thus it is that we have no manuscripts dating from earlier than the third century; thus it is that all of the extant manuscripts are remarkably similar in most of their significant features; and thus it is that the manuscript evidence can tell us nothing about the state of the Pauline literature prior to the third century."

[15] W. Willis, *Idol Meat*, 129, deals with the fallacy of the phrase "baptized into Moses."
[16] J. Hering, *I Corinthians*, 86–87.

koinonia in vss. 16ff. has long been seen as out of harmony with Paul's use of the term elsewhere (1 Cor. 1:9; 2 Cor. 8:4; Gal. 2:9; Phil. 1:5; 2:1; and 3:10). Here it has a sacramental tone,[17] there simply one of community fellowship. But the heart of the issue of the authenticity of this passage rests with an evaluation of the equation of idols and *demons*. And, although in order to evaluate the lines, "What do I imply, then? That food offered to idols is anything, or that an idol is anything? No, I imply that what pagans sacrifice they offer to demons and not to God, I do not want you to be partners with demons," we move *beyond* the issue of vocabulary and style to issues of content, literary data remain important. There is no other use of this term in the letters usually granted as Pauline. Indeed, it is only found once, in 1 Timothy 4:1, in the pseudo-Paulines. Paul was evidently not concerned with demons.

There are also a number of other cases of phrasing and word usage which render 10:1–22 suspect. Here are a few. In 10:1 the term "the fathers" is used to mean the wilderness generation, but in its three uses in Romans it is used to mean "the forefathers" or "the patriarchs" (Rom. 9:15; 11:28; 15:8). Thus the use here is uncharacteristic of Paul. In 10:6 the term ἐπιθυμητής occurs only here in Paul although he uses the noun numerous times. In 10:9 the word for "testing" of the Lord occurs only here in the New Testament. In 10:11, the adverb τυπικῶς occurs nowhere else in either the New Testament or the LXX. More strikingly, the phrase "the end of the ages" in 10:11 is found only here in Paul's letters. So, too, the term ἔκβασις (10:13) for "way of escape," occurs nowhere else in Paul's letters and only once in the rest of the New Testament.

Because the topic of 10:1–22 and its midrashic character are somewhat unique, the striking oddities of phrasing and vocabulary alone might not render 10:1–22 suspect as being non-Pauline. But taken together with the problems of content and context, they greatly increase the difficulties for holding the passage to be genuine.[18]

But the crux of the issue is substantive. Richard Horsley has recently shown that there are two distinct Jewish strategies in dealing with the issue of pagan gods. One, stemming from apocalyptic circles, viewed the gods as subordinate deities, hence demons, and urged strict abstinence from any contact with them. The other, stemming from Hellenistic Jewish

---

[17]   W. Willis, *Idol Meat*, 87, maintains that in 8 and 10 Paul is seeking to establish the reality of the pagan gods and especially their possible influence on Christians (esp. 10:19ff.), however he may regard them.

[18]   In just these 22 verses there are at least 10 cases of words found only here in material attributed to Paul, several of them *hapax legomena* in the New Testament. There are two compound phrases found only here also, and there are at least five cases where terms are used with a special meaning occurring only here, although the terms are used by Paul elsewhere with a regular, but different meaning.

Wisdom circles, like Philo and Wisdom of Solomon, argued that since "there is only one God," the idols are nothings and their worship is useless.[19] Whether or not Horsley is further correct, as I believe he is, that the best backdrop for the conversation implied in A/C is such Hellenistic Jewish thought (i.e., that the *strong Corinthians* have taken this ideology and run with it), it must be the backdrop for Paul's own usage here because Hellenistic enlightenment philosophy would never call the gods idols, nor does the eclectic Stoic/Cynic tradition discount the worth of worship of the gods.[20]

It is relatively easy to demonstrate, outside of 1 Corinthians 8 and 10, that Paul held the latter position. Romans 1:19–23 is a classic statement of the position that idols are nothing. Galatians 4:8a carefully says the same thing. 1 Thessalonians 1:9 even belongs with this point of view. Moreover, in these places and several others, where Paul had ample opportunity to condemn idol worship as trucking with demons, he did not do so. Thus it is not enough to say that the position adopted toward idols in A/C is "that of the opponents."[21] It is in fact a point of agreement between Paul and the opponents, that the idols are nothing, which he clearly acknowledges and then goes beyond:

8:4, We know that "an idol has no real existence," and "there is no God but one."

10:25, Eat whatever is sold in the meat market without raising any question on the ground of conscience. For "the earth is the Lord's, and everything in it."

On the other hand, it is very difficult to show that Paul held the position espoused in B. Willis has provided us with a solid survey of Hellenistic practice regarding meat sacrificed to idols. He establishes convincingly that there was little or no difference in the Hellenistic mind in the meaning of meal fellowship in different locations and settings. Temples, private homes, even cemeteries are all sites for sacrificial meals. "The sacrifice was the principal ceremony of all Hellenistic worship, whether domestic, civic or cultic. And the feature most characteristic of sacrifice was the meal which accompanied it."[22]

---

[19]   Richard A. Horsley, "Gnosis in Corinth: I Corinthians 8:1–6," *NTS* 27 (1980): 32–51. He says, on p. 38, "Within Judaism itself there were two distinctive traditions of polemic against idols or false gods. The one line, expressed prominently in Deutero-Isaiah, derided the heathen gods as nothing and their worship as foolishness. . . . The other attitude toward paganism, exemplified in such passages as Deut. 4.19; 29.25; Jer. 16.19 or Mal. 1.11, held that whereas God had chosen Israel for his own people, He had subjected the other peoples to the subordinate cosmic powers—hence heathen polytheism was more or less God ordained."

[20]   Ibid., 36.

[21]   W. Willis, *Idol Meat*, 112ff.

[22]   Ibid., 49.

Thus efforts to argue that B speaks only of sacrificial meals in an idol's temple while A/C speaks of private consumption of meat are only half true. B *is concerned* with eating "in an idol's temple," but A/C is concerned with private dining, with cultic dining, and with being an invited guest. And in A/C *all* are governed by the principle that meat and location are neutral so one may eat *unless* it offends a weaker brother's conscience. Moreover, the only place where Paul ventures near the position of B elsewhere is in Galatians 4:9 where he warns the Galatians of turning back, not to demons, but to "the weak and beggarly elemental spirits (ἀσθενῆ καὶ πτωχὰ στοιχεῖα)." The context implies that their following *Jewish ritual law* would so enslave them. That is hardly the argument of B which very nearly equates Jewish and Christian sacrament.[23] (One might also argue that Romans 8:38–39 signals Paul's belief in "principalities and powers" like "demons" of 10:20, but it would mean reading a great deal into an enigmatic, poetic phrase.)

To sum up this brief review of the data, 1 Corinthians 8 and 10:23–11:1 show every sign of being a coherent part of the main body of this letter. But 10:1–22 is deeply suspect. The passage exhibits non-Pauline terminology and, more strikingly, Pauline terminology used in an uncharacteristic way. It presents an ornate and flawed midrashic support unique in the Pauline corpus. It argues a position on eating in an idol's temple that is not supported anywhere else in the genuine letters. The position is contrary to one expressed earlier in Galatians and later in Romans. The passage interrupts the flow of thought from 8:1–11 to 10:23 whatever one does with chapter 9. For all of these reasons, the critic ought to consider seriously the likelihood that 10:1–22 is a later non-Pauline interpretation.

Such a view demands a further step, however. In this case one does not have to attempt to posit the occasion for a letter so strange as to contain the sectarian, Essene-like 2 Corinthians 6:14–7:1, the "anti-feminist" sections of 1 Corinthians, 1 Corinthians 11:3–16, and our passage. (What a strange letter that is?) But one must still attempt an explanation of the redactor's purpose in inserting the passage, as Robert Jewett has made us aware.[24] In this case that is not difficult. John Brunt has recently noted that the Pauline position (by which he means A/C even though he accepts B) on the treatment of idolatry was largely ignored in the church at the turn of the century. He shows that Acts 15, Revelation 2:12–17, 18–29, and *Didache* 6:3 all prohibit outright the eating of meat

---

23   Ibid., 140.
24   R. Jewett, "Redaction of I Corinthians," esp. pp. 410–411.

offered to idols. Justin, *Dial.* 35, says that Christians would rather die than worship idols or eat meat offered to idols.[25]

Thus, as Christianity took hold in the Empire it found itself in competition and conflict with traditional Hellenistic religion and developed a sharp separatist attitude. It is no major leap to posit, then, that the editor/redactor(s) of the Pauline letters wanted to bring Paul into line with the dominant anti-temple worship position of the church a generation later. How better to diffuse a libertarian or Gnostic use of Paul's advice on meat offered to idols than to insert a section condemning the practice in the middle of that advice. Not only was that the redactor's fairly obvious strategy, but it worked as well here as did the insertions on the role of women and, for the emergent early catholic church at least, Paul became an anchor for the conservative position.

---

[25] John C. Brunt, "Rejected, Ignored, or Misunderstood? The Fate of Paul's Approach to the Problem of Food Offered to Idols in Early Christianity," *NTS* 31 (1985): 113–124.

Mysteries and Sacraments

C. P. Price*

This essay is part of a larger manuscript which has been circulated to a few people, including my colleagues on the Virginia Seminary faculty. It has thus profited from prior criticism, including that of my colleague in service and now in retirement, Reginald Fuller, for whom I have the greatest affection and regard, and to whom in this revised and, I hope, improved form, it is dedicated.

I. The Problem

The essay is written in response to a nagging problem, one often addressed but never, at least in my view, satisfactorily resolved. It is this. How did the words *mystery* (μυστήριον in Greek and *mysterium* in its Latin loan-word form) and *sacrament* (*sacramentum* in Latin) come to be applied to baptism, eucharist, and, subsequently, to other Christian liturgical acts? The force of this question is indicated by two circumstances. The first is that there is no word in the Greek New Testament to cover the genus of which baptism and eucharist are instances. The second is that by mid-fourth century, μυστήριον in Greek and *sacramentum* in Latin had been impressed to do this service, and they functioned in this context without dispute or quibble.

Thus, as far as μυστήριον is concerned, about A.D. 350, Cyril of Jerusalem introduced the last five of his catechetical lectures to the newly baptized—lectures on baptism, chrism, bread and wine, and the liturgy—by saying:

I have long been wishing, O true born and dearly beloved children of the Church, to discourse to you concerning these spiritual and heavenly Mysteries;[1]

and in his Easter Sermon, *For the Lights*, Gregory of Nazianzus proclaimed:

---

* C.P. Price is William Meade Professor of Systematic Theology, Emeritus, Virginia Theological Seminary, Alexandria, Virginia.

[1] Cyril of Jerusalem, *Cat. Lect.* xix.1, *NPNF*(2) 7:144.

Jesus is here again and once again we stand before a mystery; but it is not the mystery of Hellenic intoxication; it is a mystery from above, a divine mystery.[2]

As as far as *sacramentum* is concerned, one recalls that Ambrose's lectures on the sacraments (ca. 390) have been transmitted in two forms. The longer is entitled *De Sacramentis*, and is presumably the form in which the lectures were delivered, or close to it. The shorter, *De Mysteriis*, is thought to comprise notes, either taken down by a hearer or perhaps prepared by the author beforehand.[3] In any case, the two words, mystery and sacrament, are by this time virtually interchangeable; and in this instance, both refer to baptism, chrism, and eucharist. The scope of Ambrose's lectures is virtually the same as the scope of Cyril's. Both are comments on the texts of initiatory rites.

The ground which I plan to cover in this essay traces that development. It has been done before. The number of commentators accounts for no small part of the confusion. The chief studies which underlie this paper are by Hans von Soden,[4] Odo Casel,[5] Günther Bornkamm,[6] Hugo Rahner,[7] and Raymond E. Brown.[8]

All these are instructive, but none decisive. All but Bornkamm and Brown ignore the contribution of the Old Testament even when they do lip service to it. Casel explicitly rejects it.[9] Bornkamm and Brown, on the other hand, are more concerned to establish the meaning of μυστήριον in the New Testament than to account for its application to sacraments. Bornkamm does look forward to later uses of μυστήριον and *sacramentum*, but this section of his article is necessarily compressed. None, I will argue, gives sufficient weight to the centrality of the Christian initiatory rites in the development we have in view. Rahner comes closer than the rest. In any case, I aim to present this material with different nuances.

---

[2] Gregory of Nazianzus, *Oratio I, PG* 36:336A; cited in Hugo Rahner, *Greek Myths and Christian Mystery* (London: Burns and Oates, 1963), 87.

[3] Cf. Ambroise de Milan, *Des Sacraments, Des Mystères*, ed. Dom B. Botte (Paris: Editions du Cerf, 1980), 15–16.

[4] Hans von Soden, "Mysterion und Sacramentum in der ersten zwei Jahrhunderten der Kirche," *ZNW* 12 (1911): 188–227.

[5] Odo Casel, *The Mystery of Christian Worship*, ed. Burkhard Neunheuser, OSB (Westminster, MD: The Newman Press, 1963).

[6] Günther Bornkamm, "μυστήριον," *TDNT* 4:802–827.

[7] See n. 2 above.

[8] Raymond E. Brown, *The Semitic Background of the Term "Mystery" in the New Testament*, FBBS 21 (Philadelphia: Fortress Press, 1968).

[9] "So waren die Passafeier ein Gedächtnis der Befreiung aus Ägypten und zwar ein ganz konkrete Gedächtnis . . . so schöpfte das Volk aus der rituellen Begehung des Ereignis durch das es einst als Gottesvolk geschaffen wurde, die Kraft des Weiterbestehens. Aber diese Handlung war kein Mysterium, weil sie kein Ziel im Jenseits hatte, sondern nur die Nation in ihrem irdischen Bestande berücksightige." Odo Casel, "Das Mysteriengedächtnis des Messeliturgie," *JLW* 6 (1926): 140.

Rahner outlines three stages through which this discussion has passed in this century. First, Reizenstein and his followers attempted to show that Christian sacramental doctrine really *originated* in Hellenistic mystery cults, especially in Iranian and Mandaean redemption myths.[10] Second, Casel, one of the chief figures in the liturgical revival which radiated from Maria Laach in the years between the two World Wars, elaborated a *Mysterientheologie* which denied any theory of direct, genetic derivation, but saw in the cult mysteries a "kind of imperfect and shadowy prefigurement of the reality which was brought by God to its final fulfillment in the mystery of Christ."[11]

Commentators who are at the third stage of this development, Rahner says, draw "a much sharper line of division than the other two groups between the development, on the one hand, of the fundamental Christian attitudes which we find in St. Paul and the earliest Christian writers and, on the other, the stand taken by the later and fully developed Christian Church in regard to the mystery cults of late antiquity."[12] It is a useful distinction. Yet even the earliest Christian writers took over material from the mystery cults not as borrowers, not as "seekers after treasure but as possessors thereof."[13] Rahner puts himself in this third category.

Brown's writings show that the characteristic New Testament use of the word μυστήριον is a clear development from Old Testament theological affirmations. If one takes them seriously, one has to review the whole development from the New Testament to St. Ambrose, and put it in a new light, less complacent about the influence of the mystery cults which that development reflects, more interested in the fulfillment of history.

II. *Mysterion*

Classical Greek. Within classical Greek the term μυστήριον had a developing range of meaning. The article in the lexicon of H. Liddell and R. Scott[14] indicates that this word entered the Greek language bearing a religious and cultic sense. Unlike most words in the theological vocabulary, which have an original secular use and are applied by analogy to divine things, μυστήριον belongs at the beginning (at least so far as

[10] H. Rahner, *Greek Myths*, 6–10.
[11] Ibid., 10. Cf. O. Casel, *Mystery*, 98, 100, 135, 140ff.
[12] H. Rahner, *Greek Myths*, 11.
[13] Ibid., 11.
[14] Henry George Liddell and Robert A. Scott, *A Greek-English Lexicon* (Oxford: Clarendon Press, 1968), 1156.

Liddell and Scott inform us) to the cultic sphere: ". . . mystery or secret rite; mostly in plural . . . the mysteries, first in Heraclitus 14."[15] The reference in Heraclitus is to *degenerate* mystery cults. The mysteries themselves must be far older than this fragment. Μυστεριασμός, we learn, and note well, means initiation, *initiatio*.[16]

Use of the word develops by metonomy. That is to say, things closely associated with the rite, and particular objects used in the cult, came to be called mysteries. Euripides speaks of the "holy mysteries of the garlands" (*The Suppliants*, 470), and there is a proverbial saying quoted in Aristophanes' *Frogs*, "Like an ass I carry mysteries," referring to the utensils used in the rites.[17]

By another extension it came to mean the knowledge communicated at the mysteries, the *content* of the rite, and hence a secret or hidden body of teachings. "The way of mystery," Casel remarks, "passes through initiations and the mysteries proper, in which the deeds and decrees of the gods in the first age are presented in ritual and thereby made present."[18] This description would apply to the μυστήριον in its original cultic setting. It would be only a slight step then to use μυστήριον to refer to the deeds and decrees of the gods themselves, and then only a slight further extension to refer to obscure teaching in a more general sense. In the *Theatetus*, Plato took these steps, using mysteries in an ironic way to speak of the teaching of a school of thought which reduced everything to "active" and "passive" motion. Socrates, the speaker, had little use for it:

Far more ingenious are the brethren whose mysteries I am about to reveal to you.[19]

Mysteries here refer no longer to a mystic rite but simply to a body of teaching held by a group about to be held up to ridicule by Socrates. The analogy to the hidden teaching of the mysteries is clear enough, however, and the irony depends on the association.

The Septuagint. By the time of LXX was produced, μυστήριον had this extended range of meaning. The translators made use of the word, sometimes in a purely secular sense, to mean *secret:*

Whoever betrays secrets, (ὁ ἀποκαλύπτων μυστήρια) destroys confidence and he will never find a congenial friend. (Sir. 27:16)

---

15 Ibid.
16 Ibid.
17 Ibid.
18 O. Casel, *Mystery*, 98.
19 Plato, *Theatetus* 152a.

or

Rhodocus, a man from the ranks of the Jews, gave secret information to the enemy (προσήγγειλεν δὲ τὰ μυστήρια τοῖς πολεμίοις). (2 Macc. 13:21)

But it appears also in a much more suggestive context. When the wise men of Babylon fail to tell King Nebuchadnezzar his dream and are put to death, Daniel undertakes the fated assignment. The challenge is to tell the King his dream and then to interpret it. Daniel asks his companions "to seek mercy of the God of heaven concerning this mystery (περὶ τοῦ μυστηρίου τούτου)" (Dan. 2:18). "Then the mystery was revealed to Daniel in a vision of the night" (2:1). To the king he says, "No wise men, enchanters, magicians, or astrologers can show to the king the mystery (τὸ μυστήριον . . . οὐκ ἔστι . . . ἡ δήλωσις) . . . but there is a God in heaven who reveals mysteries (ἀλλ᾽ ἔστι θεὸς ἐν οὐρανῷ ἀποκαλύπτων μυστήρια)" (2:27–28). The underlying Aramaic word is *raz*.

Mystery here refers to the *content* of something disclosed, not to a liturgy of some mystery cult. On the one hand, as we have seen, the development of the word in Greek allowed it to carry this sense easily. On the other hand, as Raymond Brown has so masterfully shown, the pattern of revelation implied in this passage from Daniel was characteristic of the Hebrew prophets from the time of Amos:[20] "Surely the Lord does nothing without revealing his secret (*sodho*) to his servants the prophets" (Amos 3:7; cf. Jer. 23:18; Job 15:8).

Daniel, in other words, does not need to reach for any Near Eastern cultic practices to demonstrate the superiority of YHWH's revelation. From the rise of the prophetic movement and before, according to Brown's study of the *sodh*, God disclosed his secret plans for the future to the prophets. They in turn taught the newly received revelation to the circle of their intimates (also *sodh*)[21] and proclaimed it to the people. Those who "had ears" were able to hear.[22]

Thus the use of the word *mystery* in Daniel is perfectly understandable Greek—the revelation of a secret of God. But it carries an unusual and characteristic Hebraic accent. It refers to God's plan for the future. To know the secret communicated to the prophet is not simply to enter into communion with the depths of God, but to know God's providential plans for human history. The prophetic message has to do with the

---

[20]   R. Brown, *Semitic Background*, 4–6.
[21]   Cf. English *counsel* and *council*.
[22]   "We believe that the background of such a concept is that of prophets being introduced into the heavenly assembly and gaining a knowledge of its secret decrees." R. Brown, *Semitic Background*, 6.

immediate future. It is not eschatological or ultimate, as it became in apocalyptic literature. But it is *a mystery of time*.

Qumran Literature. There are a number of references to "the mysteries" in the psalms at the end of the *Manual of Discipline* of the Qumran Community. In these passages, there is a deeper sense of present communion with the divine than in the canonical passages we have considered:

From the fountain of His righteousness [flows] my justification,
A light in my heart—
From His marvellous mysteries in Eternal Being.
My eye has beheld that wisdom
Which was hidden from men of knowledge
And that prudent purpose [which was hidden] from the sons of men.[23] (1QS 11.5–6)

For there is none other besides thee
To reply to Thy counsel,
And to understand all Thy holy purpose,
And to gaze into the depth of Thy mysteries. (1QS 11.18–19)

The expressions of "looking" and "gazing" into the mysteries communicate this sense of present communion; but the revelation of God's "purpose," and the enigmatic phrase "my heart is illumined with the Mystery to come (or else accomplished)" (*raz niyeh*, 1QS 11.3–4), express the same kind of mystery of time that we found in the biblical texts.

The New Testament. Μυστήριον in the New Testament presents decisive development but no surprises.

The one instance in the *Synoptic Gospels*, "to you has been given the secret (μυστήριον) of the kingdom of God, but for those outside everything is in parables" (Mark 4:11 par.), comports exactly with the prophetic use, as Bornkamm and Brown both recognize.[24] Isaiah 6:9–10 is even cited.

Paul (or the Pauline corpus) uses the word with some frequency (20 times). Particularly in Ephesians, the word acquires a precise Christian sense: *Christ* is the mystery, which has been hidden until now, but which God has revealed to his servants, the apostles and prophets, as a plan for the fulness of time to bring creation to its completion, a plan for the reconciliation of all things—Jews and Gentiles, heaven and earth (1:3–10; 3:1–6). This usage describes the ultimate case. Whereas the Hebrew and Aramaic passages we have examined represented *sodh* or *raz* as a counsel

---

[23] This and subsequent translations are quoted from William H. Brownlee, *The Dead Sea Manual of Discipline: Translation and Notes* (New Haven: American Schools of Oriental Research, 1951), 43–46.

[24] G. Bornkamm, "μυστήριον," 824; R. Brown, *Semitic Background*, 32–36.

of God for the near future and proximate fulfillment, Christ becomes the plan of God for ultimate redemption. But we still deal with a mystery of time.

Mystery is used also in a narrower sense, to mean not much more than *symbol*, although not arbitrary symbol; rather a participating symbol which draws its essential nature from the thing symbolized: "This [Christian marriage] is a great mystery, and I take it to mean Christ and the church" (Eph. 5:32; cf. Rev. 1:20; 10:7; 17:5, 7).

Present communion in the mysteries of God, so eloquently voiced in the *Manual of Discipline*, comes to expression in 1 Corinthians 2:7ff., "we impart a secret and hidden wisdom of God (σοφίαν ἐν μυστηρίῳ)." The passage continues, "no one comprehends the thoughts of God except the Spirit of God. Now we have received not the spirit of the world but the Spirit which is from God" (2:11–12). One observes the cult language in this passage: (τελείοις, ἀπεκάλυψεν, and of course, σοφία).[25] One observes also that the context of this chapter is baptism (cf. 1 Cor. 1:10ff.), especially the connection between the preaching of the cross and baptism (1:17), whose full significance can be appropriated only by the aid of the *Spirit* (2:4, 10).

Present participation in the "mysteries" is implied also in a later passage of the same epistle, where we note also the important mention of the *Spirit:* "For one who speaks in a tongue speaks not to men but to God; for no one understands him, but he utters mysteries in the Spirit" (14:2).

In all this, there is no reference to sacrament. Nevertheless, a certain similarity between the actions performed in the eucharist and actions performed in pagan sacrifice was not lost on Paul. The cup and bread make us participants in Christ. To eat of meat sacrificed to idols made pagans partners with their gods. "You cannot drink the cup of the Lord and the cup of demons. You cannot partake of the table of the Lord and the table of demons" (1 Cor. 10:21).

The issue is one of faith, of course. To a Christian, pagan sacrifice was nothing; to a pagan, the Christian eucharist would presumably be nothing. But the similarity of ritual action invited comparison, and to those whose faith was not secure, the resulting confusion could be destructive. This antipathy between Christian worship and pagan sacrifice proved to be determinative for the first three centuries of the life of the church. *Although the possibility of comparison between Christian liturgy and pagan mystery was recognized, baptism and eucharist were never referred to as mysteries,* and when comparisons were made, pagan mysteries were referred to as demonic. That is to say, they were not powerless. They were filled with distorted power. It would not be true to

---

[25]   G. Bornkamm, "μυστήριον," 819.

this insight to claim—as some theologians, both ancient and modern, do—that the mysteries were a "merely human" imitation of the Christian divine reality. More is at work on both pagan and Christian sides than is dreamed of in a secular philosophy. A later "world theology" might find it possible to say that God is at work in both, although not in the same way.

Thus μυστήριον is used in a number of senses in the New Testament. Each sense has an analogue in earlier literature. What we have called the "precise Christian sense," the characteristic Pauline usage, is prepared for in earlier Semitic texts. Its use to mean *symbol* was available in classical Greek.[26] What is striking, therefore, especially in recognition of the similarity between baptism and eucharist on the one hand, and pagan cultic practice on the other, is the absence of any reference to baptism and eucharist as mysteries.

Some Early Christian References. It is not the purpose of this section to examine the full range of uses of μυστήριον in early Christian literature, but a few are illuminating. Early on, Ignatius speaks of "three mysteries of a cry which were wrought in the stillness of God"[27]—the virginity of Mary, her giving birth, and the death of the Lord, three aspects of God's plan for reconciliation of the world, and hence not a wrenching extension of the characteristic Christian usage. By the third century Clement, in *Protrepticus*, makes a frank attempt to elucidate Christian by pagan mysteries: "Come, I will show you the Word and the mysteries of the Word, and I will give you understanding of them by means of images familiar to you."[28]

Nevertheless, even here, the word *mystery* does not appear in reference to Christian *ritual* acts. The fact is that even when theologians of the first three centuries desire to elaborate the comparison between Christian rites and pagan mysteries, the word *mystery* is studiously avoided as a description of what the Christian community engages in. Three examples will suffice:

The Case of Justin Martyr:

Which [i.e., the administration of bread and wine at the eucharist] the wicked devils have imitated in the mysteries of Mithras, commanding the same thing to be done. For, that bread and a cup of water are placed with certain incantations in the mystic rites of one who is being initiated, you either know or can learn.[29]

---

[26] ὕπνος τὰ μικρὰ τοῦ θανάτου μυστήριον (Mnesimachus 11); cited in H. Liddell and R. Scott, *Lexicon*, 1156, as an example of the metaphorical sense.

[27] Ignatius, *Eph.* 19.1. Cf. Geoffrey W. H. Lampe, *A Patristic Greek Lexicon* (Oxford: Clarendon Press, 1961), 891.

[28] Clement of Alexandria, *Protrep.* xii.119, *GCS* 1:84; cited in H. Rahner, *Greek Myths*, 3.

[29] Justin, *1 Apol.* lxvi, *ANF* 1:185.

The same charge is brought against lustrations (i.e., pagan ritual washings), that is, that they are a demonic imitation of baptism. Yet, throughout the entire discussion of baptism and eucharist (chs. 61–67), the word μυστήρια is not applied to them.

The Case of Tertullian: Tertullian, as we shall note later, had at his disposal both the word *mystery* and the word *sacrament*. Casel convincingly showed against Ghellinck that the two words share the same range of possible meanings.[30] Yet in Tertullian's discussion of Eleusinian initiation, the term is *mysteries* (μυστήρια), repeated at least three times in a single passage.[31] The treatise on baptism, however, begins, "Happy is our *sacrament* of water."[32] The word is *sacramentum*. Speaking of *Christian* heresies, he remarks, ". . . they are in no sense apostolic because of their diversity as to the mysteries of the faith." The Latin is *sacramenti apostolicae*.[33] Later in the same treatise Tertullian asks:

By whom is to be interpreted the sense of the passages which make for heresies? By the devil, of course, to whom pertain those wiles which pervert the truth, and who, by the mystic rites (*mysteria*) of his idols, vies even with the essential portions (*res*) of the sacraments of God (*sacramentorum divinorum*).[34]

The Case of Clement: There can be little doubt that the Alexandrian temperament was sensitive to the similarities between Christian and pagan mysteries, especially when mystery is understood in the sense of what is communicated and not in the sense of the *rite*. As we have seen, Clement gladly interprets the "mysteries of the Word" by means of ideas and language already familiar through pagan and gnostic use.[35] He is quite able to say, "Understand now for me the mystery of the truth. . . ."[36] On the other hand, *mystery* in this context precisely does not refer to baptism and eucharist, but to a present divine reality. And his offer to expound "the mysteries of the Word after thine own fashion" comes after a blistering attack on the pagan mysteries:

And what if I go over the mysteries? I will not divulge them in mockery, as they say Alcibiades did, but I will expose them right well by the word of truth.[37]

---

30 O. Casel, "Zum Worte Sacrementum," *JLW* 8 (1928): 225ff.
31 Tertullian, *Against the Valentinians* i, *ANF* 3:503.
32 Tertullian, *On Baptism* i, ibid., 669.
33 Tertullian, *Prescription Against Heretics* xxxii, ibid., 258.
34 Tertullian, *Prescription* lx, ibid., 262.
35 Cf. n. 28.
36 Clement of Alexandria, *Strom.* xi, *ANF* 2:502.
37 Idem, *Exhortation* ii, ibid., 175.

Even at the end of this exhortation, when he says, "Then shalt thou see my God, and be initiated into the sacred mysteries,"[38] the reference is not *directly* to baptism, but to that present relation to the depth of God's being to which baptism introduces one. There is even an allusion to 1 Corinthians 2:9: "ear hath not heard, nor have they entered into the heart of any."[39] *That is, baptism initiates into the mystery, but is not itself called the mystery.*

Nevertheless, when the comparison between Christian and pagan mysteries is drawn as closely as Clement does, it is obviously not a far step to refer to baptism and eucharist as "the Christian mysteries." Why such usage did not become general for over a hundred years can only be a matter of conjecture. The continued strength of the cults and the fact that even by Clement they were regarded as immoral and demonic must be among the chief factors at work.

In any case, as has already been observed, it was not until Cyril of Jerusalem delivered his *Catechetical Lectures* (ca. 370) that we have a free, unmistakable, explicit, unabashed reference to baptism, chrism, and the eucharist as *the Christian mysteries.* By this time the Constantinian settlement had been made and the cults were no longer a threat. I underline for future reference the fact that the reference in Cyril is to *initiatory rites.*

III. *Sacramentum*

The Latin word *sacramentum* has a very different history in classical Latin from that of μυστήριον in Greek. Although even in pre-Christian times its meaning overlapped with that of μυστήριον,[40] and although after the fourth century, both μυστήριον and *sacramentum* came to denote certain Christian liturgical acts, nevertheless the Latin development is distinctive.

There seem to be two basic meanings for *sacramentum:* (1) a sum of money deposited by both parties to a civil suit as a pledge of good faith (the loser's deposit being used for religious purposes); and (2) an oath of allegiance sworn by soldiers to their commanding officer.[41] It might be

---

[38] Idem, *Exhortation* xii, ibid., 205.

[39] Ibid. The reference in *Strom.* xxi, ibid., 435, to the mysteries which are "for the most part celebrated at night" *might* be a reference to Christian mysteries, as the editor suggests in *ANF* 2:621; and if so, it would be a very early instance of the word used in connection with Christian rites. However this interpretation is not absolutely demanded by the context, and Clement's normal usage counts against it.

[40] H. Liddell and R. Scott, *Lexicon*, 1156 (μυστήριον 3).

[41] Charlton T. Lewis, *A Latin Dictionary for Schools* (Oxford: Clarendon Press, 1901), 925.

tempting to imagine that the former sense of *sacramentum* lay behind such English hymn verses as

Approach ye then with faithful hearts sincere, and take the pledges of salvation here,[42]

which is a John Mason Neale translation of a seventh century Latin text, or the Doddridge lines,

. . . and may each soul salvation see, that here its sacred pledges tastes.[43]

To think of the eucharistic elements as a pledge of good faith left to us while history endures is attractive and compelling. At one time it tempted me. However, these hymns almost certainly have no connection with early Latin understandings of *sacramentum*. The underlying Latin word in the Neale translation is *custodiam*. No Christian Latin texts are known to me when *sacramentum* needs to be rendered *pledge*. English hymn writers are not likely to have discovered hitherto unknown Latin references but to have made a new—and striking—image.

Scholarly interest has focused rather on the second meaning, a soldier's oath of allegiance. Von Soden, Bornkamm, and Casel all cite certain passages in Livy. I quote them here for ease of reference:

After summoning all of military age to take the oath (*sacramentum*). . . .

. . . and it happened that the enemy had made their preparations for the war with the same earnestness and pomp . . . and had likewise invoked the assistance of the gods, initiating as it were, their soldiers with a certain antique form of oath (*rite quodam sacramenti vetusto*).

In this place they offered sacrifice in accordance with directions read from an old linen roll. The celebrant was one Ovius Paccius, an aged man. . . . Besides other ceremonial preparations, such as might avail to strike the mind with religious awe, there was a place all enclosed, with altars in the midst and slaughtered victims lying about, and round them a guard of centurions with drawn swords.

For their eyes beheld all that array of the secret rite, and the armed priests . . . and they could hear the baleful execrations and that dire oath (*furiale carmen*).[44]

The soldiers of the Samnite legion "were, as Livy says, initiated (*initiati*) according to the ancient rite of consecration (*ritu sacramenti*). The whole panoply of ritual was used; there were sacrifices and terrible

---

[42]   *The Hymnal 1982* (New York: The Chruch Hymnal Corporation, 1982), 327.
[43]   Ibid., 321.
[44]   Livy, *Ab Urbe Condita*, LCL; 12 vols. (Cambridge: Harvard Univ. Press, 1919), 4:370, 504–6, 516–18.

oaths, so that the whole proceeding seemed more like initiation into a mystery than a military oath-taking."[45]

This observation becomes quite helpful and suggestive when one tries to interpret the enigmatic description of Christian worship which Pliny supplied to the Emperor Trojan in his well-known letter written about 112. This text contains the first application of the word *sacramentum* to Christian worship:

> But they declared that the sum of their guilt or error had amounted only to this, that on an appointed day they had been accustomed to meet before daybreak, and to recite a hymn antiphonally to Christ as to a God (*carmen . . . dicere secum invicem*) and to bind themselves by an oath (*sacramentum*), not for the commission of any crime but to abstain from theft, robbery, adultery, and breach of faith. . . . After the conclusion of this ceremony it was their custom to depart and meet again to take food; but it was ordinary and harmless food.[46]

It is notoriously difficult to understand what is being described. Pliny's informants were lapsed Christians who testified reluctantly. Pliny himself had no first-hand knowledge of these circumstances. We do not know whether it was his idea to speak of the liturgy as a *sacramentum*, or whether that was the word applied by his witnesses. The latter seems more likely. Granted these elements of distance and uncertainty, it seems not unreasonable to suggest that what Pliny has described here *is a rite of Christian initiation.* Consider the following features of the occasion:

—Although it makes sense to read *carmen* as hymn, for the Christian community often sang "psalms and hymns and spiritual songs" (Eph. 5:19), *carmen* can also, as Bettenson's own note indicates, mean "any set form of words." It might refer to religious formula, a creed, or even a baptismal liturgy.

—The idea of an "oath of loyalty" lies very near the surface of Christian baptism. The striking insertion into the text of Acts 8, following v. 36, might well qualify as an early baptismal liturgy, and might well be described as a *carmen* and a *sacramentum:*

> -What is to prevent my being baptized?
> -If you believe with all your heart you may.
> -I believe that Jesus Christ is the Son of God.[47]

It even has the element of antiphonal response.

---

[45]   O. Casel, *Mystery*, 56.

[46]   Pliny, *Epistles* 10.96.7; quoted from Henry Bettenson, *Documents of the Christian Church* (New York: Oxford Univ. Press, 1947), 6.

[47]   Acts 8:37; cf. Oscar Cullman, *Baptism in the New Testament*, SBT 1 (London: SCM Press, 1950), 71–80.

—The fact that the assembly broke up and gathered again to take food suggests that a eucharistic celebration brought the occasion to an appropriate climax. From the *Apostolic Tradition of Hippolytus* (ca. 215) we know that the eucharist after baptism was celebrated in another place.

—The emphasis on ethical behavior in Pliny's account also suggests the preparation of candidates expressed in the *Apostolic Tradition of Hippolytus* (2.21), and the fact that the *Didache* (ca. 100?) begins with extended ethical instruction, followed by accounts of baptism and eucharist (1:1–6:3), underlines still further the connection between initiation and moral instruction.[48]

—Although Pliny makes no mention of baptism as the induction of "the Christian soldier," the fact is that the very word *sacramentum* has this connotation; and the motif of the *miles Christianus* is well established in connection with baptism.

The identification of the liturgy which Pliny describes with Christian baptism is not an open and shut case. There is no mention of water, and the implication is that the service described is a regular service, often repeated rather than annual. The weight of such considerations cannot be disregarded. Nevertheless, the preponderance of the evidence leads me to persist in thinking that at its earliest use, early in the second century, *sacramentum* may already have denoted Christian sacramental rites, *initiatory* rites.

If it were to be accepted that *sacramentum* came into the Christian vocabulary at a very early date meaning *baptism and a following eucharist*, that development would account for Tertullian's easy and explicit use of *sacramentum* to mean *the whole initiatory rite* in his treatise on baptism (hence the occasional translation as *mystery;* cf. n. 33) and his customary usage elsewhere of *sacramentum* to cover Christian and biblical symbols and μυστήρια to denote pagan rites.

We should register the fact that when the pre-Christian Roman *sacramentum* had to be translated into Greek, the word μυστήριον was used. Herodian's phrase is "the awesome oath of office of Romans" (τῆς Ῥωμάιον ἀρχῆς σεμνὸν μυστήριον).[49] And the opposite process also went on. When the Greek μυστήριον had to be translated into Latin, the word *sacramentum* was used. Thus in early Latin translations of the New Testament as well as in the Vulgate, *sacramentum* renders μυστήριον in that full range of meaning which we have already examined, *none of which refer to baptism and eucharist.*[50]

---

[48]   Texts in *Apostolic Tradition of Hippolytus*, ed. Burton Scott Easton (London: Cambridge Univ. Press, 1934), 47; and *The Apostolic Fathers*, LCL; 2 vols. (Cambridge: Harvard Univ. Press, 1912), 1:303–333; cf. Justin, *1 Apol.* lxi.

[49]   Cited in H. Liddell and R. Scott *Lexicon*, 1156 (μυστήριον 3).

[50]   O. Casel, "Zum Worte Sacramentum," 232.

III. Some Conclusions

This material suggests several conclusions.

1. Despite the graphic similarities between Christian liturgical action and pagan mysteries, and indeed probably because of these similarities, μυστήρια was not used to refer to Christian rites for a long time. Its broader reference, established in both LXX and the New Testament, was taken up earlier by Christian writers. It began with that broader reference to the depths of God's being and to God's plans for the reconciliation of the world in Christ. It referred then to a mystery of time, to the fulfillment of history. *Not till the mid-fourth century did μυστήριον refer explicitly and unquestionably to ritual acts, and then at first chiefly to baptism and eucharist.*

2. *Sacramentum,* on the other hand, was impressed to refer to baptism (including chrism and eucharist) at a fairly early date and slowly acquired virtually the same range of meaning as μυστήριον. Ambrose's twin treatises, *De Sacramentis* and *De Mysteriis* is a striking example of the eventual convergence.

3. During the whole period under discussion, there was no effort either to define or enumerate the mysteries. Because of the fluidity of reference, a large number of things eventually came to be called *mysteries,* ranging from the incarnation to the chalice and paten used at the eucharist.[51] Thanks to the influence of the New Testament, incarnation, cross, and resurrection form the palpable, if unstated, context of the Christian mysteries.[52] During the period covered by this survey, about three hundred years (A.D. 50–350), and for a long time thereafter, no attempt was made to restrict the understanding of mystery or sacrament to a material object which conferred or distributed grace to a believer.

4. We have collected a good deal of evidence to suggest that *at the beginning, the Christian sacrament or mystery denoted the initiatory rite:* baptism, chrism (certainly by Tertullian's time), and eucharist. Subsequent references to separate sacraments are derivative and dependent on Christian initiation.

IV. "Concluding Unscientific Postscript"

We have now arrived at our first goal: to understand at least something of the etymological and theological development behind the

---

[51] G. Lampe, *A Patristic Greek Lexicon,* 891–93.

[52] Cf. H. Rahner, *Greek Myths;* chapter II, "The Mystery of the Cross," is the introduction to and provides the context for chapter III, "The Mystery of Baptism."

application of the words μυστήριον and *sacramentum* to Christian rites. A concluding unscientific postscript might be in order, however, about Augustine's influential definition of sacraments as signs. "Signs when applied to divine things are called sacraments."[53] "A sacrament is an outward and visible sign of an inward and spiritual grace."[54] Heretofore the focus was on *mystery,* which (to be sure) was revealed in liturgical action, a sign. There was only one mystery—Christ. Christ might be revealed in many different ways. Many "mysteries." In the post-Augustinian West, the focus was put on the sign, often disconnected from liturgical action. To be sure, it expressed a mystery. There is water, or bread, or oil. How does one reach from the object to Christ? How is it possible? The difference in nuance is considerable. It has put the discussion of sacramental theology on a new level, and has made it difficult to recover the early relation of sacramental thought to the fundamental Christian mystery of Christ's reconciling love through the initiatory rite. By virtue of the Augustinian definition and the availability of both words in Latin, both *mysterium* and *sacramentum,* the mystery of God's act in Christ and its expression in special sacramental acts became separable. In separation the former tended to become inaccessible and the latter unintelligible, especially in a nominalist world.

The numbering of the sacraments increased this tension. Sacraments were numbered in connection with the elaboration of the sacramental–penitential system during the twelfth and thirteenth centuries.[55] As is well known, the number was finally determined to be seven, in the thirteenth century. This development moved the discussion still further away from the "mystery theology" (to use Casel's phrase) of the first few centuries and tended to obscure it. On the other hand, the attempt of the Protestant reformers to reduce the number from seven to two on the basis of Jesus' instituting words has proved unstable both because historical-critical problems in each case call the institution into question, and even more because the prevailing nominalism of the last four hundred years has attacked the very possibility of sacraments.

Casel and Rahner, through their mystery theology, represent the movement of a generation ago to recapture an understanding of the divine presence and a sense of participation in divine reality through liturgical action. Their work through the pervasive mediation of the liturgical movement has born much fruit. The widespread acceptance of the 1976 Book of Common Prayer testifies to it. By his illumination of the particular Semitic background of mystery, Raymond Brown should enable

---

[53] Augustine, *Epistles* 138.1.7; cited in Bernard Leeming, *Principles of Sacramental Theology,* 2nd ed. (London: Longman's, 1960), 562.
[54] Augustine, *Epistles* 105.3.12; cited in B. Leeming, *Principles,* 533ff.
[55] B. Leeming, *Principles,* 533ff.

us to see that the character of that mystery theology has to be altered from simple participation in the divine presence to participation in the fulfillment of history through the reconciling act of Christ.

One aim of this paper has been to bring these two ideas together. We had to treat them together in order to understand the development of mystery and sacrament language at all. Their synergism should permit further ecumenical progress in the area of sacramental theology.

William Porcher DuBose: New Testament Scholar and Systematic Theologian

JOHN MACQUARRIE*

William Porcher DuBose (1836–1918) has been described by Norman Pittenger as "the only important creative theologian that the Episcopal Church in the United States has produced,"[1] and one of my own predecessors in the Lady Margaret Professorship at Oxford, William Sanday, said that "the American Church should make much of DuBose."[2] Yet DuBose remains neglected. For instance, in the recent scholarly two-volume history by Claude Welch,[3] although there is a very full coverage of the American scene, there is no mention at all of DuBose. I wonder if this neglect is due, at least in part, to the fact that his theology is very much Anglican in its ethos, and therefore eschews extreme and sensational positions which tend to attract attention in the United States before they fade out and are forgotten. It is true that some of DuBose's views were considered daring in his day, and we quite often find him defending himself against possible misunderstandings, but on the whole it is the classical Christian tradition which he expounds. One characteristic of any classic work is a certain timelessness, and that helps to explain why those who do appreciate DuBose still find him a source of insight today, long after more sensational theologians have faded into oblivion. In this essay, I shall show how DuBose's thought follows the Anglican pattern of drawing upon Scripture, tradition, and reason, a pattern that was already stated by Thomas Cranmer when the breach with Rome took place in the sixteenth century.

That Scripture supplies the foundation for DuBose's thought is obvious. No memoir of DuBose omits to mention that he carried his Greek New Testament with him while serving with the Confederate Forces in the Civil War, and his attachment to the New Testament had a major role both in his teaching at Sewanee where he came in 1871 and in

---

* John Macquarrie is the retired Lady Margaret Professor of Divinity, Oxford University.

[1] Norman Pittenger, *Unity in the Faith*, by W.A. DuBose, ed. N. Pittenger (Greenwich, CT: Seabury Press, 1957), 21.

[2] William Sanday, *The Life of Christ in Recent Research* (New York: Oxford Univ. Press, 1907), 281.

[3] Claude Welch, *Protestant Thought in the Nineteenth Century*, 2 vols. (New Haven: Yale Univ. Press, 1972–85).

his writings. His most famous book is *The Soteriology of the New Testament*, published by Macmillan in 1892; yet that book might be better classified as a work of systematic theology than as a New Testament study. The truth is that for DuBose some of the artificial divisions that we have made are unimportant. As a Christian theologian, he believed that theology must be closely tied to the foundation documents which more than anything else define the essential nature of Christianity. Yet he was no "fundamentalist," as if the teaching and even the very language of Scripture could be uncritically repeated for the modern age. And it was toward the modern age that his teaching was directed.

His theological interest in the New Testament saved him from some of the more sterile exercises in biblical scholarship, when the New Testament comes to be regarded as primarily an object for historical inquiry, so that its soteriological or saving truth is lost sight of in disputes about the authenticity of certain sayings, the circumstances under which they were uttered, and so on. Of course, I am not saying for a moment that close investigative technical scholarship is not needed. I am only saying that the rigor of scholarship should not stifle sensitivity to the vision of the New Testament, though it is very difficult to hold these things together. In this age of specialization, systematic theology and biblical scholarship seem to get more and more separated. But this certainly could not be said of DuBose.

At an early stage in *The Soteriology of the New Testament*, DuBose offers us an explicit and quite detailed statement of the place of Scripture, as he understood it. He points out that if the New Testament contained a clear and authoritative final doctrine of the salvation effected by Christ, then a book like his would be unnecessary, for we would already be in possession of all the answers to our questions about salvation.[4] Indeed, almost two millennia of Christian thought and discussion would be superfluous. He also points out that the very word "atonement," so central in the Christian theological vocabulary, would be unknown, because it is not used in the New Testament. In saying such things, he not only rejects a narrow biblicism but seems also to indicate that if he had been living several decades later, he would have had little sympathy with that more sophisticated "biblical theology" which urged theologians to confine themselves to the biblical concepts and even words. An example of this would be Oscar Cullmann's claim that we should make a strenuous effort to conform all our ideas about time to what we find in the most ancient Christian writings.[5] Are we not then allowed to bring modern researches into time and temporality to bear on our theology? Must we

---

[4] William P. DuBose, *The Soteriology of the New Testament* (New York: Macmillan, 1892), 19.
[5] Oscar Cullmann, *Christ and Time* (London: SCM Press, 1951), 23.

142   *Christ and His Communities*

remain bound for ever to the understanding of time that was prevalent in the first century, as if that were itself part of the divine revelation? DuBose would clearly have rejected any such attempt to be purely biblical.

In an utterance which probably seemed more provocative when it was made than it does today, DuBose declared: "The New Testament no more gives us doctrine than nature gives us science. It gives us the facts but not the theory, the matter of all Christian doctrine but no finished doctrine or doctrines of the whole matter of Christianity."[6] The sentences just quoted obviously imply an analogy, namely, that doctrine or theology is to the New Testament as science is to nature. But this is not a good analogy, and it oversimplifies the relation. Nature consists of facts or phenomena which science proceeds to analyse and describe through appropriate words, concepts, and theories. But the New Testament is already at least one remove from the facts and phenomena in which theology is interested. These facts have already in the New Testament been transposed into language, and although the gospels and other New Testament writings do not (at least, for the most part) attempt the systematic theological interpretation of the facts, they certainly do introduce theological considerations. For instance, we do not find a simple chronicle of the passion and death of Jesus, but a narrative in which the events are presented as having saving significance. The word "atonement" is not there, but something like a theology of atonement (or several theologies of atonement) are already striving to find expression. So the relation of theology to the New Testament is seen to be more complex than might at first have been supposed from what DuBose says. Between the theologian and the facts stands the New Testament, which is indeed our only substantial witness to these facts, but which has already given a theological interpretation to the facts.

It is commonly recognized nowadays that all alleged descriptions of facts even in the sciences are already theory-laden, and the point has been well understood in theology for a long time. One remembers how Albert Schweitzer in *The Quest of the Historical Jesus* (1906; English trans., 1910) showed how successive attempts to provide objective scientific accounts of the career of Jesus inevitably reflect back the values and theological prejudices of the biographers. But there is still the legitimate task of trying to ascertain as far as possible the facts concerning Jesus. A recent brilliant example is the work of E. P. Sanders.[7] But this was not the task which DuBose set himself, in spite of that somewhat unfortunate analogy that theology is to the New Testament what science is to nature.

---

[6]   W. DuBose, *Soteriology*, 19–20.
[7]   E. P. Sanders, *Jesus and Judaism* (Philadelphia: Fortress Press, 1985).

Yet though history and theology are already mingled in the New Testament, and although in theory one goes to it as either primarily a historian or a theologian (Sanders says plainly he is writing as a historian, not a theologian), the two tasks cannot be kept entirely separate. Sometimes how we understand the facts may have profound consequences for the theology. For instance, if we could discover how Jesus understood his own death, this would have important implications for any atonement theory. Though I have been critical of the analogy which he mentions, I think the complex relation of theology, Scripture, and fact was indeed clear to DuBose, and we shall have evidence of this when we consider some of his actual exegesis.

But before we do that, we have still to explore some further points in DuBose's preliminary statement about the place of Scripture in his theology. He names three points which, taken together, make it clear that even if he gives a priority to Scripture as a source for theology, it remains nevertheless *one* source which has to be set alongside and seen in the light of other sources.

The first of his three points is this, using DuBose's own words:

We could not even understand, much less be able to attach their peculiar value, to the Scriptures, if we were not conscious of, and they did not speak to, those facts of universal human experience which give all their truth and all their interest to the Scriptures.[8]

These words clearly differentiate DuBose's point of view from that of the critical historian who is concerned primarily to discern the facts that lie behind the scriptural record. The Scriptures do not point us to these facts in a direct way, but already include an appropriation and interpretation of the facts as they impinged on the minds of those who wrote the Scriptures. So we are now able to see more clearly the complexity of the relation between Scripture, theology, and historical fact. The relation had been obscured by DuBose's own misleading analogy—theology is to Scripture as science is to nature. He is now showing that Scripture is neither to be identified with the facts themselves, nor is it ever a mere transcription into language of these facts. It is rather a transcript of the faith that has been brought into being by the facts, or to express the matter differently, it is a view of the facts mediated through minds which have already responded to these facts as significant for human salvation, and whose aim is just as much to enable us to see the facts in the way that they have seen them as to inform us about the facts themselves. Again, let me say that if anyone decides to use the gospels to reconstruct the main

---

[8] W. DuBose, *Soteriology*, 20.

events of the career of Jesus from the points of view of a positivist historian, this is no doubt a legitimate exercise, and the findings of such research should not be ignored by theologians. But it has equally to be said that these findings represent only a partial and one-sided interpretation of the scriptural material, and systematically miss the central ideas which the scriptural writers are trying to convey.

On the other hand, DuBose is just as far from any fundamentalist or literalist reading of Scripture. There is in fact much in common between a purely critical approach to Scripture by an uncommitted historian and the literalist approach of a biblicist Christian. Both of them have turned Scripture into an object standing there for our inspection and manipulation. In both cases, there has been a failure to grasp the true *genre* of a document claiming to be "gospel," a document which already embodies in itself the subjective appropriation of faith as well as the objective reference to the events that have awakened faith. It has sometimes been claimed that the great Reformers, in spite of their concentration on the Bible and their use of proof-texts, summed up in the slogan *sola scriptura,* were not literalists. Calvin, for instance, held that we do not understand Scripture from the bare words, the objectively given text before us, but require in addition the "inner testimony" (*testimonium internum*) of the Holy Spirit. Only so can we hear the Scriptures as a living voice. DuBose seems to have had much the same idea in mind when he uses less pretentious language and says we would miss the meaning of Scripture "if we were not conscious of, and if they did not speak to, those facts of universal human experience which give all their truth and interest to the Scriptures." If the Holy Spirit is God immanent in us, then is not this "universal human experience" at least very close to what Calvin called the "inner testimony" of the Holy Spirit? DuBose, as it seems to me, had a very good grasp of the hermeneutical problems connected with the study of Scripture, and steered a judicious course between a naive biblicism which ignores the element of receptivity both in the writers and readers of Scripture, and that supposedly scientific analysis of Scripture which screens out the central concerns of the scriptural writers.

The problem is still with us. For example, Andrew Louth has not hesitated to question whether the critical methods of New Testament scholarship are not obscuring the theological meaning of the writings.[9] But his suggestion that we reconsider the allegorical method of interpretation used in a former age seems unrealistic. DuBose shows us a better way in his balanced combination of critical scholarship and spiritual sensitivity, but this in turn is a reminder that hermeneutics is as much an

---

[9]   Andrew Louth, *Discerning the Mystery* (Oxford: Clarendon Press, 1983).

art as a science, so that it can never be fully learned from lectures and textbooks but requires also a gift of creativity on the part of the interpreter.

Of course, it is important not to claim too much for DuBose, or to pretend that he was not limited by the perspective of his time. Yet I would like to spend a little longer defending the view that he combined critical scholarship and spiritual sensitivity, for although the biblical scholar or systematic theologian of today would not be able to follow quite the same paths as DuBose, he should still share some of his aims.

For example, DuBose, like most Christian scholars of earlier generations, aimed at synthesis, at presenting the teaching of the New Testament as a unified whole, and in the process minimized or obscured the differences among the various writers. Thus, in one passage, he sets out from the Johannine saying, "Peace I leave with you, my peace I give to you" (14:27), but almost immediately he moves into the beatitudes of Matthew as a description of the life which knows inward peace, the peace that the world cannot give. Then by a bold stroke he joins Matthew and John together. Matthew gives his teaching about the way to God and to the true life, but Jesus not only taught that life but lived it, and that brings us back to the Johannine claim, "I am the way, the truth and the life." So DuBose concludes, "The work of Jesus Christ was not to teach but to be the Word of God, our way to God, because God's truth of us and God's life in us."[10] This has homiletical effect, but it would be open to criticism by the modern critic who might say that Matthew's Gospel has been subordinated to John's, and Matthew's distinctive view of Jesus as a teacher has been swallowed up in the Johannine conception of Jesus as the living Word.

This is no doubt a just criticism , but is there something further to be said? Since DuBose's time, New Testament studies have become increasingly analytic. They have stressed the differences to be found among the writings, and have branded as unscholarly any attempts at "harmonization"—a very bad word today. At the end of DuBose's life, form criticism was emerging, and its technique broke up the Synoptic Gospels into many fragments of teaching that had circulated in the early churches. At a later time, redaction criticism came along, stressing the different points of view of the editors of the gospel material. The danger is that one may be left with a collection of bits and pieces. Now, let us concede that DuBose may sometimes have been uncritical in his attempts at synthesis. Even so, that does not mean that such attempts have to be abandoned as merely mistaken. It means only that the modern scholar has to be more discriminating than was possible in DuBose's time, but that if there is

---

[10]   W. DuBose, *Soteriology*, 291.

indeed something we may call the Christian faith, and if its foundation documents are included in the New Testament, then there is still the task of setting it forth as a connected body of teaching, though this must be done with integrity. In theology as in philosophy, analysis is only one part of the task and should lead eventually into synthesis.

The second of DuBose's three points can be dealt with much more briefly than the first. It is: "The Scriptures are not Christianity, but a product of Christianity. They are a witness to it and a record of it, of peculiar value."[11] Christianity, he declares, could have been a fact of human history without the Scriptures at all. The New Testament, as indeed we have already noted, is not itself the raw material out of which the fabric of Christian truth has been formed, and it does not create this truth. This second point seems to me to do little more than link together the first and third points. It is in the first and third points that we meet the theologically significant elements in DuBose's approach to the Scriptures, while the second point is the negative corollary—we must not confuse the Scriptures with Christianity itself, or fall into any merely biblicist version of Christian theology.

The third point bears closely on some of the questions which have arisen in our examination of the first point. This third point, in DuBose's own words, is:

We cannot interpret the Scriptures apart from the mind of the Church which originally produced them, and whose subsequent historical understanding of them, on the lowest grounds, we can even less rationally ignore, than if, in studying nature, we should despise all the already attained results of natural science.[12]

This is a very controversial statement, perhaps more so than it appears at first sight. In one sense, DuBose seems to be putting merely the view of common sense. If someone today decides to study astronomy, let us say, he could conceivably proceed on a strictly "do-it-yourself" basis. He could go out tonight and begin observing the sky, taking note of the objects he saw there, their relative positions, and so on. In other words, he could put himself in the position of a pioneering Babylonian star-gazer at the very dawn of astronomy, except that the Babylonian would have been better off as an observer because there was less atmospheric pollution in his time. But frankly I do not think our hypothetical "do-it-yourself" student would live long enough to make even the most elementary progress in his science. It would be simply absurd for such a person to ignore the thousands of years of observation

---

[11]   Ibid., 20.
[12]   Ibid., 21.

of the celestial bodies that has gone on, the theories that have been developed, the instruments that have been invented, the star-atlases that have been compiled, and so on, or the assistance to be had from related sciences such as physics and chemistry. All sciences are developed in communities of investigation, and the contributions of even the most brilliant individual investigators are small compared with the heritage which these investigators have received from their predecessors. Is not then DuBose perfectly correct in claiming that the Scriptures must be read in accordance with the mind of the church?

Certainly, Anglican theology—and I am trying to show, among other things, that DuBose was a truly Anglican theologian—has never been purely biblicist. It has recognized the priority of the Bible as a theological source, but has not embraced the principle *sola scriptura*. It might seem, however, that our quotation from DuBose gives priority to the church, for he reminds us that the church produced the Scriptures and then in the course of history developed a normative understanding of them. I do not think, however, that he was deliberately shifting the weight of theological authority from the Scriptures to the church, but only recognizing their reciprocity. The church did produce the Scriptures, but having done so and having established the canon, willingly submitted itself to the Scriptures as the authoritative witness of apostolic Christianity. A possible analogy would be that of the founding fathers of the United States producing a constitution, and then conferring on it an authority which would be binding on future generations of citizens, though not without the possibility of new interpretations. This kind of reciprosity between Scripture and church was well expressed by Bishop R.E. Terwilliger when he wrote: "The New Testament is the book which the Church created, and the book which creates the Church."[13]

The much respected Report of the Commisssion on Christian Doctrine, *Doctrine in the Church of England* (1938), claimed:

All Christians are bound to allow very high authority to doctrines which the Church has been generally united in teaching; for each believer has a limited range, and the basis of the Church's belief is far wider than that of his own can ever be. An individual Christian who rejects any part of that belief is guilty of presumption, unless he feels himself bound in conscience to do so, and has substantial reasons for holding that what he rejects is not essential to the truth and value of Christianity.[14]

---

[13]   Robert E. Terwilliger, *Christian Believing* (New York: Morehouse-Barlow, 1973), 55.

[14]   *Doctrine in the Church of England: The Report of the Commission on Christian Doctrine Appointed by the Archbishops of Canterbury and York in 1922* (London: S.P.C.K., 1938), 36.

Thus Anglicans reject (in theory, at least) the individualism that has been so injurious to Protestantism.

Nevertheless, can one go quite as far as DuBose in saying that we cannot interpret the Scriptures apart from the mind of the church? In a science like astonomy there is, broadly speaking, continuous advance in the agreed findings of that science. But in Christian doctrine, it is not clear that such a straightforward development has taken place. What comes later is not always a closer approximation to the truth. What would DuBose himself have said about developments in the understanding of the Petrine office? The New Testament certainly shows that Peter had some kind of primacy in earliest Christianity. But it is a very long way from that to the dogma of papal infallibility. Would interpreting the Bible according to the mind of the church mean that one would have to interpret the Petrine texts as containing and justifying the later development?

Let me take another example which, though it may not have aroused so much passion as controversy over the papacy, is close to the heart of Christian belief. I mean the understanding of the person of Jesus Christ himself. DuBose states plainly: "That Christianity is an Incarnation in the fullest possible sense of the term is so indubitably the mind of the New Testament, as of the Church, that the only question before us is to define the meaning of that assertion." A little further on he says again that the belief that "Jesus Christ is the Incarnation of a Divine Person" is the doctrine both of the New Testament and of the church.[15] Such assertions would nowadays bring howls of protest not only from radical theologians,[16] but likewise from many moderate biblical scholars who might themselves be firm believers in the incarnation but whose scholarly integrity would not allow them to claim that this doctrine is so clearly and definitely taught in the New Testament—"indubitably the mind of the New Testament," as DuBose expresses it. Thus even a quite conservative scholar, James Dunn, who acknowledges that "historically speaking, Christian faith has been faith in the incarnation," gives a strong warning against reading the later doctrines of the church into the New Testament:

What would it have meant to their hearers when the first Christians called Jesus 'son of God'? . . . We must endeavour to attune our listening to hear with the ears of the first Christians' contemporaries. We must attempt the exceedingly difficult task of shutting out the voices of early Fathers, Councils and dogmaticians down the centuries, in case they drown the earlier voices, in case the earlier voices were

---

[15]   W. DuBose, *Soteriology,* 122, 138.
[16]   For example, the contributors to *The Myth of God Incarnate,* ed. John Hick (London: SCM Press, 1977).

saying something different, in case they intended their words to speak with different force to their hearers.[17]

This looks like an opposite prescription from DuBose's advice to study the Scriptures in conformity with the mind of the church.

Yet I do not think the two positions are irreconcilable, and it is the necessity of bringing them together that makes the question of how biblical studies and systematic theology are related so difficult. On the one hand, no one is going to deny that there takes place development of doctrine. One can see it going on in the New Testament itself, and it took several centuries of reflection before the classical Christology of the church was formulated. But on the other hand, given the long history of theological controversies, no one is going to deny either that development can go astray and that one has sometimes to go back to the sources to check whether a particular development can be deemed legitimate. Even so central and venerable a doctrine as the incarnation is not exempt from this kind of test. To read the Bible in the light of the church's teaching is justifiable provided we do not force the scriptural text to conform to concepts which may be alien to it. To search out the original meanings is justifiable, provided we relate them to the developed doctrines and do not become immersed in purely antiquarian problems. The difficulties may vary from one doctrine to another. In some cases, including Christology, much of the development takes place within the New Testament, and the incarnational model is clear when one comes to the Johannine literature. In the case of other doctrines, such as the ministry, some of the major developments occur after the completion of the New Testament, and then it is more controversial to determine whether the developments are justified in terms of the origins.

It would be a clarifying exercise if we were to take some actual example of DuBose's exegesis, and then compare (or contrast) it with the exegesis of the same text by Professor Dunn, who is, as I have said, a moderate rather than a radical New Testament scholar. In *The Gospel According to St. Paul*, a brilliant work by any standard, DuBose states: "That St. Paul realizes profoundly the truth of the pre-existence and the deity of our Lord there can be no question. The conviction of it runs through the whole texture of the Apostle's thought and knowledge of Jesus Christ."[18] I want to pay attention in particular to the idea of pre-existence. Paul's use of the idea is said by DuBose to be "beyond

---

[17]   James D.G. Dunn, *Christology in the Making* (Philadelphia: Westminister Press, 1980), 1, 13–14.

[18]   Quoted from *A DuBose Reader*, ed. Donald S. Armentrout (Sewanee: University of the South, 1984), 142. Source: W. P. DuBose, *The Gospel According to St. Paul* (New York: Longmans, Green & Co., 1907).

question," and it is said also to be a conviction that runs through all his writings. Many people would simply accept this statement as true, for have we not all to a large extent read the Bible through the eyes of the church and know that the mainstream of exegesis, from patristic times down to eminent scholars of our town time, has ascribed to Paul a belief in the pre-existence of Jesus Christ? We can think at once of passages which seem to admit of no other interpretation: "When the fullness of the time was come, God sent forth his Son" (Gal. 4:4); "God, sending his own Son in the likeness of sinful flesh, condemned sin in the flesh" (Rom. 8:3); "For you know the grace of our Lord Jesus Christ, that though he was rich, yet for your sakes he became poor" (2 Cor. 8:9); and, above all, the famous Christ-hymn in which Christ, being in the form of God, emptied himself to take the form of a servant (Phil. 2:6–11).

DuBose thinks that there can be no question that such passages clearly indicate Paul's belief in a pre-existent Christ. But we find a very different view in Dunn. He and DuBose are very close at many points. They are both fascinated by Paul's analogy between Christ and Adam, and see Christ as successfully fulfilling the human destiny which Adam had missed. But whereas Dunn thinks this analogy needs only two stages for its working out, the earthly life of Jesus and his post-resurrection existence, DuBose preceded these with a prior stage, his pre-existence. About the Christ-hymn in Philippians, Dunn says, it "certainly seems on the face of it to be a straightforward statement contrasting Christ's pre-existent glory and post-crucifixion exaltation with his earthly humiliation."[19] But he thinks that we read it this way because we have been so conditioned by long centuries of teaching and that the text can be adequately interpreted without bringing the idea of pre-existence. Being "in the form of God" is true of Adam and all human beings made "in the image and likeness of God." I cannot go into the details of Dunn's argument concerning this and other passages, though I find him persuasive. He believes that a definite belief in pre-existence and incarnation does not emerge until we come to John's Gospel.

Of course, the whole question is still debatable. One might even argue that it is a question of common sense rather than exegesis, for if God sent forth his Son in the fullness of time, must not this entail that the Son already existed? Or is one to suppose that the Son came into being in the very act of sending? But when it was suggested by a reviewer that on his own theory, Professor Dunn ought to "distance" himself from the Johannine view because of its isolation in the New Testament, he replied that John's doctrine of incarnation is the fulfillment of a dynamic already at work in the Pauline epistles, and that to "distance" ourselves from John

---

[19]   J. Dunn, *Christology,* 114.

would mean to distance ourselves also from "all the major Christian thinkers of the first as well as of subsequent centuries."[20] So it seems that DuBose, though he may have expressed himself incautiously, has not been refuted in his general position demanding that we read the Scriptures with the mind of the church. There remains also, of course, what exactly is meant by pre-existence, for this could be understood in several ways.

But that last point raises an issue which could hardly be decided on biblical grounds alone. To deal with it in any serious way would raise further questions of Christology, the Trinity, the nature of a human being, and so on—questions which continued to be debated in post-apostolic times and are still being debated today. That is why it is not enough to consider only DuBose and Scripture, for one must go on to DuBose and tradition. He stood firmly in the Anglican way of doing theology, in which tradition is accorded a place (though admittedly subordinate) alongside Scripture. A recent illustration of this is the "Agreed Statement on Ministry" produced by the Anglican-Roman Catholic International Commission. Though in that document an appeal is made to Scripture, some points can be supported only by broadening that appeal to include the teaching and practice of the church of the early centuries. In the Church of England itself, the traditional ordinal stated bluntly that "it is evident to all men, diligently reading the holy scripture and ancient authors, that from the apostles' time there hath been these orders of ministers in Christ's Church: bishops, priests and deacons." In the revised ordinal of 1980 it is simply claimed that this church "maintains the historic threefold ministry of bishops, priests and deacons." I suppose the doctrine of the Trinity is also not fully to be found in Scripture, so that the scriptural teaching needs supplementation from later sources.

These remarks bring us back to the relation of biblical studies and systematic theology in DuBose. Though he was primarily a biblical scholar, he was also a systematician. He tells us himself that at an early age he fell under the spell of St. Paul. One of his major books is *The Gospel According to St. Paul*, a detailed exposition of Paul's letter to the Romans. In this book, DuBose does not hesitate to attribute to Paul "scientific definiteness and clearness"[21] in his handling of theological themes. He points out in the same context that Paul goes about the theological task in a twofold way, asserting on the one hand certain facts about Jesus and on the other the salvific appropriation of these facts in the lives of believers. It would be going too far to say that the Letter to the Romans is a piece of systematic theology, but it is the earliest *enchiridion*

---

[20] J. D. G. Dunn, "Some Thoughts on Maurice Wiles's 'Reflections,'" *Theology* 85 (1982): 98.

[21] *A DuBose Reader*, 95.

or handbook of Christian teaching. It is, as the title of DuBose's books suggests, a gospel, but different from the four gospels commonly so-called. It is, we might say, a gospel that has undergone massive redaction so that the story of Jesus is now visible only in hints and allusions, and has been overlaid by Paul's theological teaching about sin, the human condition, the work of Christ, justification, and so on. It is worth remembering too that this *enchiridion*, as I have called it, is an older writing than any of our gospels, though of course fragments of narrative were circulating before Paul wrote.

I suppose it is just conceivable that the Christian Scriptures might have consisted only of epistles, without the narrative gospels. But such a collection of epistles, or even this single Epistle to the Romans, would still have deserved the name of gospel. I say it is just conceivable that only epistles would be written, but clearly the early church wanted something more, and so first Mark and then the other evangelists composed their narrative works. But it is certainly interesting that before these narrative pieces were written, Paul chose to express the gospel in the thematic form that we find in Romans. Why did he do that? Was it due to his rabbinic training? Or has it deeper roots in an intellectual demand (not, of course, necessarily explicit when Paul wrote) that the truths of Christianity should be stated in the form of a coherent body of teachings? No doubt it lacks the concreteness and imaginative appeal of the stories of Jesus and his sayings; yet one could also say that it has been released from the specific situation in which it arose and so made free for development in wider traditions. I think it could also be said that the move away from story to doctrine is the first step toward demythologizing. It is probably no accident that the most successful part of Rudolf Bultmann's *Theology of the New Testament* is his exposition of the thought of St. Paul, mostly in anthropological categories.[22] Bultmann, like DuBose, felt a special affinity for Paul, and both of them in different ways emphasize the anthropological or existential aspects of Paul's version of the Christian gospel.

If I am right in holding that DuBose was primarily a New Testament scholar who nevertheless was very much interested in moving into questions of systematic theology, I think one could say that he found the precedent for this in the New Testament itself, and especially in the thought of St. Paul. I think too we can say that he did a useful service in helping to break down the divisions between the two disciplines. Neither can do without the other, and it is unfortunate that in our era of excessive specialization, the two have drifted so far apart that sometimes one finds suspicion and even hostility between practitioners of the two disciplines.

---

[22] Rudolf Bultmann, *Theology of the New Testament*, 2 vols. (New York: Charles Scribner's Sons, 1951–55), 1:187–352.

The New Testament scholar complains that the systematician does not care enough about the Bible, while the systematician tends to regard the biblical scholar as overly concerned with ancient texts.

I have not said much about the third factor in Anglican theology, the use of reason. We find that too in DuBose, but I shall deal with it more briefly, since I have written about it somewhere else.[23] Especially in one of his late writings, *The Reason of Life*, DuBose directly confronted some of the problems which Christianity faces in the context of modern thought. The greatest intellectual event in his own lifetime was one which many thought to be destructive to the whole Christian position—I mean, the publication in 1859 of Darwin's *Origin of Species*. As we all know, the church fought a long rearguard action against the theory of evolution, and that action still goes on in a few areas. But some Christian thinkers speedily came to terms with the new ideas. Among them was DuBose. He said he accepted evolution both because it was the current science and because its general truth could, in his view, scarcely be questioned.[24] The masterly way in which he incorporated evolutionary ideas into his theology still repays study.

He was thinking of evolution not just as a biological theory but more as a general philosophy in which change and development belong to the essential nature of things. Although he lived before the publication of Whitehead's philosophical works, I think it would be fair to call DuBose a "process" theologan. But he drew the inspiration for his dynamic worldview from a philosopher who lived long before Whitehead and company. Man, he tells us, is spiritual in the sense taught by Aristotle, namely, he has the capacity for becoming spiritual. The important sentence from Aristotle is this: οἶον ἕκαστόν ἐστι τῆς γενέσεως τελεσθείσης, ταύτην φαμὲν τὴν φύσιν εἶναι ἑκάστου, ὥσπερ ἀνθρώπου, which DuBose translates, "What a thing is when its becoming has been completed, that we call the *nature* of the thing, as, e.g. of man."[25] The definition of a thing is not the τί ἐστι, "what it is," but the τί ἦν εἶναι, "what it were to be it."[26] It is with such ideas in mind that DuBose expounds in dynamic and evolutionary terms the prologue to St. John's Gospel in a truly remarkable exercise in which Scripture, tradition, and philosophy all make their appropriate contributions. No wonder America, and especially the Episcopal Church, should make much of him.

---

[23] John Macquarrie, "DuBose and Modern Thought," *St. Luke's Journal of Theology* 31 (1987): 15–24.

[24] *A DuBose Reader*, 149. Source: W.A. DuBose, *The Reason of Life* (New York: Longmans, Green & Co., 1911).

[25] W. DuBose, *Soteriology*, 7.

[26] Ibid., 9.

DATE DUE

HIGHSMITH   # 45220